Ibsen and the Irish Revival

Ibsen and the Irish Revival

Irina Ruppo Malone

palgrave
macmillan

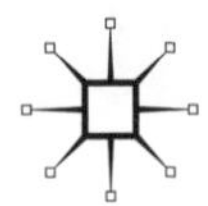

First published 2010 by
PALGRAVE MACMILLAN

Palgrave Macmillan in the UK is an imprint of Macmillan Publishers Limited, registered in England, company number 785998, of Houndmills, Basingstoke, Hampshire RG21 6XS.

Palgrave Macmillan in the US is a division of St Martin's Press LLC, 175 Fifth Avenue, New York, NY 10010.

Palgrave Macmillan is the global academic imprint of the above companies and has companies and representatives throughout the world.

Palgrave® and Macmillan® are registered trademarks in the United States, the United Kingdom, Europe and other countries.

ISBN 978–0–230–23199–3 hardback

This book is printed on paper suitable for recycling and made from fully managed and sustained forest sources. Logging, pulping and manufacturing processes are expected to conform to the environmental regulations of the country of origin.

A catalogue record for this book is available from the British Library.

A catalog record for this book is available from the Library of Congress.

10 9 8 7 6 5 4 3 2 1
19 18 17 16 15 14 13 12 11 10

Printed and bound in Great Britain by
CPI Antony Rowe, Chippenham and Eastbourne

To the memory of my father,
Yuri Aleksandrovich Ruppo

Contents

List of Figures

Acknowledgements

I would like to express my profound gratitude to Professor Adrian Frazier for scholarly advice, generous encouragement and constant support throughout my work on this book. I thank him for his kindness, wisdom, excellent guidance and, above all, for helping me develop my own voice as a scholar.

I am particularly grateful to Professor Nicholas Grene who examined the doctoral thesis from which the present book has evolved. I am greatly indebted to Dr Ros Dixon, not only for reviewing several sections of this book, but also for being a source of inspiration and support. I thank Dr Patrick Lonergan and Dr Lionel Pilkington for insightful comments on the early drafts.

I gratefully acknowledge the receipt of the NUI Galway Arts Faculty Fellowship and the funding received from the Irish Council for the Humanities and Social Sciences. I wish to thank all the everyone in the English Department, NUI Galway. I am particularly grateful to Dr Riana O'Dwyer and Professor Kevin Barry for their help and encouragement. Special thanks go to Irene O'Malley and Dearbhla Mooney. I thank all the students whom it was my pleasure to teach during my postgraduate training at NUI Galway. At Palgrave Macmillan I would like to thank especially Christabel Scaife and Ruth Willats.

My thanks go to Professor Miglena Ivanova for her generous advice at the early stage of the project and for many stimulating discussions since. I have benefited greatly from presenting my work at several workshops and conferences, and would like to thank Dr Nessa Cronin at the Department of Irish Studies, NUI Galway, the organisers of the New Voices Conference at NUI Maynooth (2006) and St Patrick's College Drumcondra (2007), the International Association for the Study of Irish Literature (IASIL), the Society for the History of Authorship, Reading and Publishing (SHARP), the International Ibsen Committee, the Irish Society for Theatre Research, and Professor Ann Heinemann and Dr Mark Llewellyn, organisers of the Third International George Moore Conference. I thank the Irish Theatre scholars with whom I was fortunate to discuss my ideas and those who encouragement: Dr Patrick Burke, Professor Joan FitzPatrick Dean Professor Kathleen Heininge, Dr Eamonn Jordan, Dr Cathy Leaney, Professor Christopher Murray, Professor Donald Morse and Professor

Anthony Roche. I also wish to specially thank Professor Joan Templeton, editor of the *Ibsen News and Comment.*

I thank the Centre for Ibsen Studies in Oslo for the opportunity to present some of the sections from this book at an in-house seminar and to carry out research at the extensive collection held at the Centre. My thanks go to all the staff at the Centre. I am particularly grateful to Dr Aina Nøding and Randi Meyer for providing me with important archival materials. During my stay in Oslo, it was an honour to discuss some of my ideas with Professor Bjørn Tysdahl. I thank Professor Frode Helland and Professor Astrid Sæther. My thanks also go to Jens-Morten Hanssen and Benedikte Berntzen at ibsen.net, Anette Storli Anderssen and Giuliano d'Amico. I would like to express my special gratitude to Professor Tore Rem for his generous interest in my work.

My thanks go to Scott Kraft, Acting Head of Special Collections at Northwestern University Library Illinois, and to Nick Munagian for providing me with materials from the Archives of the Gate Theatre of Dublin. Many thanks to the staff of the James Hardiman Library, NUI Galway, the Manuscript Department at the National Library of Ireland, and the Trinity College Manuscript Department.

All efforts have been made to secure rights for material used in this book. I gratefully acknowledge RTÉ Radio, Ireland's Public Service Broadcaster, for permissions to use transcriptions form 'The Hilton and Michael Show'. I thank the Board of the National Library of Ireland for permission to quote from the manuscripts of Joseph Holloway. I am grateful to Gerry O'Regan, editor of the *Irish Independent*, for permission to use quotations form the *Irish Independent* and the *Freeman's Journal*. My thanks to John Braine for letting me use photographs by Harry Braine. For allowing me to quote from the unpublished autobiographical piece by Shelah Richards, I thank her son, Micheal Johnston. I thank the Gate Theatre Dublin and Michael Travers, executor of MacLiammóir Estate, for permission to use Micheál MacLiammóir's sketch for *Peer Gynt*.

I thank all my friends. While unable to name all, I would like to mention with gratitude Alan Bergin, Dermot Burns, Jennifer and Tina Hannon, Val Nolan, Kinga Olszewska, Garret O'Malley, Catherine Ryan, Jennifer Smith and Áine Tierney.

My family have been a constant source of support. I would like to thank Maureen Nevin, Niall Cawley, Vladimir Ruppo, Michael and Mark Malone, Ella and Alexandra Ruppo, and especially my parents-in-law, John and Helen Malone, and my mother, Marina Ruppo. And very special thanks to my wonderful husband, Paul Malone, and our little daughter, Alice.

Introduction

Today the legacy of the Irish Literary Revival is obvious. Irish schoolchildren are taught a variety of native myths and texts by W. B. Yeats and James Joyce. Among the many mementoes of this literary movement are the statues of the legendary Cúchulainn at the Dublin Post Office and of the Children of Lír at the Garden of Remembrance, and the plaques commemorating Leopold's Bloom fictitious journey through Dublin. Yet, what is occluded in this process of commemoration is the international dimension of the Revival. For the young James Joyce, however, or at least for the protagonist of his autobiographical first novel, Dublin's streets seemed to be haunted by foreign authors. As Stephen 'walked along the North Strand Road, glancing idly at the windows of the provision shops, he would recall the dark humour of Guido Cavalcanti and smile' and 'as he went by Baird's stonecutting works in Talbot Place the spirit of Ibsen could blow through him like a keen wind, a spirit of wayward boyish beauty.[1] Joyce, moreover, was not alone in feeling the wind of Ibsen's radical dramas. On his walks to and from the National Library, he could have passed a tiny performance hall in Molesworth Street where, in 1897 (shortly before Joyce entered the university), an Irish company staged the Irish première of *A Doll's House*.

This book is concerned with two interrelated subjects: Ibsen's influence on the writers of the Irish Literary Revival and the reception of his plays in Ireland. With its several theatres, large population of keen theatregoers and vociferous theatre critics, Dublin was indeed a place where literature and daily life intermingled. The Irish Literary Revival gave literature, and in particular dramatic writing, a prominent place in Irish society. Plays by various authors of the Revival were presented as exercises in fostering national consciousness; and the public responded by viewing them as events of political significance. As the records of *The*

Playboy riots show, the audience's response to a play depended not only on its aesthetic qualities, but its relation to the wider social and political concerns of the day. Plays by foreign dramatists, such as Ibsen, were often subjected to the same broad expectations. The very appropriateness of enjoying a play by a non-Irish author who had achieved fame on the English stage was debated in the nationalist papers. Another question was whether Irish literary nationalism could benefit from studying foreign writers who, like Ibsen, had participated in movements analogous to the Irish Revival.

This book challenges the commonly held view that the Irish Revival was rooted in the rejection of Ibsen. Proponents usually refer to Lady Gregory's diary entry of early 1898: 'Yeats ... believes there will be a reaction after the realism of Ibsen, and romance will have its turn.'[2] Yet to take this comment literally and to subscribe to its apparent equation of Ibsen with dramatic realism means overlooking the stylistic diversity of Ibsen's life work. It also leads to a neglect of the significance of his romantic plays for Yeats's attempted revival of the pre-realist aesthetics in drama and the subsequent emergence of the Irish modernist tradition.

As Toril Moi has pointed out, Ibsen is all too often considered to be an outmoded realist, a classic of the pre-modernist age and of no interest to modern academics. She detects a certain critical blindness to the modernist tendencies of Ibsen's drama, namely its reflection on the status of language and self in the post-idealist world and its 'unmatched series of superbly sustained metatheatrical reflections'.[3] This limited approach, which Moi finds is prevalent in the English-speaking academic world, can be particularly harmful for the reconstruction of various aspects of Ibsen's reception. By focusing on diverse aspects of his drama, rather than merely on realism, as reflected on the Irish stage and Irish literature, I explore the role that Ibsen played in the unfolding of the Irish Revival from a naively idealistic phenomenon to a self-conscious and self-mocking version of modernism.

When Ibsen's plays were first produced in London, the result was, as G. B. Shaw puts it, that he

> attracted one section of the English people so strongly that they hailed him as the greatest living dramatic poet and moral teacher, whilst another section was so revolted by his works that they described him in terms which they themselves admitted to be ... all but obscene.[4]

Shaw described this reaction as a 'phenomenon, which has occurred throughout Europe whenever Ibsen's plays have been acted'.[5] It did not occur in the country of Shaw's birth, however. As I argue in Chapter 1, Ireland's incongruous status as a cultural province of England conditioned its initial response to Ibsen. While in England and on the Continent Ibsen's literary influence began to be felt after the public had seen his plays, in Ireland the situation was different. Dublin first saw Ibsen in 1894 when Herbert Beerbohm Tree presented *An Enemy of the People* at the Gaiety Theatre. By that time most of Ibsen's works were available in several English translations and some Irish authors had already been subjected to his influence. Shaw's *The Quintessence of Ibsenism* (1891) is one example; George Moore's *The Strike at Arlingford* (1893) is another.

With the foundation of the Irish Literary Theatre in 1899, a new chapter opened in the story of Ireland's reception of Ibsen. In his promotional speeches and articles Yeats shuffled a few facts of Ibsen's biography to present him as a romantic nationalist of worldwide fame, and consequently a role model for Irish playwrights. However, Ibsen's early plays, which Yeats lauded at the expense of the better-known plays of the realistic phase, remained unstaged in Ireland; and the first offerings of the Irish Literary Theatre fell short of the ideal that Yeats sought to associate with Ibsen. The resulting confusion in the public's perception is outlined in Chapter 2.

In *The Anxiety of Influence*, Harold Bloom depicted literary works as battlefields on which writers fight to overcome the influence of their masters.[6] The main premise of this study is that such battles are not waged in isolation but amid the multiple incidents and influences of everyday life, and, importantly, in the midst of other readers, who may or may not be writers. Yeats's assessment of Ibsen (if we take his word for it) radically changed following a conversation he overheard between a washerwoman and a small child. Moreover, neither Yeats nor John Millington Synge, whose *In the Shadow of the Glen* (1903) was branded 'Irish Ibsenite propaganda', could engage in a purely literary relationship with Ibsen. Their society's responses to him influenced their private interpretations, just as these writers, in turn, influenced contemporary views of Ibsen through their critical and literary works. I therefore address the question of Synge's Ibsenite allusion in *In the Shadow of the Glen* in the context of the public reception of *A Doll's House* (both plays were produced in Dublin in 1903). In dealing with Yeats's literary relationship with Ibsen, I illuminate the immediate context for his conflicting remarks on the playwright – his squabbles with George Moore, his befriending of Synge, his confrontations with Mrs Patrick Campbell. In writing *The Player Queen* (begun in 1907; published in 1922) Yeats voiced anxieties associated with Ibsen's influence and analysed his shifting attitudes to dramatic realism.

Chapter 3 deals with Ibsen's influence on the dissenters from the traditions of the Irish drama established by Yeats and Synge. Edward Martyn, who parted company with Yeats in 1901, and Padraic Colum, who left the Abbey Theatre in 1905, openly expressed their admiration for Ibsen. The Cork Realists, a group of playwrights who rose to prominence in the early 1910s, rebelled against the image of peasant Ireland propagated by the Abbey. They prided themselves in following in the footsteps of the Norwegian playwright. Ibsen's influence on the early twentieth-century Irish realists is undeniable. Rather than outlining the obvious similarities between his plays and those of the Irish realists, however, this chapter is concerned with their differences. In *Ibsen and the Great World*, Naomi Lebowitz observes how frequently Ibsen has been misread and underread.[7] Shaw, whose *The Quintessence of Ibsenism* is sometimes cited as precisely such a misreading, was in fact the first to notice that Ibsen's critique of idealism is often misunderstood. This chapter discusses the problems inherent in the Irish realists' attempts to reconcile Ibsenism with nationalism. While they refused to idealise their countrymen, seeing the realistic drama as a particularly poignant form of social critique, they did not always subscribe to Ibsen's rejection of the ideal of redemptive sacrifice.

While Chapter 3 analyses the difficulties involved in accepting Ibsen's criticism of idealist ethics, Chapter 4 considers the problem of Ibsen's challenge to the aesthetics of idealism.[8] Ibsen's exploration of the relation between language, superstition and the everyday was not always understood or welcomed by Irish audiences, critics and writers. A comparison of *Ghosts* with T. C. Murray's *Maurice Harte* (1912) suggests that Ibsen's unique approach to the interaction between the myth and the everyday – an approach that constitutes the beginning of literary modernism – failed to register in the plays of the Cork Realists. Their attitude to Ibsen's symbolism was thus similar to that of the majority of theatre critics. They were baffled by plays such as *The Master Builder, The Lady from the Sea, Little Eyolf* and *Rosmersholm*, performed in Dublin between 1908 and 1915. *Little Eyolf*'s blending of realism and symbolism is approximated in Edward Martyn's *An Enchanted Sea* (1904) and *Grangecolman* (1912) and paralleled in James Joyce's 'An Encounter'.

Chapter 5 addresses the question of whether in the twenty years following the first production of an Ibsen play in Ireland, attitudes to his plays changed. It examines the contrasting reception of Ibsen's dramatic works and those of his Irish followers. What is at stake here is not merely Ibsen's dramatic reputation, but the relevance of his radical ideas to the changing Ireland from 1911 to 1926. During this period, Ibsen's dramas were not only explored by several Irish writers, they were also played out in the Irish political arena. The first section looks at the reception of *A Doll's House*, produced in Dublin in 1911, in the context of the history of the Irish suffragist movement. The second section examines the conflicting responses to the productions of *Ghosts* (1917), *An Enemy of the People* (1917), *John Gabriel Borkman* (1918) and *Blight* (1918), a realistic play by Oliver St. John Gogarty and Joseph O'Connor. The third section develops the subject of nationalist attitudes to Ibsen and Ibsenism through a discussion of the Abbey's 1923 production of *A Doll's House* and the 1926 première of Sean O'Casey's *The Plough and the Stars*. While the production of *The Plough and the Stars* provoked nationalist riots, the press made no mention of its indebtedness to Ibsen. Yet O'Casey's Norah Clitheroe does not merely exhibit similar character traits to her Norwegian namesake; both characters are used by the dramatists to expose the harmful idealism of the societies they inhabit. The affinity between Ibsen's play and O'Casey's *The Plough and the Stars* is a point of departure for a discussion of the relation between feminism and anti-idealism as manifested in politics and in drama.

The concluding chapter presents the Gate Theatre's *Peer Gynt* (premièred in 1928 and revived in 1932) as a turning point in the Irish reception of Ibsen and a departure from the spirit of the Irish Revival. Unlike the earlier productions of Ibsen's plays, the Gate's expressionistic *Peer Gynt* broke away from romanticised approaches to stage setting. It was the first Irish Ibsen production to be a commercial success. Moreover, for the first time since 1894, people saw in Ibsen's play a reflection of their own concerns. Some reviews compared Peer to the Irish Taoiseach Eamon de Valera; others pointed to the parallel between the controversial reception of *Peer Gynt* when it was published in Scandinavia and the Irish controversies over the plays of Synge and O'Casey. Through a consideration of the parallels between *Peer Gynt* and such revisionist texts of the Irish Revival as Yeats's late poetry, the 'Circe' episode of *Ulysses* and Synge's *The Playboy of the Western World*, this chapter investigates the emergence of the humanist and the modernist traditions in Irish writing and its criticism of the cultural policy of the Irish Free State. The Epilogue deals with George Moore's retrospective examination of the Irish Revival as it emerged through his engagement with Ibsen's last play.

The only book-length study of the reception of continental drama in Ireland is Miglena Iliytcheva Ivanova's doctoral dissertation 'Staging Europe, Staging Ireland: Ibsen, Strindberg, and Chekhov in Irish Cultural Politics 1899–1922'.[9] As its title suggests, Ibsen is only one of the dramatists examined by Ivanova. Yeats's 1899 articles on the Irish Literary Theatre and the Ibsenite resonances of Lennox Robinson's *Patriots* are the only two points where our studies cross paths; in both cases my perspective differs from Ivanova's. Until the entirety of Joseph Holloway's papers are digitised, annotated and cross-referenced with the Irish newspapers, Abbey Theatre Scrapbooks and W. A. Henderson's Scrapbooks, *The Documentary History of Irish Drama* by Robert Hogan, James Kilroy and several other scholars remains indispensable for any study of the theatre of the Irish Revival.[10] The same can be said of William J. Feeney's *Drama in Hardwicke Street: A History of the Irish Theatre Company*.[11] Feeney's list of Ibsen's productions in Dublin from 1897 to 1916 was particularly useful in the early stages of my research.[12] The majority of reviews of Ibsen's productions used in the present book, however, were collected from various Irish newspapers and periodicals.

Ibsen's impact on the writers of the Irish Revival has been a subject of some critical interest. In *Ibsen and the Beginnings of Anglo-Irish Drama* Jan Setterquist analyses his influence on Martyn and Synge.[13] Ibsen's influence on Joyce is examined in detail in Bjørn J. Tysdahl's study *Joyce and Ibsen – A Study in Literacy Influence*.[14] The study continues to attract scholarly interest,[15] along with the question of Ibsen's influence on Synge and Shaw.[16] However, I devote more space to the question of Ibsen's influence on Yeats, which by comparison remains under-researched.

Yeats's ambivalent attitude to Ibsen has given rise to critical confusion which I hope to help clarify by placing his conflicting statements in their immediate contexts. Ibsen's influence on O'Casey has not attracted much attention, and my section on *The Plough and the Stars* and *A Doll's House* is only a small contribution to this potentially important subject. Ibsen's influence on the minor playwrights of the Irish Revival is well known, even though these playwrights themselves have not received much attention. Robert Welch, Ben Levitas and Albert DeGiacomo (in his study of T. C. Murray) agree on the Irish realists' indebtedness to Ibsen.[17] In concentrating on the Irish realists' divergence from Ibsen, I hope to start a debate on what is thus often taken for granted.

For Joyce, as for Stephen Dedalus, the spirit of Ibsen was omnipresent. In *Scribbledehoble*, Joyce suggested that Yeats's *The Land of Heart's Desire* was similar to *Little Eyolf*.[18] He once said that the last scene of Synge's *The Playboy of the Western World* reminded him of *The Master Builder*.[19] The thrill that one feels when confronted with the interplay of literary texts was part of the motivation for the current project. However, rather than merely listing the Ibsenian resonances in the works of the writers of the Irish Literary Revival, this book examines them in their historical context.

1
Dublin's First Introduction to Ibsen: The Realist Plays

English controversy – Irish reactions, 1889–93

> There is no other explanation of the momentary craze for Ibsen's dramas in this country than that they represent the views of certain advanced thinkers in their hostility to the permanence of domestic ties. Their teaching may be summed up as a crusade against marriage as an intolerable wrong to a woman who happens to get tired of her husband in the inevitable friction of the fireside. So ardent are the votaries of these improved ethics, that they have gone to the length of hiring a theatre in London for the performance, as a free representation, of a play too repulsive in subject to be licensed as a public spectacle.[1]

Such was the opinion expressed anonymously in the review of Edmund Gosse's translation of *Hedda Gabler*, which appeared in the *Dublin Review* in 1891. Rumours of Ibsen's moral depravity and of Ibsenism as a dangerous social addiction began to circulate in Dublin three years before the public had a chance to see one of his plays. Dublin's status as a cultural satellite of England meant that plays that excited London reached Dublin sometimes after a time lag. This, however, did not apply to the flow of opinions. English papers were on sale in Dublin; Irish papers published London gossip; and Irish communities in London ensured the swift transference of ideas to Dublin. The story of the Irish reception of Ibsen begins, therefore, with the London controversy over his plays, an event that affected differently Irish people who were in England and those who stayed at home. The future authors of the Irish Revival, Yeats, Edward Martyn, George Moore and Lady Gregory, as well as their later opponent, D. P. Moran, witnessed at first hand the rage over the first professional production of *A Doll's House* (1889) and the outcry against the public performance of the unlicensed *Ghosts* (1891). Moore and Shaw, moreover, were directly involved in the debates that surrounded these productions and the later premières of *Hedda Gabler* (1893) and *The Master Builder* (1893).

The critical battle over Ibsen generated a host of topics: female suffrage and emancipation, free speech, censorship and socialism.[2] The overriding subject, however, was the future of the English theatre. The established system of the long run ensured the prosperity of actor-managers at the expense of playwrights. As Shaw pointed out, 'unless you could get 100,000 people to see a play in London, it was not worth putting on'.[3] This arrangement, argued such Ibsenites as Shaw, Arthur B. Walkley and William Archer, hampered creativity and exposed the theatre (and aspiring playwrights) to the dictates of the compact majority of amusement seekers and the tyranny of the actor-manager. The success of Ibsen's problem plays proved that the theatre could be turned from a site of mere amusement into a place where the public could be made to think and playwrights could be free to express minority opinions.

In the hands of the Ibsenites, especially the most prominent translator of his plays, William Archer, and the founder of the Independent Theatre, Jacob T. Grein, Ibsen became a symbol of the emancipation of the English theatre. Dublin, however, was excluded from the debate. None of the professional pioneers of Ibsenism on the English stage, such as Elizabeth Robins, or Janet Achurch and her Irish husband, Charles Charrington, was interested in an Irish tour. Grein, who defied the censor by producing *Ghosts* in his subscription theatre, might have been aware that the censor was powerless in Ireland, but the battle over Ibsen was waged on English ground, in the name of the English public. Provincial Dublin had to wait until the end of the controversy marked by the 1893 production of *An Enemy of the People* by a well-established professional actor-manager Herbert Beerbohm Tree. This production reached Dublin in 1894 and was the first of Ibsen's plays to be performed in Ireland.

Until then, a peculiar incongruity characterised Irish reactions to Ibsen. England trapped Ibsen's name in a web of various social and artistic issues from which he could not be easily disentangled, but which also made little sense in the very different context of Dublin. There was no tyranny of the long-run actor-managers or state censorship in Ireland. The relatively small size of Dublin's population ensured a quick succession of plays at its main theatres – the Queen's and the Gaiety.[4] In the former, the manager, J. W. Whitbread, cultivated Boucicault-style melodrama on patriotic themes, along with musical comedies and dramas by touring companies. The Gaiety was run by John Gunn and hosted English and continental operatic and dramatic companies. The plays were often self-censored in order to avoid upsetting the sensibilities of the Catholic members of the audience.[5] The Ibsenites' crusade against the theatre of commerce would seem out of place in Dublin.

Neither Ibsenism nor Ibsenphobia (terms coined during the London Ibsen controversy) reached Ireland in its pure form. The split between the conservatives and the 'younger generation' which Ibsen symbolised in London was not replicated in Dublin. There all such distinctions were secondary to political and religious divisions. Dubliners observed the 'Ibsen wrangle' from a distance. They displayed occasional cautious interest in Ibsenism as a social phenomenon and interpreted it according to their own beliefs.

The main Dublin dailies, the *Daily Express*, the *Irish Times* and the *Daily Independent*, published a few reports of Ibsen's productions in England, but abstained from discussing the merits of his plays. The *Irish Times* readers might have admired the star of the English stage, Ellen Terry, for proposing (wrongly as it later emerged) having nothing to do with Ibsen's 'preposterously unreal' plays.[6] Some readers would have been horrified to hear that a Finnish woman who poisoned her husband was 'wonderfully like some of Ibsen's creations'.[7] They might also have come across an occasional anecdote about Ibsen's life.[8] Yet, the newspaper did not consistently engage with the Ibsen controversy.

The Catholic quarterly *Dublin Review* attacked Ibsen in terms worthy of some of its most vociferous English opponents. Father Tom Finlay, founder and editor of *Lyceum*, the journal of University College, Dublin, was antagonistic to Ibsen. In 1893, he published two articles on 'The Norwegian Literary Triumvirate', dealing with Bjørnstjerne Bjørnson and Alexander Kielland, but not with Ibsen. Constantine P. Curran, then a student at the university, recalls his dismay when he discovered that 'complimentary reference to Ibsen [in these articles], degenerated in a later hand to a grotesque slating of *The Master Builder*'.[9] The anonymous writer of that review (published in 1893) declared: 'It is a strange thing that such stuff as this should be regarded as dramatic literature in a country which has produced Shakespeare and where his plays are still acted.'[10]

Conversely, the Unionist *Dublin Evening Mail* viewed Ibsen favourably. The first time Ibsen is mentioned there appears to be in a review of George Moore's *Impressions and Opinions* (1891). In that book, Moore includes his 'Note on *Ghosts*', in which he describes the 1890 production of *Les Revenants* (*Ghosts*) at the Théâtre Libre in Paris and calls for a similar independent theatre in England.[11] Moore recalls how he had once tried to read *A Doll's House* and 'could make nothing of it – nothing, nothing, nothing'; but seeing *Ghosts* in performance proved a different experience:

> before half the first act had been read nothing but the play existed for me. The remorseless web that life had spun, and the poor boy entangled in it, I watched, even as a child watches the fly that chance had thrown into the spider's web.[12]

The *Dublin Evening Mail* review of Moore's book appeared on 18 March 1891 – five days after *Ghosts* was produced by the Independent Theatre, a society newly founded in London in defiance of the censor's order and public opinion. The founder of the society was Grein with Moore on the committee, however, the *Dublin Evening Mail* did not mention either of these facts. Nor, indeed, did it describe the critical uproar that followed the production of *Ghosts* or the demands to close the theatre and prosecute the managers for 'infecting the modern theatre with poison'.[13] The author of the review did single out Moore's article on *Ghosts* for special attention, however, and mentioned Moore's advocacy of the Théâtre Libre in Paris and the nascent Independent Theatre in London. 'One of the dramatists taken up by these new Theatres, both in London and Paris is Ibsen', noted the reviewer;

> and we think that most of those, whose acquaintance with Ibsen is confined to a close perusal, will be enabled to realise his merits much more adequately by reading Mr. Moore's papers on the subject. His description of *Les Revenants* (*Ghosts*) is really a very clever performance, and makes the reader anxious to see the drama performed by competent artists.[14]

It is not certain whether the review had been submitted to the newspaper before the English première of *Ghosts* (13 March 1891) or whether the author adopted a pose of naïve curiosity while implicitly declaring his allegiance to Ibsen and the Independent Theatre movement. In any case, the timing of the review makes it easier to see the incongruous position of Dublin theatregoers in relation to the Ibsen controversy. London newspapers were full of excitement. Ibsen was being denounced as 'an egotist and bungler'; his play was called 'an open drain: a loathsome sore unbandaged'; his supporters were accused of 'Ibsanity' and 'Ibscenity',[15] whereas the Dublin paper merely speculated on the desirable possibility of seeing the play.

Later notices in the *Dublin Evening Mail* likewise reveal a bemused fascination with Ibsenism. On the occasion of the première of *The Master Builder* (1893), a day before Moore's *Strike at Arlingford*, it was noted that the week 'has been one of joy we should suppose for the "intellectual" playgoer'.[16] The plan proposed by Janet Achurch (who had played Nora in the 1889 *Doll's House*) and her husband, Charles Charrington, to devote Saturday matinées at the Royalty to Ibsen was also duly noted in March 1893:

> under the new auspices, [the Royalty might] become the home of the New Drama – in the best sense of the phrase. The 'literary' drama will probably be always welcome there, because the new lessees appear to be genuinely desirous not to subsist upon long 'runs' but to diversify their work as much as possible.[17]

Two weeks later the following notice appeared:

> The genuine vogue of Ibsen is a notable sign of the times. It has been found impossible to crush him, either by declamation or by ridicule. He has succeeded in catching the ear of the thoughtful playgoer, and has acquired a certain fashionable cachet. Serious as are his limitations – doubtful as at times is his taste, and wholly destitute as he seems to be of humour – one can only be pleased that a public should have been found for his productions. These will act as a valuable solvent. Passing by the purely fanciful and the purely artificial in our drama – with which they have nothing to do – the Ibsen pieces will have the effect of remodelling the serious native plays of the future. After this, the English play which professes to deal seriously with life will need to act up to its professions. The day has gone by for mere conventionality either in characterisation or plot.[18]

The *Dublin Evening Mail* might have played to local curiosity about Ibsen. Yet its articles probably intensified readers' sense of provincialism. The day was over; the battle had been won; and the Irish public had been excluded from the excitement. William Fay recalls the frustration which might have been shared by many literary-minded Dubliners:

> although [Frank and I] had ... fair opportunities of seeing first class acting, we who were enthusiasts for the art of drama knew its latest developments and experiments only by hearsay. ... But with only newspaper reports and articles to help us we could not really find out how the new plays differed from the old.[19]

Fay's experience reveals the problem of Dublin's position as a cultural satellite to London.

As Vivian Mercier explains, '[p]ossessing two universities and such old established cultural institutions as the Royal Irish Academy and the Royal Dublin Society, Dublin could rival any provincial city in the British Isles, Edinburgh included, in its literary culture'.[20] In terms of its cultural relations to London, however, Dublin was disadvantaged both geographically and politically. As late as 1906, an article in the *United Irishman* satirised that situation, suggesting that England should find a means to get Ireland attached to Britain so that the Irish would get the benefits of civilisation. 'On average', the writer expostulated,

> it requires eighteen months for a new piece of English literature to reach Merrion Square from London – two years for it to reach the common people of Dublin, three years to have asserted its existence in the hinterland, and from four to five years to establish itself along our western littoral. Our fate is as melancholy in regard to the drama. Our newspapers, no doubt, do their best to let us know what London is revelling in, but it is only when London has been satiated that No 2. Provincial Company permits us to see with the bodily eye.[21]

An Enemy of the People and Irish politics, 1894

The architect Joseph Holloway was passionate about the theatre. Problem plays and melodramas, plays Irish and foreign, could give him equal pleasure – as long, of course, as the acting was up to his standards. And if the performance itself did not please him, then the gossip in the lobby, the overheard conversations in the pit and chats on the way home provided ample material for his journals, which he kept all his life, writing at the rate of five pages a day.

As far as the journals tell us, Holloway was unperturbed by the Ibsen wrangle or the struggle for the freedom of the English theatre; he had always been conservative in his tastes. However, shortly before the Dublin première of *An Enemy of the People* given by one of the most prominent actor-managers of the London stage, Beerbohm Tree, Holloway decided to read the play. He told the playwright John MacDonagh twenty-three years later: 'I was struck by its profound tragedy ... I was sadly disappointed to find that Tree conceived Dr Thomas Stockmann in a farcical spirit that robbed the play, for me, of most of its real significance.'[22]

Indeed, there are two ways of reading Ibsen's satirical parable of a doctor whose discovery of bacterial contamination in a health spa embroils him in politics and turns him into an outcast persecuted by the very people who earlier glorified him. *An Enemy of the People* (1882) was Ibsen's answer to the outcry over *A Doll's House* (1879) and *Ghosts* (1881). Like these two plays, *An Enemy of the People* exposes the clash between individual morality and the hypocritical formulae that go by the name of public morality; but it does so in a light-hearted way. It seems wrong to make a tragic figure of Stockmann with his naïve optimism, quixotic sense of justice and bumbling pomposity. Besides, while at the end of the play Stockmann may have lost his home, he has still his life, his sanity and his family's love. When Nora in *A Doll's House* finds out that her eight years of happiness have been a sham, the horror of this discovery emerges like a decomposing corpse from beneath the ice (an image from the play). In *Ghosts*, Mrs Alving realises her life-long struggle to hide her husband's depravity from the public eye was a needless sacrifice. The orphanage erected in his honour goes up in flames and her son descends into madness due to hereditary syphilis. In *An Enemy of the People* Stockmann learns from his quarrel about drainpipes that the 'strongest man is he who stands alone' and that 'a man should never put on his best trousers when he goes out to battle for freedom and truth'.[23] The hero of the play, its symbols and its dialogue are marked by farcical bluntness. Ibsen was heaping ridicule on the political right and left equally, as well as satirising himself in the figure of Stockmann.[24]

As a Dubliner who had just lived through Charles Stewart Parnell's downfall, Holloway might have been less inclined to see the comical side of the play. Ben Levitas notes how similar the Parnell affair, occurring in the midst of the London Ibsen wrangle, was to an Ibsen play. The politician who had made extraordinary advances in the cause of Irish Home Rule was rejected by the very people he represented. He was abandoned by his close political associates, Michael Davitt, William O'Brien, and Timothy Healy, and condemned by the Irish Catholic hierarchy for what had long been an open secret – his cohabitation with Katharine O'Shea. Parnell's death on 6 October 1891 turned this political débâcle into a tragedy. 'When in 1891, the West End debut of *Ghosts* provoked a rancorous public row reminiscent of that already begun in Ireland', Levitas writes, 'Ibsen and Parnell both appeared as Dr Stockmann, enemies of the people forced on to the back foot of righteous unpopularity'.[25] Holloway's response to Beerbohm Tree's Stockmann might well have been influenced by his inability to regard political persecution as a laughing matter.[26]

Tree's comedic interpretation of *An Enemy of the People* (premièred in London on 14 June 1893) brought together the two sides of the Ibsen controversy. It was a commercial, professional production, intended for the amusement of the masses, rather than the amusement of the intellectual few. Made up like 'a young Ibsen, with horrent hair',[27] Tree appeared as a living embodiment of the caricatures of the playwright that had abounded in the English magazines. He rolled his eyes; he gesticulated wildly.[28] To the horror of serious-minded Ibsenites, Tree included some '"comic business" with Little Mr. Robson [who played Aslaksen] turning on the diversity of their statures'.[29] There was 'some foolery, too, over the burgomaster's hat'.[30]

Yet Tree's approach was not all burlesque. He seemed to have emphasised the quixotic pathos of Stockmann – a comical character caught up in a tragedy. As one eyewitness later recalled, he was 'perfect in the impassioned, indignant harangues, in representing Stockmann's incredulous distress of mind, his readiness to drop any number of points if only people will listen, a readiness which looks so like want of dignity but which springs from sincerity'.[31] The general consensus in London was that Tree's interpretation was contrary to Ibsen's conception of the character – and for once Ibsenites and their opponents were in agreement with each other. Shaw wrote that Tree's Stockmann 'though humorous and entertaining in its way, is a character creation, the polar opposite of Ibsen's Stockmann'.[32] The writer for *The Theatre* believed Tree to have improved on Ibsen: 'Broader, more human, and more sympathetic, the new Stockmann drives home the truth of the play with immeasurably increased force.'[33]

Whether or not Tree might have come closer to Ibsen's Stockmann than was believed by his contemporaries, his production proved that Ibsen could be less tragically shocking and mystifying than his opponents had assumed. As *The Times* observed, '[w]hether [the play's] perfect lucidity will be recognised as a merit by the devotees ... for whom puzzles like *The Master Builder* are pregnant with meaning, is a question admitting of doubt. The average playgoer ... is grateful for this total absence of obscurity.'[34] After this production Ibsen gradually began to lose his status as a social shibboleth. Tree had taken Ibsen away from the Ibsenites by showing that his plays could appeal to the general public.

The Dublin public were not fully aware that Tree's production of *An Enemy of the People* differed from the infamous plays they had heard about. They eagerly awaited their long-time favourite Beerbohm Tree to shock them with Ibsen's unwomanly women, unmanly men and stage suicides. The Gaiety was 'crowded from floor to ceiling' and 'numbers were turned from the doors'.[35] Dubliners had grown tired of hearing rumours about the battles over Ibsen – they were ready to join the fray.

For the majority, however, the evening was a failure. 'I had never seen before or since', recalled William Fay, 'an intelligent audience so completely flabbergasted.'[36] Instead of being shocked, they were bored. One reviewer reported that there was enthusiastic applause at the end of the play, [37] but most reviewers vied with each other in describing their disappointment.

'For more than a year we have been deluged with articles on Ibsen and his dramas', complained the *Irish Times*. 'Men have philosophised, have declaimed about Ibsen to a degree that would tempt one to say that they had been Ibsenised, or to venture the suggestion that a new disease has appeared – say Ibsanity. So much turmoil about so little.'[38] The verdict of the Dublin *Daily Express* was much the same: 'One tribute is due to [Beerbohm Tree], and that is that the worst actor on the stage could not have made a more perfect representation of an absolutely uninteresting man. There is no plot in the play, no scenery, and no dresses.'[39] Tree was famous for his lavish stage sets and extravagant effects; the naturalistic style he adopted for Ibsen's play could not but disappoint.

In London, Tree's *An Enemy of the People* was a commercial success because it appeared as a comment on the Ibsen controversy. But it did not fare well as Dublin's introduction to Ibsen. In London, Tree's production was appreciated for having the intellectual appeal of naturalist drama, while also working as pure entertainment. In Dublin, it was neither entertaining nor provocative. In London, it was a light-spirited antidote to the tragic naturalism of *Ghosts* and *Hedda Gabler* and the alleged mysticism of *The Master Builder* (premièred on 20 February 1893 and revived on 29 May 1893). Dubliners had not been given an opportunity to see these plays. If a provincial tour is supposed to bring the peripheries into a closer contact with the metropolitan centre, Tree's Dublin production of *An Enemy of the People* achieved the opposite. Instead of integrating Dublin into the dialectics of the London controversy, his production heightened the sense of Dublin's alienation from the English capital.

'To fail to find transcendent beauty in Ibsen was to confess oneself vulgar and stupid', read the review of the *Freeman's Journal*. 'So people admired him in self-defence. But a Dublin audience have a way of seeing with their own eyes and having the courage of their own thoughts.'[40] The *Freeman's Journal* reconstruction of Ibsenism as a mark of philistinism and Ibsenphobia as a mark of national distinction is the first indication of the attitude to Ibsen that would later emerge in the nationalist press. D. P. Moran and Arthur Clery would later present him as an 'English' item of interest, a symptom of West Britonism and a favourite playwright of the 'seonini'.[41] These views can be understood better when we consider their relation to Ibsen's initial failure with the Dublin public, a failure that stemmed from Dublin's long-time exclusion from the English controversy.

Dubliners expected *An Enemy of the People* to be what it certainly was not – the epitome of Ibsen's work. Its production left the public disillusioned. They had acted like provincial fools and had rushed to a theatre and scrambled for seats so they could prove themselves as fashionable as the London followers of Ibsen. Irish nationalist disapproval of Ibsen is rooted, among other things, in the incongruities involved in receiving Ibsen via England.

While most critics were content to recount the wrong done to them by Tree's unfortunate production of Ibsen's play, two critics spoke favourably of the play and noted its relevance to Irish politics. The Parnellite *Daily Independent* commented:

> Dr Stockmann discovers amongst other things that 'the confounded Liberal majority does not always make for truth and freedom that if it ever came to a serious National struggle, public opinion would be for taking to its heels, and the compact majority need scamper for their lives.[42]

Writing three years after Parnell's death, the critic presented Ibsen's play as a critique of the British prime minister William Gladstone and the Liberal Party, who had refused to support Parnell following the exposure of his relationship with Katharine O'Shea.

After the recent defeat of the second Irish Home Rule Bill in September 1893, Parnellites' frustration with the Liberal Party must have reached a new climax. 'Dr Stockmann discovers', continued the critic quoting from the play 'that party programmes wring the necks of all young and vital truths; that considerations of expediency turn justice upside down; that a party is like a sausage machine, it grinds all brains together in one mash, and that's why we see nothing but porridge heads and pulp heads all round, that self reliance is the only real security.'[43]

The *Independent* was not the only newspaper to turn a review of *An Enemy of the People* into a political commentary. In its leading article, the *Dublin Evening Mail* accused all the Dublin newspapers of moral blindness and cowardice for failing to acknowledge that the play 'deals with the greatest, the most fundamental, the most pressing question of the day – with Democracy and the arts by which it can be hocussed and blinded and befooled'.[44] Like the *Independent*, the *Dublin Evening Mail* reinterpreted *An Enemy of the People* as an attack on Gladstone, but its perspective was unionist:

> On the production of the play in London, Mr. Gladstone, as we read in the London papers of that day, went to witness its performance, curious, no doubt, to see what a Norwegian dramatist – a bit of the 'civilized world' – thought of the enemies, and of course, of the true friends of that darling 'People' of his, with a big P, the 'Masses' who were so far superior in 'political sagacity' and in 'moral integrity' to the Classes who laboured under the corrupting influences of education and property. And the same papers told us that Mr. Gladstone left the theatre at the end of the first act. It was natural that Mr. Gladstone should dislike the play. But it is to his credit that he did not understand it. [45]

Neither the split within the Irish parliamentary party, nor Parnell's death in 1891 or Gladstone's resignation in March 1894, had quite ended unionists' fear of the spectre of Home Rule. As the autumn campaign approached, it became clear that Home Rule needed to be addressed by the government and either 'forced or hung off'.[46] It could not 'lie another year, another six months as it [was]'.[47] And while separatists remained pessimistic, unionists lived in fear of the 'great wave of darkness that threatens to engulf us in confusion and ruin'.[48]

In its defence of *An Enemy of the People*, the *Dublin Evening Mail* transformed the play into a eulogy of conservative unionism and presented Stockmann as a victim of nationalist agitators. An educated man fighting for the truth and the common good, he is branded by the public as an 'obnoxious person, first to be boycotted, then exterminated'.[49] The *Freeman's Journal* called him a 'sanitary Don Quixote'. But the *Dublin Evening Mail* considered such a judgement unforgivable:

> We may judge ... what the *Freeman* would call political Quixotism, and in what respect it holds persons who tell popular untruths. Murder, whether by poisoned water or by bludgeon and blunderbuss, becomes quite respectable when it serves the temporary interests of a 'vast majority' and of the scoundrels who manage it. The *Irish Times* is against agrarian murders, but murder by poisoned water, it thinks, is quite pardonable when it brings grist to the mill of a majority of ratepayers.[50]

The *Dublin Evening Mail* suggested that the daily newspapers' rejection of the play was similar to the townspeople's castigation of Stockmann: it

was a symptom of their political blindness and moral depravity. Too cowardly to expose the vested interests of the Liberal Party, they would leave Irish landlords exposed to agrarian outrages and Irish Protestants subjected to the will of the Catholic majority. While the review of the *Daily Independent* reinforces Levitas's point about the connection between Parnellism and Ibsenism, the (more favourable) review of the *Dublin Evening Mail* suggests that Ibsen found even greater support in the opposite camp.

Indeed, the first mention of Ibsen in relation to Ireland seems to have been made in 1889 by a certain Mrs Henry Fawcett, who quoted at the Liberal Unionist Women meeting in Birmingham the following from Ibsen:

> Mere democracy cannot solve the social question; an element of aristocracy must be introduced into our lives. Of course, I do not mean aristocracy of birth or purse, nor even of aristocracy of intellect, I mean the aristocracy of character, of will, of goodness. That can only free us [*sic*]. From two groups will this aristocracy, I hope, come to our people – from our women and from our workmen.[51]

In his role as a radical harbinger of the new age, Ibsen seems to be naturally aligned to the turn-of-the-century revolutionary movements such as the one that led to the foundation of the Irish Free State. However, upon his entry into the highly politicised milieu of Dublin, Ibsen was more readily welcomed by the unionist than the nationalist section of the audience.

The brief upsurge of interest in Ibsen that followed Beerbohm Tree's *An Enemy of the People* soon subsided. However, the sentiments that emerge in the reviews of the play resurfaced in 1899 when the Irish Literary Theatre brought Ibsen to the centre of public attention.

A Doll's House and the beginnings of the Irish Literary Theatre, 1897

As George Moore recounts in *Ave,* his involvement with the Irish Dramatic Revival began when Edward Martyn 'great in girth as an owl ... blinking behind his glasses, and Yeats lank as a rook, a-dream in black silhouette on the flowered wall-paper',[52] presented themselves at his London apartment with the news that a change had come over Ireland. 'Dublin', insisted Martyn, 'was no longer a city of barristers, judges, and officials pursuing a round of mean interests and trivial amusements, but a capital of the Celtic Renaissance'.[53] Their plan was to found a theatre in Dublin. 'A forlorn thing it was surely to bring literary plays to Dublin!'[54] Moore protested. 'Tell me, do you think you'll find an audience in Dublin capable of appreciating *The Heather Field*?' Moore asked in reference to Martyn's as yet unpublished play. 'Ideas are only appreciated in Ireland,' Edward answered, somewhat defiantly.[55]

The story of the three Anglo-Irishmen's search for an ideal audience is well known. There is one episode, however, that is not emphasised in most accounts of the foundation of the Irish Literary Theatre – the Irish première of *A Doll's House* on 14 December 1897.

Ibsen's controversial play was an unusual choice for the first public performance of the little amateur group that called themselves the Dublin Players' Club. However, they received good notices. The *Daily Express* review, penned by an 'Ibsenite', called the production 'an oasis in the desert' and 'an educational treat', noting Dublin's 'constant deprivation and isolation from the new sources of art'.[56] The *Irish Times*, while far less enthusiastic about the play, welcomed the company. 'Composed of enthusiasts whom the question of receipts does not trouble, and who are prepared to make some sacrifices for their favourite hobby, it might play a most important part in the life of a community', the reviewer asserted, suggesting also that the company could act as a 'feeler to test ... public opinion', make people acquainted with lesser-known dramatic works and even 'furnish opportunities for trying new works by its own members'. [57]

Very little is known about the members of the group which, like the Irish Literary Theatre, aimed to reform the dramatic tastes and further the growth of dramatic literature of the capital. Flora MacDonnell (in notices of later productions sometimes referred to as MacDonald), who played Nora, and George J. Nesbitt, who played Torvald Helmer, remained with the Dublin Players' Club until its last production in 1909. But Harold White, who played Dr Rank, J. W. Mahood, who played Krogstad, and Miss Lily and Mr S. W. Maddock, who played the servant and the porter respectively do not appear in later Dublin productions. It is unknown whether Martyn, who participated in MacDonnell and Nesbitt's Ibsenite experiments in 1903–4, had been involved in the 1897 production.[58] It is not unlikely, however, that he was the anonymous 'Ibsenite' of the *Daily Express* review. In 1913–15, when Martyn was again involved in amateur productions of Ibsen's plays in Dublin, he was careful to draw attention to the performances and praise the actors in the newspapers. This habit might have been acquired early. Who else but Martyn had in 1897 a reputation as the

Dublin Ibsenite and could compare the Dublin production to the French production of Mme 'Rejane, who failed ... so dismally in Paris', or to the version of 'Janet Achurch, who ... is a haunting vision still'?[59] Martyn is one of a few likely to have seen those productions in Paris, London and Dublin.

While it cannot be proved that Martyn did in fact participate in the production, or whether he indeed reviewed it, it is almost certain that he knew about it. Therefore, his assertion to Moore that ideas, that is, the drama of ideas, 'are only appreciated in Ireland', might have been less the attitude of a romantic idealist, blissfully unaware of the obtuseness of his countrymen, than a comment born out of experience.

The performance was a moderate success, though some things did go wrong. The *Irish Times* complained that the Molesworth Hall was unsuitable for the performance. The scenery, according to Holloway 'was bad'.[60] Worse still, 'the prompter had a fairest sized part to play' while 'the curtains had to behave in an eccentric manner', causing Nora to make her exit the wrong way.[61] Besides, the four pieces from the *Peer Gynt* suite 'played in really good style as a species of overture',[62] seem poorly suited for *A Doll's House* (even though no one seemed to notice the stylistic clash at the time). These mistakes were forgiven, however, for the audience was captivated by the talent of Flora McDonnell. According to the reviewer of the *Daily Express*, her Nora was

> surprisingly good, to a great extent, especially in psychological moments, she was Ibsen's Norah [*sic*], her weakest part being in the transition period, or rather the doll epoch. In her impersonation there was the foreshadowing of an awakening, too ripe a promise of mind and soul still undeveloped; she was not sufficiently the lark and squirrel which Helmer addresses in his ponderous way.[63]

McDonnell's strong-willed, intellectual Nora was offset by a particularly unpleasant Torvald. Nesbitt's creation was 'an enervated brute of an animal, and his voice was painfully monotonous. Even a selfish, narrow-minded prig daren't call his wife 'lark' and 'squirrel' in the same tone as [he] discusses his bank account!'[64]

Nesbitt and McDonnell's interpretation of *A Doll's House* seems similar to Charles Charrington and Janet Achurch's in 1889. The production that sparked the London Ibsen controversy seemed to onlookers 'less a play than a personal meeting – with people and issues that seized us and held us and wouldn't let us go'.[65] Dublin amateurs attempted a similar effect (albeit less successfully), hence Holloway's comments on the 'bad' (or simplistic) scenery and that '[n]ature was the keynote of the entire enthusiastic little company'.[66] Moreover, in both productions, Nora is more convincing as the New Woman ever-ready to leave her husband than as a pliant doll woman, while Torvald is a stage villain. In an early interview, Achurch suggested that Nora might return to 'try again the experiment of living with [Torvald] Helmer. But it will fail. That man is impossible, utterly impossible. She did right to leave him.'[67] Such an approach to *A Doll's House* may be simplistic;[68] however, it was instrumental in awakening the British public. By recruiting the audience's sympathy for the heroine who leaves her family, this production made audiences re-evaluate their belief in the sanctity of marriage and woman's place within the home.

Even though it resembled the 1889 London production in its conception, if not in its execution, the Dublin *Doll's House* proved a remarkably easy pill to swallow. As he was leaving the Molesworth Hall, Holloway heard

> a gentleman observe in a mystified manner to the lady who accompanied him: 'What are all the hubbub made about him, and calling him all sorts of bad names ...? I could see nothing wrong. His other plays must be worse?' 'I didn't think so', answered his fair companion; 'They are all conceived on the same lines.'[69]

As the couple went into the night, Holloway was left to meditate on the discrepancy between the public opinion of Ibsen in Dublin and the actual experience of his plays:

> Any who earnestly study his social dramas know that he is not the monster of inequity his traducers wish to make him out to be, and the public (who never think for themselves) take for granted that he must be without further inquiry. ... I am sure many were disappointed at not seeing something shocking in the play.[70]

Like *An Enemy of the People*, staged three years earlier, *A Doll's House* failed to confirm the rumours of Ibsen's immorality. 'How disappointed they must have been with *A Doll's House*, as their evil-searching minds had nothing to feed on in that way in the piece,' Holloway continued. 'Instead of filth they had presented before them an excellent moral lesson.'[71]

There may be several explanations as to why the play that started the Ibsen controversy in England was received with amused indifference in the more conservative Dublin. The amateur nature of the single performance is one. The first performance of *A Doll's House* in London (which was acted by amateurs in 1885, four years before the outbreak of the Ibsen wrangle) likewise produced very little reaction in the theatrical world. A better cast was needed, or at least one less dependent on the prompter, to launch the Ibsen boom in Ireland. And more people needed to see the production. Besides, it was simply too late for Dubliners who had been exposed to ten years of rumours of Ibsen's depravity to be shocked by his plays. That the controversy was truly over is demonstrated by the appearance of an article on *Little Eyolf* in the January 1897 issue of the *Dublin Review*. In that article, A. F. Spender qualified his objections to the play by acknowledging Ibsen's genius and praising *Hedda Gabler*, *Brand* and *Peer Gynt*. The article is symptomatic of the change in critical attitude to Ibsen. Some critical hostility remained and the English press still published complaints (often reprinted in the *Irish Times*) about the 'dull, tiresome, and often indelicate productions' of Ibsen's plays.[72] Yet, occasional conservative outbursts notwithstanding, Ibsen was by then accepted in England as a distinguished world dramatist. The Irish journals followed suit. Finally, Ibsen's problem play was not a novelty for audiences that had already seen plays influenced by Ibsen, such as Alfred Wing Pinero's *The Second Mrs Tanqueray* (first staged in Dublin in 1893) and Herman Sudermann's *Magda* (first seen in Dublin in 1896).

The Irish première of *A Doll's House* took place only a few months after Lady Gregory, Martyn and Yeats first discussed the possibility of establishing a literary theatre in Dublin. At that meeting, the view was advanced by Yeats and Martyn that in Dublin they would find an audience less sophisticated and therefore more receptive to their literary drama than the English public. Adrian Frazier has pointed out the erroneousness of Yeats's pastoral view of the Irish audiences. While Yeats hoped 'to find in Ireland an uncorrupted and imaginative audience trained to listen by its passion for oratory',[73] he in fact faced intelligent, critical urbanites who 'had seen at the Gaiety the best and worst of the global entertainment market'.[74] The reception of the Dublin Players' Club Ibsen experiment reinforces the point.

Dubliners resented having been forced into the position of London's cultural satellite. As Clery put it in 1898 in a 'Theatre – Its Educational Value', a paper read before the Literary and Historical Society of the University College Dublin: 'it is the most unsatisfying feature of the present day stage that there alone is Ireland consistently and unblushingly treated not as a country, but a province'.[75] When it came to Ibsen, Ireland's provincial status was felt particularly keenly, for English professional companies avoided bringing Ibsen to Ireland. There were five Ibsen productions in London in 1897: the New Century Theatre opened with *John Gabriel Borkman* on 3 May; a week later Charles Charrington, as the new manager of the resurrected Independent Theatre, launched five matinées of *A Doll's House* and *The Wild Duck*; and on 24 June he organised a private performance of *Ghosts*. Charrington's efforts also extended outside London. That year he produced *Ghosts* in Manchester and toured the provinces with *A Doll's House*. But Ireland was outside his range. Possibly, it was regarded as too provincial and Catholic to understand Ibsen. After all, Beerbohm Tree never again brought *An Enemy of the People* to Dublin following the disappointment of 1894.

While Yeats aimed to prove that 'Ireland is not the home of buffoonery and of easy sentiment, as it has been represented, but the home of an ancient idealism',[76] the Players' Club performance aimed to prove that Ireland, while viewed in England as a provincial backwater, was capable of enjoying the drama of ideas. Given Martyn's passionate interest in Ibsen and his possible involvement in the production, it is likely that the other founders of the Irish Literary Theatre knew that the change that they sought to bring from without had already been manifested within the Dublin community.

It was also around this time that Ibsen found one of his strongest supporters among the 'younger generation' of Dublin: James Joyce. It is uncertain whether Joyce had seen the 1897 production of *A Doll's House*. However, his discovery of Ibsen 'through the medium of hardly procured translations'[77] had occurred either, as Richard Ellmann believes, between 1897, which ended his 'period of piety' and his enrolment in University College in September 1898,[78] or, as Tysdahl believes, after the summer of 1898.[79] Given Joyce's familiarity with the Irish press, his interest in the theatre and the minutiae of Dublin popular culture, it is likely that he would have known about the Players' Club production even if he had not seen it. Yet there is no mention of it in *Stephen Hero* or, even more surprisingly, in Stanislaus Joyce's *My Brother's Keeper*. When, in 1903, the enthusiastic Padraic Colum asked his opinion about the recent revival of the Players' Club production of *A Doll's House*, Joyce replied curtly: 'Of course it will remain interesting, as a post-card written by Ibsen will remain interesting.'[80]

Joyce's passion for Ibsen was possessive. He gloried in opposition and jealously guarded his master from others. Clery's criticism of the problem play as a 'product of dilute Ibsenism' (in 'Theatre – Its Educational Value') was more welcome to Joyce than Francis Skeffington's avowed admiration of Ibsen.[81] Joyce impressed many students with the eloquence of his attack on Clery's paper, the night promptly entering student lore as Joyce's 'Ibsen Night'.[82] However, this incident also goes unmentioned in *Stephen Hero*. Instead, Joyce presents an exaggerated account of the antagonism and misunderstanding that greeted his paper 'Drama and Life' (read on 20 January 1900). In Joyce's epic of artistic martyrdom, individual failures were more important than collective victories. For such a man to admit that he was not Dublin's only apostle of Ibsen was impossible – hence his disregard for Players' Club *A Doll's House*.

The coincidence of the Irish première of *A Doll's House* with Joyce's discovery of Ibsen is an instance of Joyce's ability to reflect the concerns of his age through his individual experiences. In the mid-1890s, a change of direction occurred in the course of the Irish reception of Ibsen. Shortly after the commotion over the 1896 production of *Little Eyolf*, English papers lost interest in him. Subsequently, their power to affect Irish opinion of Ibsen diminished. At around the same time, the typical five-year period needed for the diffusion of new literature and drama from London to Dublin had passed. Dublin intellectuals, students and newspapermen grew more curious about the playwright who had so excited England. As his name began to be hea`rd more often in debates on Irish drama, Ireland responded to Ibsen as a country and not as a province.

2
Ibsen and the Early Abbey Tradition

Ibsen's early plays and the revival of Irish myths, 1899–1902

In September 1898, the critic and essayist John Eglinton (William Kirkpatrick Magee) and Yeats debated the future of Irish drama in the Dublin *Daily Express*. Eglinton proposed that a truly national drama should be based on the writer's personal experiences and must therefore be realistic. He was sceptical of the Irish legends as a proper subject for national drama, doubting 'whether the mere fact of Ireland having been the scene of these stories is enough to give an Irish writer much advantage over anyone else who is attracted by them'.[1] Dramatic works based on legends would be faithful neither to the lost beauty of the myth nor to the spirit of the modern age. 'Ireland must exchange the patriotism which looks back for the patriotism which looks forward,'[2] he insisted.

In defence of revivalism Yeats cited Wagner, 'whose dramas ... are becoming to Germany what the Greek Tragedies were to Greece', and Ibsen, 'whose *Peer Gynt* ... is not only "national literature" ... but the chief glory of "the national literature" of its country'.[3] Yeats also pointed out that Ibsen's *The Vikings at Helgeland* (which is, unlike the largely satirical *Peer Gynt*, a revivalist drama) was a 'great influence ... in the arts of Europe'.[4] In his reply, Eglinton declared his dislike for *Peer Gynt*, which he called '*Faust* in nubibus'.[5] He believed Ibsen's real strength lay in his realist dramas: 'Ibsen appears to have found himself in a drama which is not ideal drama, because neither in its form nor in its dominating ideas is it poetical, but which seems the nearest thing to a distinctive drama reached in this century.'[6]

This was not the first time that a debate on the appropriate subject of Irish drama was aired in the Irish press. In March 1895, the *New Ireland*

Review published William Barrett's article 'Irish Drama?' Like Eglinton, Barrett hoped that future Irish drama would be realistic. He was looking for an 'Irish Jones, Pinero, or Grundy': 'Studying life in the cities and villages, the man in the street, and the man at the plough, he will ... discover something which is characteristic of Ireland and Irishmen, and of no other country or people.'[7]

Barrett's article received several responses which appeared in the next issue of *New Ireland Review* under the heading 'Irish Drama: A Symposium'. Ibsen was mentioned, but in a different context from that in the Yeats–Eglinton debate. Surveying the shortcomings of dramatic literature of other countries, James A. Scanlan declared that 'Ibsen gives us works supposed to represent Norwegian and Scandinavian life, in which the characters converse on topics which the Apostle Paul tells us should not even be mentioned amongst men'.[8] The debate between Yeats and Eglinton is thus unusual in two respects: first, Ibsen was mentioned without sanctimony; and second, Ibsen's name was employed on both sides of the realist/romanticist divide.

Ibsen himself had once defended myth as an appropriate subject for drama and argued that 'to draw it up from its sea-depths, to study it on the plane of speculation, is not in any respect a violation of the sanctity of the poetry of myth ... [but] an essential phase in its ... development'.[9] He argued that the literature of the modern, reflective age might liberate the ideas that lie hidden in the naïve forms of the mythopoetic age. But this aspect of Ibsen's thought was unknown to Yeats and Eglinton, his sparse critical writings being unavailable in translation. To the majority of the English-speaking public, Ibsen was primarily the father of realist drama, the author of *A Doll's House*. Those who, like Yeats, knew of Ibsen's earlier romantic nationalist and poetic works were few in number. In 1901 William Archer estimated that among the English public 'ten people know Ibsen's prose plays for one who has read *Brand* or *Peer Gynt*'.[10] *The Vikings at Helgeland, Lady Inger of Ostrat* and *The Pretenders* languished in obscurity. In Ireland, the playwright was barely known and was associated almost exclusively with the London controversy. By foregrounding Ibsen's romanticist and revivalist works in the pages of a Dublin paper, Yeats opened new channels for his reception in Ireland.

William Larminie and 'AE' (the poet and artist George Russell) soon joined the debate. According to AE, the argument about romanticism and realism was really about literary nationalism and cosmopolitanism. He equated realism with the 'cosmopolitan spirit' that dispenses with what is 'distinctly national' in order to use the 'immense wealth of universal ideas' and engage the interest of a wider circle of readers. 'The Tolstois and

Ibsens', wrote AE, 'are conscious of addressing a European audience.'[11] AE dismissed Eglinton's contention that 'a national literature, or any literature of a genuine kind, is simply the outcome and expression of a strong interest in life itself'.[12] He proposed that the 'province of national literature' was to 'create the Ireland in the heart'.[13] Through the revival of heroic figures, the restoration of 'Cuculain, Fionn, Ossian, and Oscar' to the common imagination, the national writer would create an ideal of Ireland for which '[e]very Irishman works and makes sacrifices'.[14]

AE's reinterpretation of realism and romanticism as, respectively, cosmopolitanism and nationalism was to plague Irish literary discourse for many years. It provided the basis for future attacks on such Irish dramatists as Padraic Colum, Lennox Robinson and Sean O'Casey. Their nationalist critics would contend that not only were these realists wrong in exposing the flaws of the Irish people, but that the very form of their drama was somehow anti-national. AE's conclusion also further complicated Ibsen's image: he appeared at once as a realist, romanticist, cosmopolitan and national writer.

On 6 May 1899 members of the National Literary Society met at 6 Stephen's Green to hear Yeats speak on his latest public endeavour – the establishment, with Moore, Martyn and Lady Gregory, of the Irish Literary Theatre. Yeats started by saying that 'the promoters of the present movement wished to make a kind of ark in which the faithful few could take refuge until the tide of vulgarity sank' and that their objective was to 'spread enthusiasm for the legends and the great figures of Irish history'. [15] To the sound of applause, Yeats declared that in thus 'leaning upon the national feeling of the country' the founders of the theatre were 'doing what had been done in every country in Europe, but especially in Norway'.[16] Ibsen, 'a great European figure, about whom there were such endless disputes', said Yeats, 'produced dramas founded on the heroes and legends of Norway' and participated in a movement 'which in almost every way resembled the national literary movement that was going on in [Ireland]'.[17]

Yeats made the same point in the first issue of *Beltaine*, the magazine of the Irish Literary Theatre. It opened with the words: 'Norway has a great and successful school of contemporary drama, which grew out of a national literary movement very similar to that now going on in Ireland.'[18] An article on 'The Scandinavian Dramatists' by Charles Harold Herford (reprinted from the London *Daily Express*) was also included. It described Ibsen's involvement with Norwegian literary nationalism. The founders of the Irish Literary Theatre laboured hard to impress on the public the fact that their particular form of nationalism had found expression in another country. Moreover, in reviving Irish legends they had a famous predecessor who – and this was to be the main source of confusion – had since abandoned romantic nationalism and became a controversial and cosmopolitan writer.

Yeats's campaign attracted some enthusiasm, as well as a fair measure of bewilderment and resentment. But there was plenty of scope for humour too. The *Evening Herald* highlighted the inherent snobbery of Yeats's speech: 'in course of time ordinary playgoers will be educated up to the standard at which the Literary Theatre aims ... they will fully appreciate the praiseworthy efforts which the promoters are making namely to do for Ireland something like what has been done for the Scandinavian drama, which is thoroughly racy and national.'[19] The tongue-in-cheek attitude of this reporter contrasted with more direct criticisms. Writing in the Gaelic League journal *An Claidheamh Soluis*, the ardent nationalist (soon to found *The Leader*) D. P. Moran seized on Yeats's evocation of Ibsen as proof that 'as an "Irish" or "National" affair [the Irish Literary Theatre was] fixed on a false basis'.[20] The ILT catered for no other than the 'seonin' or West Briton, a 'Mr. Nobody ... who affects things which he does not understand, all things within the ordinary ken being necessary low ... Mr. Nobody from Dublin, who reads Ibsen and tries to persuade himself that he likes it [and who] wouldn't touch the [Gaelic] League with a forty-foot pole.'[21]

The first offerings of the Irish Literary Theatre, Martyn's *The Heather Field* and Yeats's *The Countess Cathleen*, must have struck the public as oddly inconsistent with Yeats's promotional speeches and articles. Instead of reviving the world of the saga as Ibsen had done in *The Vikings at Helgeland*, Yeats presented his audience with an Ireland populated with Catholics ever-ready to sell their souls to the devil and dependent on Protestant landowners for their spiritual salvation and material well-being. Devils freely roamed the land, along with fairies and angels. This was hardly a realistic image of Ireland in the sixteenth century or the nineteenth.[22] It was also a far cry from AE's 'Ireland of imagination' for which Irishmen were expected to make sacrifices.

As for Martyn's play, it struck some of the public as 'Ibsen with an Irish accent',[23] even though (as some critics have since noted) the play owes as much to Strindberg as it does to Ibsen.[24] Holloway delighted in the 'clever and splendidly characterized' play influenced by 'the great Norwegian dramatist'. *The Heather Field* reminded him of *Enemy of the People*, which he had seen in 1894.[25] The reviewer of the *Irish Times*, however, was less enthusiastic: 'Is it seriously put forward by the promoters of the Irish Literary Theatre that this country of ours, which has laughed in the midst of pain, where the joke has always reigned supreme is to be subjected to Ibsenism?'[26] The writer of this article contended that Martyn could 'do much better work ... if he forgets the Land Commission, the Board of Works, Drainage Loans and Ibsen, and applies his dramatic instinct to Irishmen and Irish women apart from land legislation and mortgages, neither of which ever made, and never will, an interesting or entertaining dialogue'.[27]

The Heather Field bore no relation to Ibsen's early plays, described by Yeats. It was modelled on the plays to which Ibsen owed his notoriety: *The Master Builder, The Wild Duck, Ghosts* and, to some degree, *An Enemy of the People*.[28] Yeats's words on Ibsen and the new theatre appeared to be false advertising.

The Irish Literary Theatre never became the Ibsenite-Celtic theatre of Yeats's 1899 articles and speeches, even though he continued to cultivate the idea of a close similarity between the Irish and the Norwegian Dramatic Revivals. As late as 1911, for instance, Yeats told a reporter that in creating the tradition of a folk drama, he and Lady Gregory were following in the footsteps of 'Ibsen and Bjørnson [who] said that to understand the peasant you must know the Sagas, and to understand the Sagas you must know the peasant'. [29] He added that the 'Abbey Theatre did not propose to stop at the peasant, and proposed to give plays, either romantic and poetical drama, like Ibsen's *Brand*, or studies of the small seaboard towns of Norway, like The *Enemy of the People* and *The Pillars of Society*'.[30] Yet in spite of these promises, it was not until 1923 that the Abbey actually staged an Ibsen play, by which time Yeats had withdrawn from the active running of the theatre.

Still, Yeats, Martyn and Moore of the Irish Literary Theatre drew more attention to Ibsen than either Beerbohm Tree in 1894 or the Players' Club in 1897. Without staging any of his plays, they engaged audiences in their contrasting views of Ibsen, challenged established attitudes to the playwright and made the subject of his relation to the Irish Literary Revival a focus of public interest. Yeats's speeches and articles on Ibsen, moreover, mark the beginning of what Tore Rem describes as 'the particular tension within the early Irish reception of Ibsen ... the dichotomy between the national writer and the international writer'.[31] Dubliners now had a choice among a variety of conflicting perceptions of Ibsen that emerged in the discourse on the Irish theatre. Was Ibsen primarily a realistic playwright whose influence on Irish writing was both inevitable and desirable? Was he a romantic playwright and a model patriot? Was he, a Norwegian writer, a forerunner of future Irish-language geniuses who would win world-wide fame although writing in their native tongue? Or was he the favourite playwright of the seonini, who liked him much as they liked all things imported from England? In the absence of the frame of reference that frequent productions of Ibsen's plays would have provided, conflicting ideas about the playwright and his significance for Irish literature continued to develop freely.

In 1901, James Joyce, who had hitherto supported the Irish Literary Theatre, made an unanticipated attack on its management in 'The Day of the Rabblement'. The pamphlet accused the theatre of betraying its mission of 'protest against the sterility and falsehood of modern stage'[32] by staging second-rate local plays instead of foreign masterpieces such as *Ghosts*. In addition to the reference to *Ghosts*, the pamphlet included two allusions to Ibsen. The image of a younger artist, a successor of Ibsen and Hauptmann who '[e]ven now that hour may be standing by the door',[33] echoed a line in Act 1 of *The Master Builder*; and Act 2 of *Peer Gynt* provided Joyce with a metaphor for the Catholic nationalists: 'The Irish Literary Theatre by its surrender to the trolls had cut itself from the line of advancement.'[34]

Hogan and Kilroy observe that '[i]n 1901, these judgments sounded harshly intolerant to the point of stupidity; now despite their ardour they do not seem unsound'.[35] To Frank Fay, Joyce's assertions seemed 'grossly unjust': 'Mr. Joyce sneers at Mr. Yeats, Mr. George Moore and Mr. Martyn; but sneering at these gentlemen has become so common that one wonders why Mr. Joyce should fall so low.' [36] Indeed, even though Joyce's position was diametrically opposed to that of the nationalists, his use of Ibsen's name was similar. Like Moran, Joyce used Ibsen's name as a stick with which to beat Yeats. Like Moran, Joyce equated Ibsen and continental drama with cosmopolitanism and art independent of nationalist propaganda or populist considerations. He implied, moreover, that foreign masterpieces, should they be produced, would cause a riot among the non-intellectual nationalist patrons of the theatre: '[T]he directors are shy of presenting Ibsen, Tolstoy or Hauptmaun [*sic*], where even *Countess Cathleen* is pronounced vicious and damnable.'[37]

In his reply, Fay insisted that should Joyce read *Samhain* (which in 1901 replaced *Beltaine* as the official organ of the Irish Literary Theatre) he would see that the directors were indeed hoping to produce foreign masterpieces. Through an allusion to *An Enemy of the People*, Fay pointed out to Joyce that his anger was misplaced:

> One would be glad to know in what way the Irish Literary Theatre has pandered to popularity. Is it by producing a play in Irish? [Douglas Hyde's *Casadh an tSugáin*] ... I have yet to learn that either the Irish Literary Theatre or the Irish Language movement is popular. Surely

they both represent the fight of the minority against the 'damned compact majority'.[38]

Ensuing events proved Joyce wrong. In 1903, Martyn and Moore produced *A Doll's House* at the Queen's and *Hedda Gabler* the following year. Also in 1903, Yeats vindicated himself from the accusation of pandering to popular tastes by staging *In the Shadow of the Glen*.

In the Shadow of the Glen and popular images of Ibsen, 1903

Performed on 8 October 1903, *In the Shadow of the Glen* drove Yeats's famous love, the Irish independence activist Maud Gonne, as well the actors Dudley Digges and Máire Quinn from the Irish National Theatre, infuriated the nationalist critics of *The Leader* and the *United Irishman* and upset its audience. Synge's Nora, who leaves her peasant cottage to wander the land with a tramp, seemed an extravagant fabrication rather than 'a bit of real Irish life'.[39] Holloway recalls that while most present 'applauded the ... literary merits of the play, [they] had little to say in favour of the nature of the "story" contained therein'.[40]

The nationalist press showed less reserve than the audience. The editor of the *United Irishman*, Arthur Griffith, denounced *In the Shadow of the Glen* as a libel on the Irish character. 'Nora Burke', Griffith insisted, 'is a Lie'. 'Men and women in Ireland marry lacking love, and live mostly in a dull level of amity. Sometimes they do not – sometimes she dies of a broken heart – but she does not go away with the Tramp.'[41] While Griffith pointed to *The Decameron* as the source of the play, Arthur Clery of *The Leader* saw a direct connection between *In the Shadow of the Glen* and *A Doll's House*. '[T]he play is an evil compound of Ibsen and Boucicault', he declared, '[t]hat it should be put forward as true picture of Irish existence and worse still as an embodiment of Irish reflections on life, is a species of misrepresentation that cannot be tolerated'.[42] 'There is every opening for a healthy National Theatre in Ireland', Clery insisted in a later article; 'there is none for Irish Ibsenite propaganda.'[43]

Indeed, in 1903, the Ibsenite resonance of Nora Burke's name was impossible to miss. With the assistance of Martyn, the Players' Club produced *A Doll's House* twice that year, on 16 April in the Antient Concert Rooms, and on 25–27 June at the Queen's Theatre. On the latter occasion Holloway complained that he had never 'sat in a more disturbing and unruly audience ... "Savages" was the only title applicable to most of them'.[44] The audience drowned the actors' words with their whistling, disrespectful laughter and chatter. Nervous attendants scuttled to and fro, banging doors and distracting those few who attempted to enjoy the play. Police tried to help, but only added to the general commotion.[45]

The audience was not malicious – '[h]earty applause followed the fall of the curtain after each act'[46] – but they were restless and bored. They were accustomed to the Queen's staple fare of musical comedy and patriotic melodrama and were bent on getting an evening's enjoyment, albeit on this occasion at the expense of the actors. Possibly some were drawn to the theatre by newspaper reports of the highly praised but sparsely attended Madame Rejane's French production of *A Doll's House*, performed at the Theatre Royal only a week earlier, on 18 June.

The unprecedented 'profusion' of Ibsen productions on the Dublin stage coincided with the increased interest in his works among the Irish *literati*. Yeats (and possibly Synge) attended the Incorporate Stage Society's London production of *When We Dead Awaken* (staged on 25 and 26 January 1903).[47] In March 1903, Joyce published a review of Ibsen's early work *Catilina*. In April, Martyn and Moore were busy fighting at the Players' Club rehearsals of *A Doll's House*, while Yeats was negotiating the inclusion of his verses in Edward Gordon Craig's forthcoming London production of *The Vikings at Helgeland*.[48] 'More than any ancient or modern, Ibsen was then the exemplar,' wrote Padraic Colum, who recalled Martyn's fascination with *The Wild Duck*, Yeats's guarded praise for Ibsen in the original (which he had never read), Joyce's rejection of *A Doll's House* as a mere postcard and Moore's exclamations on the night of the Dublin Players' production: 'Shakespeare, Sophocles! What are they to this man?'[49]

It was evident to the Ulster critic Robert Lynd that Ireland was undergoing the process of 'Ibsenising'. 'In the chaos that followed the death of Parnell, the Irish brain began to reassert itself',[50] he wrote, noting that, with the publication of *Where There Is Nothing* (October 1902), Yeats had joined the Ibsenites' ranks headed by Moore and Martyn. Moore's *The Untilled Field* (June 1903) was conceived as an imitation of Turgenev's *A Sportsman's Sketches*. However, Maurice Joy, who reviewed the book for the *United Irishman*, detected an indebtedness to Ibsen and supplemented his interpretation of the collection with a phrase from *Ghosts*: 'All the stories tend towards the one conclusion, that Ireland is suffering from a National euthanasia, dying away without a struggle either in emigration or in apathy at home, because the "joy of life" is absent.'[51] Joy's mild objection to Moore's realism was counterbalanced by his weariness at 'the tendency for unreality of the Anglo-Irish Literary Movement'.[52] The conservative and nationalist Joy begrudgingly welcomed modernity and Ibsenism, citing Frederick Ryan's *The Laying of the Foundations* (which was staged by the Irish Literary Theatre in 1902) as a particularly successful alternative to the Celtic twilight visions of Ireland.

There is a myth in the history of the Revival that the controversy over Synge's plays, like the English controversy over Ibsen, was related to his realism. In her autobiography *The Splendid Years*, the Abbey actress Máire Nic Shiubhlaigh writes of *In the Shadow of the Glen* as 'the first of the Irish "realist" dramas'.[53] She believed that Synge offended his critics by refusing to romanticise the peasantry:

> Ireland was on the threshold of a renaissance. Everybody, writer, politician, artist, was at pains to eulogise over the beauty of the Irish character. The advent of a comparatively unknown writer who painted an unpleasant if realistic picture of the peasantry at such a time was, to say the least unwelcome.[54]

Similarly, Yeats, writing to the American supporter of the Irish theatre, John Quinn, predicted that a fight for Synge would 'be ... like that over the first realistic plays of Ibsen'.[55]

It is tempting to see Synge as the first Irish realist and to compare the Irish controversy over Nora Burke to the English wrangle over Nora Helmer. Yet Synge was not Ibsen's first ambassador to Ireland. He was preceded by Martyn and Ryan, whose *The Heather Field* and *The Laying of the Foundations* were closely modelled on Ibsen's dramas yet drew less opposition than *In the Shadow of the Glen*. The contrast between the hostile reviews of Synge's play and the commendatory reviews of the three 1903 productions of *A Doll's House* likewise indicates that it was not merely Synge's realism or his alleged Ibsenism that offended his nationalist critics. Arthur Griffith, who was so bitterly opposed to *In the Shadow of the Glen*, described *A Doll's House* as 'Ibsen's great play' and praised the Dublin Players for staging it.[56] Notably, the part of Dr Rank in that production was played by Dudley Digges, who had resigned, along with Máire Quinn, from the Irish National Theatre Society over the production of *In the Shadow of the Glen*. What did Synge do in *In the Shadow of the Glen* that was more controversial than staging *A Doll's House* or writing *The Laying of the Foundations*? Why did Nora Burke seem more of a 'lie' than Nora Helmer or even Carden Tyrell in Martyn's *The Heather Field*?

Synge's play was extensively examined in the nationalist press; by contrast *A Doll's House* was reviewed in the Irish dailies. (Generally the

Leader, An Claidheamh Soluis and the *United Irishman* abstained from commenting on the productions of Ibsen's plays, even though nationalist journalists attended these performances.) The Irish play was regarded as a literary aberration, while Ibsen's play was seen as a cultural curiosity – an insight into the aberrant life of Norwegian families. In a review of Rejane's *La Maison de Poupée*, for instance, the critic of the *Dublin Evening Mail* commented:

> We are not accustomed in these temperate countries to see the domestic happiness of an agreeable family sacrificed on the altar of an attack of nerves. The denouement leaves the 'plain man' altogether out of sympathy with Nora, and altogether in sympathy with her forsaken children and with that 'plain man' and rather decent fellow, her husband.[57]

Similarly, the *Irish Times*, in a review of the Dublin Players' version of the play, called Nora 'the well meaning but somewhat imprudent wife of Helmer'.[58] Ibsen's status as a classic international author allowed the people to view the play with detachment, to judge it on its artistic merits and to overlook the social problems it addressed. The *Irish Times'* approach to *A Doll's House* was representative:

> Ibsen ... has taken as his themes social and moral problems, and has worked them out according to his own system of ethics in a series of dialogues, no doubt ingeniously conceived and admirably bound together, but at the same time unreal and unconvincing.[59]

Ibsen's Norwegian characters were allowed to be eccentric, whereas Synge's Irish characters were expected to behave according to idealised Irish moral standards. The contrasting reception of *A Doll's House* and *In the Shadow of the Glen* suggests that rural Ireland was seen as profoundly different from the bourgeois society of the Continent.

It is also important to note that, unlike Ryan or Martyn, Synge did not, in fact, imitate Ibsen. *In the Shadow of the Glen* is closer to the various early parodies of *A Doll's House* than to Ibsen's play. Synge's Nora does not go alone, leaving a beloved husband on discovering the falsity of her marriage. She is thrown out of her house by a drunkard whom she had married for security, and leaves with a tramp because her lover has also rejected her. In fact, the connection between *In the Shadow of the Glen* and *A Doll's House* only becomes apparent because of Nora Burke's name. Synge's contemporaries saw her name as a provocative admission of the Continental origins of his writing. Modern critics also see Synge's choice of name as a point of departure to discuss the plays' common themes: their exploration of the idea of freedom and their feminism.[60] Given Synge's life-long interest in Ibsen (he read most of his plays in German and French translations and saw at least one of them on stage)[61] and the fact that *A Doll's House* had been performed three times in Dublin only a few months earlier *In the Shadow of the Glen*, it is indeed possible that the allusion is deliberate. It allowed Synge to confront his reservation about using the Irish countryside as a setting for his plays, to challenge the artistic norms of the Irish Revival and to shatter the idealistic expectations of contemporary audiences.

It is possible that by naming his peasant heroine after Ibsen's Nora, Synge was attempting to forge a link between the world of the peasantry and the metropolitan societies of England, France and Germany. *In the Shadow of the Glen* dramatises one of the central themes of Synge's *The Aran Islands* – the confrontation between two different modes of experiencing life: the emotional and the physical. On the islands, Synge's loneliness was caused by an inability to make the islanders understand the depth and significance of his life, lived primarily on the emotional and intellectual plane. The primitive quality of life on Inishmaan challenged Synge's habitual romanticism and *fin-de-siècle* melancholy. His lifestyle seemed inadequate, undignified and incomprehensible. He was like a 'waif among the people':[62] 'I can feel more with them than they can feel with me.'[63] Albeit set in Wicklow rather than the Aran Islands, *In the Shadow of the Glen* is Synge's experiment in bringing the world of the European cities closer to the world of the Irish peasantry. As she leaves her husband, the peasant Nora begins to resemble her Continental namesake. Synge thus imagines the Irish countryside into closer affinity with his city-bred worldview.

The Ibsenite name of the heroine is a device that allows Synge to establish a form of communication between the peasant way of life and that of the upper middle classes. On the one hand, *In the Shadow of the Glen* satirises the world of *A Doll's House*. Nora Helmer's unhappiness appears almost ridiculous in comparison to the misery of Nora Burke's existence. The woman whose husband pretends to be dead to spy on her would hardly be able to understand a woman who leaves a comfortable house and a good provider because her marriage is supposedly based on a lie. On the other hand, *A Doll's House* serves as a point of reference within Synge's play. Through the Ibsenite allusion, he implies that false standards, duplicity and broken marriages are not unique to the bourgeoisie. In this one-act play, Synge achieved what he had found difficult on

Inishmaan. The play discloses the possibility of humorous communication between the world of the metropolis, symbolised by Ibsen, and the world of the peasantry. Each way of life, the emotional, and the physical, is parodied, analysed and ultimately understood by the other.

Possibly, it was Synge's rejection of the widely accepted belief in the clear distinctions between the world of Irish peasantry and that of the city that so infuriated his critics. They dreaded Synge's play even more than Yeats's early plans to stage Ibsen's plays. In 1901 Moran explained his objection: 'talking of performing the masterpieces of the world to the debilitated Irishman of to-day, to the respectable traders of Khaki Cork, to the huxters of Dublin, to the resolution mongers all over the country is only talking of further provincialising the country'.[64] The fear that diffusion of continental works might be damaging to the country was often expressed in the nationalist press. In a 1903 article entitled 'Immoral Literature at Popular Prices', Hugh Kennedy, who would later become Chief Justice of the Irish Free State, urged a ban on sixpenny 'Rationalist' publications with such titles as 'The Riddle of the Universe', 'The Question of Human Origins', 'The Origin of the Idea of Religion', 'The Ape's Parentage to Man' and, notably, 'A Norse Playwright's Way out of Old Difficulties'.[65] The last title appears to be Kennedy's satirical reference to Shaw's *The Quintessence of Ibsenism*. Kennedy explained that his objection to the publication of these works and French novels was not based on their literary merits:

> it may be that one of these novels is a masterpiece ... I, who am not a Frenchman, do not venture to criticise it as a work of French literature. But it has been translated into English and distributed at a popular price in Ireland, and therefore I, an Irishman, have something to say to it.[66]

Performing *In the Shadow of the Glen* was a worse offence than popularising Ibsen's ideas. In this play, Synge presented Irish peasant life as already as impure as the world of Ibsen's drama.

Kennedy and Moran were not alone in the belief that patriotism should override artistic considerations and that Ireland was not ready for continental ideas. Synge's closest friend, Stephen MacKenna, expressed a similar concern in a letter written a few months after the production of *In the Shadow of the Glen*:

> I do not know which of yez is in the right. You should be free as an artist ... whether you should be played I do not know ... I like the

> philistine idea of a purely fantastic unmodern ... ideal, breezy – spring-dayish Cuchulainoid etc. national theatre ... I believe in the ripeness and unripeness of nations and class Ireland blessedly unripe ... Give us our own literary nationhood first, then let us rise to our frieze-clad Ibsens. (I know of course, you hate the word Ibsen ...) I would like to see your play in book form, not on boards ... not for myself, but for the people ... The stage might regenerate Ireland, used Cuchulainly.[67]

For MacKenna, as for Moran and Kennedy, the Irish people and Nora Helmer existed on different planes of consciousness. Synge, however, refused to believe in the immature purity of Irish public: 'The Dublin audiences who see Mde Rejane in Ibsen, Mrs P. Campbell in Sudermann, Olga Nethersloe in Sappho etc., are hardly blessedly unripe.'[68] Yes, the Irish countryside was different from the city, but Synge did not see why this should prevent productions of his plays: 'Do you think the country people of Norway are much less blessedly unripe than the Irish?' he asked MacKenna:

> If they are not, should Ibsen never have been played in Norway, and therefore never have become an efficient dramatist? Do you think that because the people I have met with in the valleys of Wurzburg and the Rhein are quite as unripe as those of Wicklow or Kerry, that Sudermann and Hauptman [*sic*] should be driven from the boards of Berlin?[69]

The false belief in the unripeness of the Irish audience has its roots in Yeats's 1899 speeches and articles promoting the Irish Literary Theatre. While addressing a city audience, trained in modern drama, Yeats contended that the theatre would educate and re-nationalise the imaginative and naïve people of Ireland. By 1903, this idea has become entrenched in the public imagination. For the Dublin nationalists, Nicholas Grene points out, 'the very concept of a nation involved an idealising vision of the difference between their own modern middle-class lives and a pure, crimeless peasantry of the West of Ireland'.[70] The theatre was expected to act as a one-way channel of communication between the countryside and the city. Dublin audiences required revivalist plays to inspire them through the idealised image of the countryside. What Synge did in *In the Shadow of the Glen* (and later in *The Playboy*) was just the opposite. The countryside is presented as an imaginary place where city-bred ideas such as the Ibsenian notion of individual responsibility and feminism are tried out. Synge's play is not a critique or indeed an accurate representation of Wicklow life. Nor is it a problem play. The problem it dramatises is not a social but an aesthetic one. It is an experiment in revivalist imagination and demonstrates to the audience that one cannot and should not abandon modern ideas as one approaches peasant life. As Gregory Castle explains: 'Synge's attempt to translate traditional folklore into stage drama altered the nature of the dialogue by suggesting that the crucial issue was not the *right* representation but rather the *right to represent*'.[71]

Critical hostility to Synge's Nora was thus not merely an echo of Ibsenphobia; nor was Synge's play, as MacKenna implied, an Ibsenite experiment in a rural setting. *In the Shadow of the Glen* was one of the first revisionist works of the Irish Revival as well as a parodic inquiry into Ibsen's ideas. Synge's mature reassessment of the Revival, however, was rejected because of the critics' belief in the naivety of the audience and the insufficient development of the movement.

The inconsistent Ibsenism of W. B. Yeats, 1902–6

Most critical barbs flung during the *In the Shadow of the Glen* affair (as well as the *Playboy* riots which it prefigured) were aimed not at the play's author but at its producer and defender, Yeats.[72] *In the Shadow of the Glen* shared some problematic aspects with the first plays staged by the Irish Literary Theatre. Like *The Countess Cathleen*, it presented an allegedly false picture of Irish life and, like *The Heather Field*, it alluded to Ibsen. Moreover, Synge might have given the impression that he was following Yeats's controversial advice to the young Irish playwrights: 'If Irish dramatists had studied the romantic plays of Ibsen, the one great master the modern stage has produced, they would not have sent the Irish Literary Theatre imitations of Boucicault, who has no relation to Literature,' Yeats wrote in 1901, noting that '[w]e Irish ... have ... far greater need of the severe discipline of French and Scandinavian drama than of Shakespeare's luxuriance'.[73] Through his frequent praise of Ibsen, Yeats had contributed to what the playwright and critic W. P. Ryan perceived as an Irish obsession with Ibsen: 'I am getting just a little bit weary of the blessed word Scandinavia,' he wrote in a 1903 review of Synge's *Riders to the Sea* and Hyde's *Teach na mBocht* (*The Poorhouse*). 'Some of our literary friends point every moral and adorn every tale by something from Scandinavia ... Yet, it is better that even now our writers should endeavour to give us the life of Ireland and of their own souls in drama rather than try, with the best intentions, to Norwegianise us.'[74]

In his history of the Abbey Theatre, Lennox Robinson writes of Yeats's resistance to his own attempts to stage Ibsen's plays. Apparently oblivious to Yeats's frequent praises of the Norwegian playwright, Robinson says simply: 'Yeats hated Ibsen'.[75] Elsewhere, Robinson suggests that Yeats and Synge's dislike of Ibsen's 'flat and colourless dialogue' was due to their insufficient knowledge of his works: '[Synge] and Yeats cannot have been aware of *Peer Gynt*; compared with its fantasy and poetry, *The Playboy* itself seems a little pallid.'[76]

Robinson was wrong. Yeats's first article on Ibsen appeared in 1894. It was a review of a verse translation of *Brand* by F. E. Garrett. Yeats quotes from Garrett's translation and compares it to the earlier versions by William Wilson (1891) and C. H. Herford (1894). He alludes to *Peer Gynt* and refers to recent critical judgements of that work. Yeats makes clear his preference for Ibsen the poet, rather than the author of the realistic plays. He does not, however, fully condemn the realistic plays: 'because prose is more syllogistic than poetry and because the theorist and the preacher have devoured the land like the locust, the later and less imaginative though *profoundly interesting* plays have been acted and expounded to the neglect of the works of his prime'.[77] Yeats knew his Ibsen; his preference for the two dramatic poems, as well as the earlier historical dramas, was an informed choice.

Padraic Colum, whose dramatic talents came to Yeats's attention in 1902, was in a sense a forerunner of Robinson. Like Robinson, Colum was a devotee of Ibsen and a realistic playwright. He was also one of several young men of talent – Joyce, Robinson, and later O'Casey – to be 'fostered' by Yeats and Lady Gregory. At Christmas 1902, Yeats made Colum a present of a volume of Archer's translations of Ibsen's early plays, *Lady Inger of Ostrat, The Vikings at Helgeland* and *The Pretenders*. In the note inserted in the front cover of the book, he urged the young playwright 'to make a real good study of *Lady Inger*' and to read *The Pretenders*, 'a very fine play, but ... not so fine as *Lady Inger*'.[78] Nonetheless, the image of Yeats as someone who hated Ibsen was passed on to future historians while Yeats, the Ibsenite proselytiser, is forgotten. Thus Jerry Nolan, in his recent study of Edward Martyn, asserts that '[f]or Yeats, Ibsen was little more than an effective journalist'.[79]

Yeats's remarks on Ibsen range from sincere expressions of admiration to equally sincere articulations of distaste. As the well-known story in *The Trembling of the Veil* suggests, Yeats's attitude to Ibsen fluctuated according to external circumstances and public opinion.[80] Yeats tells how at a performance of *A Doll's House* at the Royalty Theatre, Deane Street in 1893,[81] he could scarcely overcome his revulsion: 'art is art because it is not nature', he kept murmuring to himself. His opinion would have remained hostile had not a 'washerwoman' (who, as Tracy C. Davis has pointed out, had probably thought the play would be suitable for the small child that was with her)[82] 'said in a very loud voice: "Timmy, if you promise to go home at once, we'll leave now"'. After the play was over a certain critic grumbled: 'what is it but a series of conversations terminated by an accident?' While he 'hated the play', Yeats writes that he became convinced that while 'Ibsen and I had not the same friends ... we had the same enemies'. Yeats admitted that his generation could not 'escape' Ibsen – as soon as they were available in English,[83] he purchased Ibsen's collected works and studied the plays on his travels around Ireland.

This was not the only time that Yeats let his enemies' opinions influence his attitude to Ibsen. In 1904, readers of *Samhain*, who had been accustomed to Yeats's exaltation of the Scandinavian theatre 'where the mind goes to be liberated',[84] would have been puzzled by the following remark:

> Ibsen has sincerity and logic beyond any writer of our time, and we are all seeking to learn them at his hands; but is he not a good deal less than the greatest of all times, because he lacks beautiful and vivid language?[85]

In a direct contradiction of his earlier assessment of Ibsen as the 'one great master of modern stage',[86] Yeats now described his art as 'terrible, satirical, inhuman'.[87] What seems to have caused this abrupt attack on Ibsen was an article on 'Stage Management in the Irish National Theatre' by George Moore, published in September 1904 in the anticlerical journal *Dana*.

In this article Moore suggested that the supposedly unprofessional manager of the Abbey Theatre, Frank Fay, should learn from the founder of the French Théâtre Libre, André Antoine. To explain that '[w]ords are dependent on the position of the actor on the stage',[88] Moore added a description of a scene from *Ghosts* in which Oswald asks his mother to poison him and says (in answer to her protestations 'I who gave you life'): 'a nice kind of life you gave me.'[89] 'To speak these lines rising destroys the author's meaning', wrote Moore. 'The lines should be spoken pensively, looking across the room, almost as one speaking in a dream: "A nice kind of life it was that you gave me."'[90]

The pseudonym 'Paul Ruttledge' that Moore chose for the occasion indicates that the overt criticism of Fay's staging methods was also an implicit attack on Yeats. Paul Ruttledge is the protagonist of *Where There Is Nothing* (1902), a play that, Moore claimed, was based on his own original idea and a lengthy draft and should not have been published under Yeats's name. The pseudonym is symbolic of the rift that had occurred between the one-time dramatic collaborators and co-founders of the Irish Literary Theatre. Through a contrast between Fay's stage management and that of Antoine, Moore suggested that, as president of the National Theatre Society, Yeats betrayed the ideal of the Irish theatre movement. In the 1899 issue of *Beltaine* Yeats had described Antoine's Théâtre Libre and the Independent Theatre as 'associations ... [that], in the face of violent opposition, have trained actors who have become famous, and have had a powerful influence even upon those plays which are written to please as many people as possible'.[91] He declared, moreover, that

> the Irish Literary Theatre will attempt to do in Dublin something of what has been done in London and Paris ... The plays will differ from those produced by associations of men of letters in London and in Paris, because times have changed, and because the intellect of Ireland is romantic and spiritual rather than scientific and analytical, but they will have as little of a commercial ambition.[92]

Yeats's vilification of Ibsen in 'The Play the Player and the Scene' in the 1904 issue of *Samhain* was a reply to Moore. He emphasised that telling Fay 'to study the stage management of Antoine ... is like telling a good Catholic to take his theology from Luther'. Yeats then attacked realistic stagecraft, dramatic realism, and Ibsen's *Ghosts*:

> At the first performance of *Ghosts* I could not escape from an illusion unaccountable to me at the time. All the characters seemed to be less than life-size; the stage, though it was but the little Royalty stage, seemed larger than I had ever seen it. Little whimpering puppets moved here and there in the middle of that great abyss. Why did they not speak out with louder voices or move with freer gestures? What was it that weighed upon their souls perpetually? Certainly they were all in prison, and yet there was no prison. ... May not such art, terrible, satirical, inhuman, be the medicine of great cities, where nobody is ever alone with his own strength?[93]

Moore, however, was not the only reason for the change in Yeats's attitude to Ibsen. In the same article, Yeats writes of his hope 'to rediscover an art of the theatre that shall be joyful, fantastic, extravagant, whimsical, beautiful, resonant and altogether reckless'.[94] If this is not an actual reference to Synge, it is a statement that reveals the reasons for Yeats's deep fascination with that playwright.

In the introductory note distributed at the première of *The Playboy of the Western World* in 1907, Synge pointed out the superiority of Elizabethan idiom over modern speech, and accused Ibsen and Zola of 'dealing with the reality of life in joyless and pallid words'.[95] The ideas expressed in Synge's preface first appear in the 1904 *Samhain* article, where in a reversal to his 1901 advice to young playwrights to study Ibsen rather than Shakespeare, Yeats points out that Ibsen does not possess the vivid beauty of the Elizabethan language.[96] In the 1905 issue of *Samhain*, Yeats again notes that 'it is always Shakespeare or Sophocles, and not Ibsen, that makes us say "how true, how often I have felt as that man feels" or "how intimately I have come to know those people on the stage"'.[97] Was it Synge who in 1904 persuaded Yeats to go back on his earlier advice to the young playwrights and praise the Elizabethans? Or was it Yeats who inspired *The Playboy*'s introductory note?

The poet Ella Young suggested in her memoir that at least some ideas in Synge's introduction can be attributed to Yeats: 'Everyone would have taken *The Playboy* as an extravaganza, a fantasy, if Yeats had not prevailed upon Synge to write a little notice explaining that the play represented real life in the Gaelic parts of Ireland, studied at first hand by the author.'[98] Whether or not Young is a reliable source in this instance, Synge and Yeats did influence each other, and Yeats's revised attitude to Ibsen in 1904 was a result of this collaboration.

During the *Playboy* riots '[t]he stage became the spectators and the audience the players'.[99] To his surprise, Yeats found himself in the role of a character in an Ibsen play – an enemy of the people. The author of the satirical piece entitled 'Aping Ibsen at the Abbey' poked fun at Yeats's (and Synge's) professed dislike of dramatic realism, suggesting that the riots were a better play than anything Yeats had produced. 'Messrs. Yeats and Synge have out-Ibsened Ibsen', he wrote,

> the realistic situations when some one in the audience whispers 'rotten!' and the glorious charge of the police and the delightful change of scene, at a wave of W. B.'s hand, to the Police Courts and the mirth-provoking magistrate, with his 'forty shillings or a month!' must be ranked among the dramatic wonders of the age.[100]

'No, William Butler', the critic continued, 'never in your most glorious "Countess-Cathleen-Pot-o'broth" nebulous incoherence did you attain the transcendent attitude on which your latest performance has pinnacled you.'[101]

From *Hedda Gabler* to *The Player Queen*: the transformations of Yeats's attitude to dramatic realism, 1907

On 24 October 1907, nine months after the *Playboy* riots, Mrs Patrick Campbell, a star of the English stage, presented *Hedda Gabler* at the Gaiety Theatre. 'All literary Dublin' was present, Holloway observed; '[n]o matter where your eye rested, there was some one you knew who "carried the literary bee in their bonnet". Ibsen had the same effect of attracting them, as the summer has on flies; so they all were there.'[102] Sitting in the front row next to Holloway was Fred Ryan, one-time secretary of the Irish Literary Theatre and author of one of the earliest Irish Ibsenite plays, *The Laying of the Foundations*. Frank Fay 'slipped in his gloomy way'[103] and found himself a seat behind a pillar. In the top box, on the right, Holloway could see Synge's fiancée, Molly Allgood, in the company of James Starkey and Mary Walker, who had a year earlier left the Abbey for the Theatre of Ireland. Their colleague George Nesbitt, who had played Lovborg in the Players' Club production of *Hedda Gabler* in 1904, occupied the second row of the upper circle. And further to the back loomed Arthur Clery; evidently his scorn of 'Irish Ibsenite propaganda' did not stop him from attending an Ibsen play.

As he was running down the Gaiety stairs, J. H. Cox of the *Irish Independent* overheard three reactions to the play:

> An elderly lady said: 'I was never so bored in all my life'. A gentleman declared to somebody – 'I call it a perfectly idiotic piece – perfectly idiotic'. Lastly, I overheard – very wrong of me, of course – Mr. W. B. Yeats remarking: – 'It's one of the best of Ibsen's plays – but you have to get used to his methods'.[104]

Yeats's conflicting remarks on Ibsen made his attitude to the playwright a subject of some public curiosity. Moreover, there was an apparent discrepancy between his position as an artist and his actions as a director of his theatre. The arch-romanticist and opponent of realism, Yeats became known as a pioneer of Irish Ibsenism through his support of Synge, and indeed Ryan, Colum and William Boyle (whom Griffith commended for 'suggest[ing] what an Irish Ibsen might be').[105] Not long before that, Yeats had compared the *Playboy* riots to the controversial reception of Ibsen's plays, saying that 'Ibsen's *League of Youth* created a most powerful uproar when first produced, but eventually it became the most popular of all the Norwegian's plays'.[106] It is no wonder that Yeats's pronouncements and actions were closely monitored by the press during Mrs Campbell's visit to Dublin. The public wanted to know whether the romantic poet approved of the realistic plays. They also wanted to hear his answer to the question which the *Freeman's Journal* reporter asked Mrs Campbell: '[Was] the Abbey theatre likely to go as far as Ibsen has gone?'[107] They were curious to know whether Yeats's ambition to surpass Ibsen's achievement could be reconciled with his position as an Irish Revivalist.

At the end of the actress's visit, the *Irish Times*' 'Books of the Week' section advertised *Kathleen Ní Houlihan* (6d) next to *Hedda Gabler* (1s 3d) and Pinero's *The Second Mrs Tanqueray* also performed by Mrs Campbell (1s 3d). Plays by Yeats and Ibsen displayed side by side in Dublin bookshops provided a fitting conclusion to the week-long contest between romanticism and realism. Arriving in Dublin on 22 October, Mrs Campbell gave four problem plays that had once shocked the English audiences: Pinero's *Notorious Mrs Ebbsmith* and *The Second Mrs Tanqueray*, Sudermann's *Magda* and Ibsen's *Hedda Gabler*. On 25 October, the actress was invited to a special 'professional matinée' at the Abbey. The plays shown were *The Gaol Gate, Spreading the News, Kathleen Ní Houlihan* and *In the Shadow of the Glen*. During the entr'acte, Mrs Campbell announced that she greatly admired the plays and that she had 'asked Mr. Yeats and Lady Gregory to be allowed to play on the Abbey boards, in an Irish play'.[108] At the end of the production, Yeats appeared on stage to announce that Mrs Campbell had promised to return to Ireland the following year time to perform in his *Deirdre*.

It is plausible that Yeats felt that by converting an Ibsenite actress to romanticism, by transforming Hedda into Deirdre, he would achieve a symbolic victory over Ibsen and, by implication, over realist drama. Indeed, Campbell's performance in *Deirdre* (a year later on 7 November 1908) was a greater success with the audience than *Hedda Gabler*. Holloway, who was 'bored to death' at the Ibsen play, remarked that the applause was 'not general or very enthusiastic'.[109] The only positive review was from Colum. *Hedda Gabler* was denounced by most as 'an unpleasant play about an irritating and abnormal woman'.[110] By contrast, Yeats's tragedy, which also ends with the heroine's suicide, received extensive applause and commendatory reviews. It was described as Yeats's 'masterpiece', 'his best achievement in dramatic construction'.[111] It 'put new life into the Irish dramatic movement'.[112]

Yeats seemed to have triumphed over Ibsen and his dramatic followers. He rescued Mrs Campbell from insipid realism (he once described her as a 'volcano cooking eggs')[113] and gave her a role that suited her passionate personality.

However, the victory was not complete. Several contemporary reviewers noticed that Yeats failed to escape Ibsen's influence completely. Thus a scornful review of *The Unicorn from the Stars* (performed on 21 November 1907) detected the play's similarity to *Brand*, 'from whom Mr. Yeats has consciously or unconsciously absorbed a good deal'.[114] *Deirdre*, moreover, reminded Francis Sheehy-Skeffington of 'Ibsen in its fastening on the closing scene of Deirdre's history. Like Ibsen's play it is really a fifth act.'[115]

In late 1907, after seeing Mrs Campbell in *Hedda Gabler*, and inspired by her offer to play Deirdre, Yeats began writing what he originally intended as another verse tragedy for the actress, but which eventually emerged as *The Player Queen*. This play, which was fifteen years in the writing, blends the circumstances of Mrs Campbell's visit to Dublin with the plot of *Hedda Gabler*.

The play revolves around a fight between two married members of a travelling theatre. Decima, the leading lady of the company, is enraged when the poet Septimus (in earlier drafts called Martin) casts her as a stubborn old woman in an uninspiring play about Noah's ark. Decima refuses to act unless she is given a role that suits her passionate and ambitious personality. 'The only part in the world I can play,' she declares, 'is a great queen's part.'[116] Yeats's conception of Decima as a headstrong, self-enamoured woman owes much to his experience of working with Mrs Campbell. The Abbey actor Gabriel Fallon recalls how Yeats described Mrs Campbell 'as having an ego like a raging tooth and spoke of her habit of throwing tantrums at rehearsals'.[117] However, in the quarrel between Septimus and Decima, Yeats inverted the situation in which he found himself with Mrs Campbell. In the play, the poet tries to force a realistic role on the actress who longs to restore romanticism to the stage. In the final version, Decima refuses to play Noah's wife out of personal vanity – she had sworn that 'she would rather drown herself than play a woman older than thirty'.[118] In earlier drafts, the obstacle is not merely Decima's pride but her abhorrence of dramatic realism. She objects to playing 'dull women with nothing to commend them except that they were like people one knew and pitied'[119] and begs her husband to revive his old play about the Queen of Babylon, 'a wild thing full of oratory and poetry, the kind of thing the pagans wrote long ago'.[120]

This inversion reflects Yeats's ambivalence about casting Mrs Campbell, then famous for her impersonations of Ibsenian characters, in a romantic role. Was he right to insist on the supremacy of romanticism as a dramatic genre? Or was he as stubborn and vain as Decima in refusing to acknowledge the significance of realism for contemporary drama? The drafts of the play suggest that at the time of its composition Yeats was unable to decide whether the emergence of dramatic realism was a symptom of cultural decline or a new kind of courageous literary idealism. Yeats's disgust with realism as a favourite genre of the mob is reflected in the words of Decima's husband, later deleted from the play: 'The public is the vainest of all hobgoblins, for it loves nothing but its own face in the mirror ... they [are] all cattle, no, pigs; loving the straw they lie on better than the clouds of dawn.'[121] But in an even earlier draft his mistress (in the final version called Nona) offers a different view of the genre and its popular appeal:

> now it's real people, [who] would seem to gather up all the life of the land, who spring into the unknown like a dive into the sea – no mere maker of laws nor leader of battle – but the flavour of life, thirst for what exists, sheer life, the flame that comes from us that are its fuel, people like themselves, pettish, troublesome, ordinary people like Noah's wife, they want to see.[122]

The play, moreover, retraces the plot and examines some of the ideas found in *Hedda Gabler*. The action of *The Player Queen*, like that of *Hedda Gabler*, is based on a love triangle. Septimus, Decima and Nona resemble, respectively, Lovborg, Hedda and Thea. In both plays, a seemingly docile and simple-minded woman challenges a passionate and intellectually superior heroine over the right to control a man's destiny. The characterisation of Decima and Nona matches that of Hedda Gabler and Thea Elvsted. Decima, Septimus's wife, is described as someone who 'would pull the world to pieces to spite her husband and her lover';[123] like Hedda she is tormented by jealousy and longs for incontestable power over her husband, even though she denies feeling any love for him. Nona, Septimus's mistress, like Thea, is outwardly a meek, unsophisticated woman who bestows all her care on a man rejected by the stronger woman. She betrays her true strength by assuming control of his life, even as she claims to put herself in his command. Finally, like the weak-willed debauchee and supposedly gifted historian Eilert Lovborg, Septimus is revered by his mistress as 'a great genius that can't take care of himself'.[124]

In Ibsen's play, the sexual attraction between Lovborg and Thea is sublimated in literary cooperation. Lovborg's manuscript, written under

Thea's guidance, is referred to as their 'little child'.[125] Yeats also explores the connection between sex and literary work. Septimus's poetry, which Decima cherishes as evidence of his unrequited love for her, was composed while making love to Nona; he literally used her back as a desk. Provoked by Decima's boastful recitation of Septimus's poems, Nona says to her: 'They have lain upon your heart, but they were made upon my shoulder. Ay, and down among my spine in the small hours of the morning; so many beats a line, and for every beat a tap of the fingers.'[126] The idea that literature, like a child, is conceived through the union between a writer and his beloved is presented even more explicitly in an earlier draft. In what might be a direct allusion to Ibsen's play, Yeats had the then nameless Decima speak of the poet's early work and literary ambitions as a child. 'I was never so much yours', the actress tells the poet in that version; 'for now that I have lost your love I have your dream. I sing to it, it murmurs to me, I rock it [in] my arms like a child, and I am going with it to my death, and my death shall be but the dream.'[127]

Decima's fascination with death also suggests that she is a reincarnation of Ibsen's heroine. The motives for Hedda's suicide are complex. One way to see it is as her last attempt to instil in life her vision of romance. Like Decima, who longs for a queen's part in a romantic drama, Hedda attempts to make the people of her circle act according to her idea of tragic grandeur. She tempts Lovborg with drink, burns his manuscript and gives him a gun. She then rejoices at the news of his reported suicide: 'It gives me a sense of freedom to know that a deed of deliberate courage is still possible in this world, – a deed of immutable beauty.'[128] She kills herself when she discovers that she has not only failed to inspire Lovborg to a 'deed of deliberate courage', but that she has unwittingly embroiled herself in a disgraceful intrigue and exposed herself to blackmail.

Like Hedda, Decima views death as liberation from the unbearable boredom of living. She is 'dead sick' of her husband[129] and indicates that she is 'weary of the world'.[130] Like Hedda, who, in one sense, shoots herself to escape scandal, Decima holds her 'good name ... dearer than [her] life'.[131] Above all, she is enraged by her loss of power over her husband and the theatre. 'I have been betrayed by a man, I have been made a mockery of. Do those who are dead ... make love and do they find good lovers?' she says before trying to plunge a pair of scissors into her heart.[132]

The relation between Hedda and Decima is apparent in the drafts. In one version, (the still unnamed) Decima gives vent to her romanticism when she hears the news of the execution of the Old Beggar, a prophet possessed by a spirit of the dead king (in the final version, the Old Beggar predicts the coming of a new monarch by braying like an ass).

'I would that my mother had brought me to haunted rooms and to old gentle places when I was young,' she exclaims. 'I dare say now from that on he's gone bravely and been all king.'[133] The soldier contradicts her: 'No, no, no, for they dragged him towards the tree, and he wept.'[134] Decima is shocked that someone she idealised could have died so ungracefully: 'So he was all beggar with [the] noose about him, and now he's dead he'll but consort with beggars.'[135]

This exchange echoes Hedda's last conversation with Judge Brack, during which she hears the facts of Lovborg's death. Like Decima, Hedda is inspired by the news of Lovborg's alleged suicide: 'Eilert Lovborg has had the courage to live his life after his own fashion. And then - the last great act, with its beauty! Ah that he should have the will and courage to turn away from the banquet of life - so early.'[136] This illusion is broken by Brack. He coldly informs Hedda that Lovborg died accidentally; he 'was found shot in ... in Mademoiselle Diana's boudoir ... . With a pistol in his breast pocket discharged. The ball had lodged in a vital part.'[137] Hedda and Decima are both denied their fantasy of a man dying a romantic death. Their attempts to make real life conform to an ideal are frustrated; as Hedda exclaims: 'Oh, what curse is it that makes everything I touch turn ludicrous and mean.'[138]

Even Hedda's last act of despair is rendered ridiculous by the reactions of her husband and Judge Brack: 'Shot herself! Shot herself in the temple!' shouts Tesman, adding his comic catchphrase, 'Think of that!'[139] 'Heaven help us,' Brack exclaims in incomprehension: ' – people don't do such things.'[140] In one of the early drafts, the reactions to Decima's rumoured suicide echo the closing words of *Hedda Gabler*. 'Hush, impossible. Women do not drown themselves for things like that,' says the Chancellor when he is told that the actress has killed herself to avoid playing Noah's wife.[141]

Thus the first part of the play reiterates the plot of *Hedda Gabler*. In the drafts, the resemblance is more obvious than in the final version, suggesting that Ibsen's play was Yeats's initial source of inspiration. However, while Ibsen's heroine loses her battle for heroic beauty turning her death into a grotesque farce, in the fantastic world of Yeats's play Decima emerges triumphant and lives up to her romantic ideals. A riot breaks out in town. The mob threatens to kill the queen and the little troupe of actors. Decima approaches the queen; the two exchange clothes and Decima pacifies the crowd, who then swear allegiance to the actress.

Decima not only proves herself worthy of a queen's part, but also demonstrates the validity of her romantic idealism to the sceptical members of her theatre. In the closing scene of the play, the roles of the actors and the spectators are reversed. Decima puts on the mask of Noah's sister, summons the players and makes them dance as they listen to her final farewell:

> You are banished and must not return upon pain of death, and yet not one of you shall be poorer because banished. That I promise. But you have lost one thing that I will not restore. A woman player has left you. Do not mourn her. She was a bad, headstrong, cruel woman, and seeks destruction somewhere and with some man she knows nothing of; such a woman they tell me that this mask would well become, this foolish smiling face! Come, dance.[142]

This elegant ending had evaded Yeats for nearly fifteen years. In some early versions, Decima returns to her troupe, chastened by her experience and resolved to play Noah's wife. Yeats had to overcome his own romantic yearnings – he had to transform the play from heroic blank verse into prose and adopt a comic mode – before this solution of the conflict between romanticism and realism became apparent.

In its final version, *The Player Queen* echoes another play, which in addition to *Hedda Gabler* had plagued Yeats's imagination for the duration of its composition: *The Playboy of the Western World*. Like Synge's Christy Mahon, Decima succeeds in bridging the gap between a gallous story and a dirty deed, between the mask and the self, and becomes transformed into a romantic heroine. The ending of *The Player Queen*, in its fusion of the boundaries between theatre and reality, and the role reversal between actors and spectators, is a reminder of the *Playboy* riots. It is fitting that Yeats's dramatic exploration of Ibsen's drama and impact ends with an evocation of the moment when the romantic poet found himself transformed into a character of an Ibsenite play. When, fifteen years after the events that inspired it, the play was finally finished, Yeats no longer wished Mrs Campbell to act in it. Instead, the part of Decima was filled by Molly Allgood – the original Pegeen Mike.

Anthony Roche has recently noted that 'Synge's attitude to Ibsen is a complex, ambiguous one and has frequently been misconstrued as entirely or mainly negative'.[143] The same can be said of Yeats. Even though he admitted that Ibsen had a profound impact on his own writings, there is a tendency among present-day critics to believe Robinson's assertion that 'Yeats hated Ibsen'. Joyce's accusations in 'The Day of the Rabblement', however unfair, also still resonate in current criticism. Thus Joan FitzPatrick Dean has recently observed that 'Joyce had

hoped for Ibsenite works in Dublin, but in its earliest years the Abbey rarely offered, in fact, systematically excluded the social realism and well-made dramaturgy identified with Ibsen's middle period'.[144] This, of course, is true – the founders of the Irish Literary Theatre made an implicit promise to stage Ibsen, but they failed to do so. However, when a promise is made it is important to consider not only what is meant by breaking it, but also what it meant to make it. The notoriety of the Irish Literary Theatre and the Abbey ensured that Ibsen's name, hitherto a dull reminder of the London controversy that Dublin had missed, acquired a new importance in Irish literary discourse. Yeats, through his speeches and articles, and Synge, through the production of *In the Shadow of the Glen*, drew the public into their complex literary relationship with Ibsen. And the public in turn influenced Yeats's attitude to the Norwegian playwright and dramatic realism.

Dean further argues that Ibsenism flourished in the Theatre of Ireland, founded in 1906 by several of the actors and playwrights who had left the Abbey. She emphasises in particular the Ibsenite tendencies of the plays of Padraic Colum and Seumas O'Kelly. To some extent it is true that in the Irish theatrical world, wherever Yeats's influence diminished, Ibsen's influence increased. The Cork Realists, who had revolted against Yeats's revivalist theatre, are indebted to Ibsen. The Theatre of Ireland produced Act 4 of Ibsen's *Brand* in 1906; and the lesser known Metropolitan Players produced several of his later plays in 1912–16. However, as the next chapter shows, in staging and imitating Ibsen, representatives of the 'alternative' dramatic tradition[145] sometimes misinterpreted his plays and, unlike Yeats, neglected the poetic and symbolist aspects of his art.

3
Irish Nationalism and the Ideology of Ibsen's Plays

Nationalist approaches to Ibsen, 1904–6

The Players' Club performance of *Hedda Gabler* on 20–21 April 1904 was their second and last Ibsen production. The little amateur company had been having some disagreements between their two more famous members. One of the actors, P. J. Kelly, recalled that during the rehearsals of *A Doll's House* and *An Enchanted Sea* in 1903, 'Martyn and Moore fought so many intellectual battles that it was impossible for the company to understand what it was all about. It seemed to me almost a miracle that the plays were successfully produced'.[1] Martyn and Moore's involvement with this company was not widely advertised; their names did not appear on the programme. Martyn's later references to the company are dismissive. 'Although I met with considerable talent, it was not accompanied with any sort of taste,' he wrote in 1914. 'I suppose I have no right to be surprised that the only thought of those amateurs was to show themselves off. Any idea of discovering a native work of art and interpreting it with understanding was as far from their minds as from the mind of an average English actor or actress.'[2] Martyn was particularly disgruntled by the supposed philistinism of Flora MacDonnell, the first Irish Nora:

> Would it be believed that one day when I was discussing the possibilities of a society for producing native drama and Continental masterpieces, the leading lady proposed that I should produce *Madame Sans Gene* at the Antient Concert Rooms, with an elaborate series of dresses for herself in the title part? That poor lady evidently thought that the fascination of silly players was the real motive of my interest in intellectual drama.[3]

MacDonnell's attitude to Martyn is not recorded. She was praised for her portrayal of Hedda, although the play itself received mixed reactions. 'R. M.' in the *Dublin Evening Mail* summed up Hedda as 'one of those curiously morbid female creatures who throng the pages of Ibsen's dramas, a woman who would drive the average man to drink or the Divorce Court – impossible to live with, impossible to understand'.[4]

> Those who kow-tow with superstitious reverence before the shrine of Ibsen will not accept this estimate of Hedda, and will continue to believe that from the tangled strings of her soul the dramatist has struck tragic music ... Miss Flora MacDonnell did some extremely good work last night ... If she did not give us a clear idea of what Hedda really was that was not her fault.[5]

The *Irish Times* also eulogised the acting of MacDonnell, and praised Kathleen O'Neill in the role of Thea, W. J. Tunney as Tesman, James Edgar as Judge Brack, Eileen Whitney as Aunt Julia, Agnes Plunkett as Berta (the servant) and George Nesbitt as Lovborg. The author did not get off as lightly: 'the community from which Ibsen's notions of human nature are derived is something more insane and inconsistent than the population of an average lunatic asylum.'[6]

The *United Irishman*, by contrast, published a review which called *Hedda Gabler* 'a miracle of dramatic construction – a superb specimen of stage technique': 'Not a line is misplaced; points are made and thrust home with inexorable strength and rapier-like poignancy; the whole proceeding unflinchingly to an end, unforeseen but inevitable in retrospect.'[7] Also provided was a photograph of 'Henrik Ibsen, the Famous Norwegian Dramatist, who is seriously ill'. The author of the review was James H. Cousins, who might be said to have joined the ranks of the Irish realists with the production of his tragedy *The Racin' Lug* (first staged on 31 October 1902). This was not the first time that Cousins mentioned Ibsen's name in print. In his negative review of Padraic Colum's *Broken Soil* (produced on 3 December 1903), Cousins described one of its characters as an 'Irish Hedda Gabler'.[8] On that occasion, Cousins had provoked the anger of Oliver St. John Gogarty, a medical practitioner, writer and a famous Dublin wit, who thought Cousins's criticism 'destructive and invidious'.[9] Gogarty spoke of Colum's play as 'a national drama in a fuller sense ... than any yet presented'.[10] In Gogarty's opinion, dramatic realism would become a liberating force in Irish life:

> when symbolism, that cancer of Art, shall have been extirpated, and mysticism, misunderstanding and folk-smoke cleared away, the great

> work of our poets ... may sooner bring to a focus the spirit of our nation. We will be content no longer to have our peasantry lie mere coprolites of a race once mighty for the interest of English geologists, nor as a drowsy remnant for the interest of foreign litterateurs, but we will have them once more a vital and breathing people with hate – for holiness – hate for all that tends to enslave, emasculate, or deprive them of that national identity by which alone they may hold a place among the nations of the earth.[11]

Cousins's 1904 appraisal of *Hedda Gabler* briefly alluded to the argument with Gogarty. In order to set things right and prove himself no enemy of realism, Cousins favourably reviewed a play whose author had, after all, been the first to use drama to fight holiness and 'all that tends to enslave'.

Cousins's review of *Hedda Gabler* and its publication in the *United Irishman* point to a new dimension in the Irish nationalist reception of Ibsen. While some nationalists, such as Moran, had identified Ibsen with West-Britonism, others, such as Griffith, saw Ibsen as representing a nationalist ideal. During the controversy over *In the Shadow of the Glen*, Griffith objected to Yeats's statement that the Irish National Theatre Society had 'no propaganda but that of good art'. 'If so', wrote Griffith, 'the society is no more Irish and National than the Elizabethan Stage Society, and it has ceased to follow in the footsteps of the Scandinavian Theatre, which had it started out with "no propaganda save that of good art" would never have created a Scandinavian drama'.[12]

During the years that had elapsed since Yeats had misleadingly suggested that Ibsen's world-wide success was due to his early dramas presented at Ole Bull's Norwegian Theatre at Bergen, the public image of Ibsen had undergone a sea-change. In 1899, his influence on the emerging Irish drama was but dimly perceived. By 1906, the year of Ibsen's death, such playwrights as Ryan, Colum, Boyle, Martyn and Synge had turned Ibsen into a buzzword in Irish theatre criticism. 'Ibsen influenced the modern drama, and the modern stage more than any other man of his day, and perhaps some of his influence may be seen even in some of the plays of our Anglo-Irish writers,' wrote John O'Toole, a contributor to the *Leader*. 'For this reason, if for no other there is some need to notice him and his work.'[13]

Ibsen's death on 23 May 1906 got only a brief mention in the daily papers. The unionist *Dublin Evening Mail*, formerly a source of Ibsen-related gossip, observed merely that the 'death of Henrik Ibsen, the famous Norwegian dramatist, opens anew the controversy as to whether he was really great'.[14] By contrast, the nationalist weeklies, *Sinn Féin* (which had succeeded the *United Irishman* in 1906), *An Claidheamh*

Soluis and even Moran's *Leader* published extensive obituaries. In his survey of Ibsen's dramas in the *Leader*, O'Toole revealed his conservative taste. O'Toole liked The *League of Youth*: 'I wish we had a comedy of Irish life equal to it.'[15] He dismissed *An Enemy of the People* as 'simply a parable in reply to [Ibsen's] critics, and not a legitimate drama at all'.[16] He considered *A Doll's House* 'brilliantly written and the psychology very true up to the point of Nora Helmer's "revolt": 'The petted little kitten-girl was not the person to suddenly develop into an Amazon champion of "woman's higher destiny".'[17] *Ghosts* he described as 'a terrible play, a study of heredity'. 'In *John Gabriel Borkman*,' wrote O'Toole, 'the dramatist ingeniously brings out the dominant point of egotism and selfishness in each of his characters. In *Rosmersholm* we have the seamy side of the free-thought world. In *The Pillars of Society* we get a pretty good conspectus of the forces of corruption in the trading world.'[18]

There is a similarity between O'Toole's approach to Ibsen and the nationalist responses to the plays of the Irish Ibsenites. Synge, who 'restored the sex-element'[19] to the Irish stage, was not tolerated any more than *Ghosts*. The heroine of *In the Shadow of the Glen* seemed to nationalists even less plausible than Nora Helmer. By contrast, political satire like *The Pillars of Society* was welcome, especially if, like *The League of Youth*, it took the form of comedy. William Boyle's *The Building Fund* (25 April 1905), *The Mineral Workers* (19 October 1906) and *The Eloquent Dempsey* (20 January 1906) did fit the bill and were extremely popular. Griffith's attitude was typical: 'We do not think of Ibsen when we are witnessing Mr. Boyle's plays, yet, nevertheless, he suggests what an Irish Ibsen might be.'[20] The underlying conservatism of nationalist criticism notable in O'Toole's approach to *Rosmersholm* and *John Gabriel Borkman* – his concern that the play should have a clearly defined moral message – was also one of the factors in the opposition to Synge. As Nicholas Grene points out, *The Playboy* was rejected not only because of its alleged immorality, but also because the critics were confused as to its meaning or genre. 'If it is an allegory, it is too obscure for me,' wrote one opponent of *The Playboy*, 'I cannot stalk this alligator on the banks of the Liffey.'[21]

The unsigned obituary of Ibsen in *An Claidheamh Soluis* as well as Colum's *Sinn Féin* article on 'Ibsen and the National Drama' provided coherent, positive images of the playwright who had become an acknowledged influence on Irish dramatists. *An Claidheamh Soluis* portrayed him as a language revivalist:

> A hundred years ago the language in which the greatest dramas of our time have been written was a mere patois. It had practically no modern

> literature, and was spoken only by a few thousand peasants and seafaring folk who lived far off from the world on the shores of lonely northern fjords. Wergeland and Asbjornsen and Bishop Moe arose and gave this dying speech the dignity of literary expression. Ibsen and Bjørnson followed, and for the past thirty years Norway has exercised a greater influence on the mind of Europe than any other nation.[22]

In a sense this is true, Ibsen's writings, like the plays of Bjørnstjerne Bjørnson or Peter Christen Asbjørnsen and Jørgen Moe's *Folk Tales of Norway* (1842–3),[23] contain many idiomatic expressions peculiar to Norway. Yet, neither of these writers used Norwegian Landsmaal, a language based on the Norwegian peasant dialects developed by Ivar Assen (1813–96) and claimed by its adherents to be the authentic Norwegian untainted by Danish. Ibsen's satirical response to the Landsmaal movement was the madman Huhu in *Peer Gynt* who aims to restore the dead language of the apes:

> But in long departed ages
> There the orang-outang was the ruler.
> He, the forest's lord and master,
> Freely fought and snarled in freedom.
> He was ruler of his kingdom. ...
>
> Ah, but then the foreign yoke came,
> Marred the forest-tongue primeval.
> Twice two hundred years of darkness
> Brooded o'er the race of monkeys.[24]

The writer of the *An Claidheamh Soluis* article was either unaware of what Ibsen thought of language revival and indeed the particulars of the language question in Norway, or simply concealed those facets of Ibsen which did not conform to his image of a patriotic playwright who 'showed the world what the "little" nations can do'.[25]

In 'Ibsen and National Drama', Colum adopted a similar tactic. He strove to change the popular perception of Ibsen as a symbol of cosmopolitanism. And he too extolled Ibsen as 'the great representative of a small nationality'.[26] He stressed that while in 'the public mind [Ibsen] is associated with all that is cosmopolitan in literature ... [he] has given a strong impulse to national drama'.[27] Colum's article reads more like an artist's statement than an obituary. 'The dramatists whom Ibsen liberated will find material in their street and townland,' wrote the author of *The Land* and *Broken Soil*; 'henceforward the people one meets in cabin and drawing room, in studio and committee-room, have tragic possibilities.'[28] By proving his master's significance for Norwegian nationalism, Colum hoped to show the importance of his own work to the nationalist cause. Like Yeats in 1899, Colum emphasised Ibsen's involvement as a young man with the Theatre of Ole Bull. In 1850 Bull started 'a Norse theatre in Bergen ... went with peasant dialogues, "raw Norse" peasant dances, and native music [and] succeeded in making the peasants conscious of "Norway's theatre"'.[29]

At the time of writing this obituary, Colum had reason to resent the Abbey Theatre. He left when it became a limited liability company. Along with fellow seceders from the Abbey, such as Mary Walker, Frank Walker, Honor Lavelle and Emma Vernon, Colum joined Martyn, Cousins, Thomas Kettle and others to set up an alternative national theatre – one that was more nationalist and better suited to Colum's realistic plays than the Abbey. 'Ireland of to-day is far more advanced dramatically than the Norway of Ole Bull and his colleagues,' Colum declared, 'and yet the idea of "Ireland's Theatre" has not been formulated.'[30] Neither the 'effective dramatic societies ... in Dublin ... Belfast and Cork' nor the 'plays in Irish and English which have grown around the Gaelic League', nor the 'theatre with which Mr. Yeats is associated', which had 'attained astonishing maturity', achieved the ideal of Bull's Norwegian theatre. Colum skilfully turned the obituary into a critique of the Abbey and a manifesto for the new Theatre of Ireland. 'Ireland's Theatre,' he declared, 'must not be an attempt to meet the people half way, it should arise out of the people, at least the people must be made feel that it is something to them.'[31]

Less than a fortnight after this article was published, Colum met Holloway by chance in O'Connell Street and told him that a 'new society had been formed under the title of The Theatre of Ireland'.[32] Martyn was president, with George Nesbitt as stage manager, Colum as honorary secretary, Thomas Keohler as honorary treasurer and Desmond French, Helen Laird, Cousins, Padraic Pearse and Thomas Kettle on the committee. The theatre opened on 6 December 1906 with the productions of Douglas Hyde's *Casadh an tSugáin*, J. H. Cousins's *The Racin' Lug* and Act 4 of Ibsen's *Brand*.

The Theatre of Ireland's *Brand* and the ideal of sacrifice, 1906

The plays chosen for the opening night of the Theatre of Ireland reflect the company's desire to revive the ideals of the now commercialised

Abbey. Hyde's Irish-language play, first performed on 21 October 1901, was part of the third and last season of the Irish Literary Theatre. Its revival harked back to the time when collaboration between the Gaelic League, Irish nationalists and Yeats's theatre seemed possible. Cousins's well-liked, inoffensive tragedy likewise embodied the Abbey's unfulfilled promise to become a people's theatre. Moreover, as Vandevelde points out, this play about a northern Presbyterian fishing family 'bridged the gap between the North and South of the country'.[33] It was first performed on 31 October 1902, shortly after the foundational event in the history of the Abbey Theatre – the amalgamation of the amateur group of Frank and W. J. Fay with what remained of the Irish Literary Theatre. The Irish première of Act 4 of *Brand* may also be seen as the Theatre of Ireland's attempt to return to the original values of the Irish Literary Theatre, as set out in the first number of *Beltaine* and in Yeats's 1899 speech at the National Literary Society. At the time, Yeats promised that the plays of the new theatre, like the early plays of Ibsen, would be 'leaning on the national feeling of the country'.[34]

In 1906 it was obvious that Yeats's theatre no longer wished 'to do for Ireland something like what has been done for the Scandinavian drama, which is thoroughly racy and national'.[35] For Colum and Martyn, both of whom combined admiration for Ibsen with nationalism, the Abbey's was a double failure. Instead of invigorating Irish literary nationalism through the staging of Ibsen's romantic plays, the company contributed to the image of Ibsen as a dangerous foreign influence. By producing Act 4 of *Brand*, therefore, the founders of the Theatre of Ireland might have hoped to restore Ibsen to his rightful place as a model for Irish drama. Like *Peer Gynt*, *Brand* is a dramatic poem, composed before Ibsen turned to realistic prose drama. It was a fitting choice for the theatre, which aimed to challenge the public perception of Ibsen as a controversial writer of problem plays.

In England, Act 4 of *Brand* had been performed only once, as part of Elizabeth Robins's Ibsen season of 29 May–10 June 1893. (The entire play was staged there for the first time in Wilson's prose translation on 10 November 1912 by none other than W. G. Fay, who had by then left the Abbey and joined the Ibsen Club.) A five-act verse drama, whose action takes place for the most part among the mountains and glaciers, *Brand* was written not for the stage but for the 'theatre of the mind'. Act 4, however, like Ibsen's prose dramas, is set within three walls of the protagonist's house. Act 4 seems to be a self-contained unit, allowing for an easy transformation into a one-act performance. The problem is, however, that such fragmentation of the play undermines its carefully balanced and self-reflexive exploration of idealism.

Brand is a tragedy of a priest who calls for complete, willing and unconditional sacrifice of earthly affections in the service of God. Brand rebels against the complacent, middle-class Christianity of his countrymen, who have turned God into a 'dotard and a dreamer / Verging on second infancy', a being 'stern enough to fright / A pack of children in the night'.[36] Brand's grandeur is expressed in his fearless rhetoric:

> Mine is another kind of God!
> Mine is a storm, where thine's a lull,
> Implacable where thine's a clod
> All-loving there, where thine is dull;
> And he is young like Hercules,
> No hoary sipper of life's lees!
> His voice rang through the dazzled night
> When He, within the burning wood,
> By Moses upon Horeb's height
> As by a pigmy's pigmy stood.
> In Gideon's vale He stayed the sun,
> And wonders without end has done,
> And wonders without end would do,
> Were not the age grown sick, – like you!
>
> (25)

Brand regards faith as the highest form of heroism, a battle against the spirit of compromise that has degraded his generation:

> Try every man in heart and soul
> You'll find he has no virtue whole,
> But just a little grain of each.
>
> (23)

His unwillingness to compromise leads Brand to refuse his mother her last rites (because she cannot bring herself to leave all her money to the Church), to cause his little son's death (he dies after Brand refuses to leave his northern parish for a warmer climate) and to break his wife's will and cause her die of grief. Brand himself dies heartbroken, pursued by his enraged parishioners, tormented by doubts, yet still adamant in his struggle with compromise. As an avalanche engulfs him, a voice is heard through the thunder with a message contradicting Brand's insistence that mankind shall be saved by will alone – 'He is the God of love' (262).

In 1922, in the midst of the Irish Civil War, Lady Gregory wrote in her diary: 'I have been reading act III of *Brand*. It has much of Ireland's contest of wills today.'[37] The contest of wills that erupted in 1921 had begun long before the Easter Rising of 1916; and the play, even though none of the reviewers could see it at the time, had a particular relevance to pre-1916 Ireland. Brand's uncompromising sense of duty and his distaste for the spiritual weakness of his generation make him similar to the emerging revolutionary Padraic Pearse. Through exposing the inhumanity of Brand's actions, however, the play critiques the core ideal of Irish nationalists – redemptive sacrifice.

In the most popular play of the Irish Revival – Yeats and Lady Gregory's *Cathleen Ní Houlihan* (1902) – Michael Gillane leaves his bride and parents in order to die for Ireland. The play does not dwell on the hardships and grief of Michael's abandoned family. We somehow doubt that he will survive the massacre to return home, but nor do we see him bayoneted by British soldiers. Instead, the play ends with an ideal, a dream of old mother Ireland transformed through the sacrifice of her sons into a young woman 'with the walk of a queen'.[38] *Brand*, by contrast, brings into view the wreckage left in the wake of raging idealism – the deaths of Brand's mother, his little son and his wife and the transformation of the parishioners into a raging mob. Yet, as Shaw pointed out, Ibsen's deep sympathy for his anti-hero raises the play 'at once far above the criticism that sneers at idealism from beneath instead of surveying it from the clear ether above which can only be reached through the mists'.[39] *Brand* was an important play for the makers of the New Ireland. However, by reducing it to a fragment, the founders of the Theatre of Ireland subverted the play's implications for Irish nationalism.

Act 4 focuses on Brand's wife, Agnes, who tries to overcome her grief at the death of her son and to live up to her husband's ideal. 'Thou art my wife: I crave thee all / To live according to our call' (163), Brand says to Agnes. He demands that she give the clothes of their dead son to an itinerant gypsy woman. Brand perceives Agnes's grief as idolatry: she must sacrifice her entire self to God and must do so willingly. After a tortured struggle, Agnes obeys. She rejoices in her newfound freedom, thanks Brand for saving her soul and happily tells him that her own death is now imminent: 'Whoso sees Jehovah dies' (176).

'Sinn Dicat', who reviewed the production for *Sinn Féin*, remarked, 'it is outwardly a gloomy, heart-rending scene, but it is ... justified by the irradiating sense of spiritual triumph that underlies it'.[40] 'Sinn Dicat's' reaction indicates the degree to which Ibsen's ideas were altered by the Theatre of Ireland. Act 4 is indeed apt to be misunderstood as a celebration of Christian sacrifice if one is unaware that Brand has caused the child's death. To understand Ibsen's conception of Agnes's sacrifice, it is essential to hear first the play's strongest indictment of Brand's ideology. It is uttered by the Doctor in Act 3:

> Each Age in its own way will walk;
> Ours is not scared by nurses' talk
> Of hell-bound soul and burning brand; –
> Humanity's our first command!
>
> (110)

By choosing to stage a mere fragment of *Brand*, the Theatre of Ireland followed the method laid out by the *An Claidheamh Soluis* writer and Colum in their obituaries of Ibsen. *An Claidheamh Soluis* falsified Ibsen's feelings about the Landsmaal idiom and turned him into a language revivalist. Colum avoided writing about Ibsen's emigration and his dissatisfaction with Ole Bull's theatre and portrayed him as a nationalist writer. The text of *Brand* was similarly fragmented, revised and made to conform to the Theatre of Ireland's ideal of Irish drama.

In fact, Act 4, when produced on its own, resembles the staple fare of the Abbey Theatre. Featuring a little peasant hut interior (albeit Norwegian and not Irish), a tramp intruder and the suggestion that the ghost of a dead child lurks behind the dark windows, the fragment resembles Synge's *In the Shadow of the Glen* and *Riders to the Sea* and Yeats's *The Land of Heart's Desire*. It becomes a typical 'stranger-in-the-house' play of the Abbey, which as Grene points out derives from Ibsen.[41]

This resemblance may have been noticed by those who had seen Emma Vernon, who played Agnes, and Mary Walker, who played the gypsy woman, in *Riders to the Sea* and *In the Shadow of the Glen*, respectively. Thus Holloway, who was charmed by Vernon's Agnes, recalled the beauty of the moment when 'sorrow slipped from her and like the sorrowing mother in *Riders to the Sea* when her last son was drowned, she could rest ... at last'.[42] Indeed, if Holloway had not been so displeased by Joseph Goggin's acting, he would have also heard an echo of Maurya's final speech in Brand's words to Agnes:

> Listen, Agnes; thou shalt know
> What to me our loss has brought.
> Oftentimes my light is low,
> Dim my reason, dull my thought
> And there seems a kind of gladness
> In immeasurable sadness.
>
> (129)

Through its affinity with the plays of Synge and Yeats, Act 4 is integrated into the dramatic tradition of the Irish Revival. Moreover, in comparison to Synge's plays, Act 4 emerges as a play better suited for nationalist purposes. In *Riders to the Sea*, Maurya, in an attempt to save her son Bartley, defies the priest and the tradition which dictates that '[i]t's the life of a young man to be going on the sea'.[43] Human life and earthly affections are valued above the call of duty. By contrast, Agnes of the Theatre of Ireland's *Brand* embodies that ideal of Irish nationalism – a female figure beatified by her suffering for the sake of a grand cause. She is at once Cathleen Ní Houlihan and her champion Michael Gillane. Through this production, the Theatre of Ireland drafted Ibsen for Ireland's cause and subverted the meaning of his play.

Joyce's friend, Thomas Kettle, was one of the founders of the Theatre of Ireland. Richard Ellmann describes him as 'an intellectual Catholic, a nationalist, and a spokesman for the younger intellectuals. As a student he already formulated the idea that "If Ireland is to become a new Ireland she must first become European."'[44] When *Brand* was produced, however, the Theatre of Ireland seems to have acted on the unconscious principle that 'if Ireland is to become open to Europe, Europe must first become Irish'.

Their production suggests, moreover, that Theatre of Ireland, at least in its early days, was not quite the radical Ibsenite alternative to the Abbey Theatre. This production reinforces Vandevelde's argument that in spite of its 'wide ambitions', the Theatre of Ireland 'chose to mirror that NTS [National Theatre Society]. The Abbey stage had become their performance space, and the Abbey play their prototype'.[45] The Theatre of Ireland was not, therefore, an answer to James Joyce's vision in 'The Day of the Rabblement'. On the contrary, as Vandevelde points out, the repertoire was 'less controversial and received more support from the nationalists than that of the NTS'.[46] In its benign way, the Theatre of Ireland was firmly on the side of the 'trolls' of popular opinion.

The Theatre of Ireland *Brand*, moreover, contrasts with other contemporary reverberations of this play in Ireland. Paul Ruttledge, the protagonist of Yeats's *Where There Is Nothing*, is like Brand in his uncompromising quest for truth and purity. He abandons his home to join the 'tinkers', then leaves them to become a monk, a priest and a miracle worker, and finally an outcast. Brand persuades his parishioners to build a magnificent new church and then denounces the costly edifice as a false temple and leads the people to look for God in the snow-capped mountains. Similarly, Paul, at the pinnacle of his career as a priest, summons his brethren to undertake a destructive crusade against the state, the church and the laws – all social mechanisms preventing true individual freedom. Like Brand, Paul is pursued by an angry mob. Unlike Brand, he meets his death at their hands.

Where There Is Nothing is not one of Yeats's best plays. However, it reveals his interest in Brand-like idealism, an interest shared apparently by the play's co-authors: Moore, Lady Gregory and Hyde. Their fascination with such an idealist figure was not unqualified. There is an underlying hunger for violence in Paul's search for truth; the violent aspect of his anarchism becomes even more apparent in *The Unicorn from the Stars* (1906), a later adaptation of the play by Yeats and, mostly, Lady Gregory.

A subtler exploration of idealism and its significance for the Irish Revival is Moore's *Hail and Farewell* (1911), a work that, as Frazier observes, develops the central idea of *Where There Is Nothing*, the 'idiot messiah', into a 'leitmotif'.[47] In this satirical account of the Revival, the author proclaims himself to be the saviour of Ireland who would restore its national language and free it from the oppression of Catholicism. Like Brand and Paul, Moore becomes an outcast; *Hail and Farewell* ends with his exile from Ireland. In his self-portrait, Moore combined a confessional style with parody, casting himself as a tragi-comic impersonation of the idealist spirit of the Revival. Like the poet, journalist and visionary AE, Moore claims to be haunted by visions and beset by voices speaking to him of his mission in Irish history. Yet the message that this prophet reads in the vast deep is anything but the nationalist ideal: 'as in a vision I saw Ireland as a god demanding human sacrifices, and everybody, or nearly everybody crying: Take me Ireland, take me ... But how can they work for Ireland without working for oneself.'[48] Moore was similar to Ibsen in his rejection of the ideal of sacrifice and its replacement with a belief in the importance of one's duty to oneself. In 1906, however, there were few who shared his ideas. Idealism and not individualism was the dominant force in the politics and aesthetics of the time.

The rise of the realists and the myth of Ibsen's nationalism, 1908–12

Between 1908 and 1912, realism emerged as the predominant trend in Irish drama. The strongest new Abbey playwrights – Lennox Robinson, T. C. Murray, R. J. Ray and Seamus Kelly – were nicknamed the 'Cork Realists' by Yeats. They were dedicated to expounding the generic social limitations of Irish dramatic writing. Instead of Yeats's poetic plays or Lady Gregory's peasant sketches, they offered stark critiques of Irish life. At the risk of public disapproval, they set out to show that Ireland was not home to 'ancient idealism' but to provincial corruption. Robinson summed up their position in his autobiography: 'We were very young and we shrunk from nothing. We knew our Ibsen and the plays of the Lancashire school, we showed our people as robbers and murderers, guilty of arson, steeped in trickery and jobbery.'[49]

The drama of the Cork Realists, Colum and the playwrights of the Ulster Literary Theatre (founded in 1904) – Rutherford Mayne and James Winder Good (who wrote under the pseudonym Robert Harding) – had a greater impact on Irish attitudes to Ibsen than the few productions of his plays. The public were less interested in the foreign playwright, who had by now lost his notoriety, than in the work of their contemporaries who dared to apply Ibsenite methods to Irish subjects. Indeed, the expansion of Irish Ibsenism was one of the factors explaining the dearth of Irish productions of Ibsen's plays. In 1910 Robinson persuaded the directors of the Abbey to stage *Little Eyolf*. 'Yeats grudgingly agreed' and the rehearsals were going ahead, but then 'along comes a play by an unknown fellow called Murray, and the name of the play is *Birthright*, and so, of course, poor *Little Eyolf* was put on the shelf'.[50]

While some negative associations with Ibsen's name persisted, he was by now regarded primarily as a literary classic. Nevertheless, those Irish authors who seemed to imitate him were often criticised. The Ulster playwright and journalist J. W. Good, whose *Leaders of the People* was produced in Dublin on 24 April 1908, was reprimanded for his 'ill-digested Ibsenism'[51] by Michael O'Dempsey, a contributor to the *Leader*. 'When the author treads the stage of Molière,' wrote O'Dempsey, 'he is entertaining, but when he attempts to mount the slopes where Ibsen towers alone, his step falters and his vision fails pitiably ... When he attempts after the manner of the Scandinavian Master, to search the deeps of a soul, he lapses rapidly and unforgivably into the commonplace.'[52]

O'Dempsey was well aware of the controversy over Synge's *Playboy of the Western World* which had taken place a year earlier. Indeed, he placed himself within the tradition of nationalist opposition to the Abbey, noting that the

> superficial ... Ibsenism [of the play] is reminiscent of one period in the history of the National Theatre Society when certain leading lights of that curious and occasionally lurid constellation were wont to draw unconvincing parallels between the Abbey and Ibsen's Theatre, between (exempla gratia) Ibsen's *Ghosts* and Mr. Synge's *Playboy of the Western World.* [53]

The tone of O'Dempsey's review is reminiscent of Clery's attack on *In the Shadow of the Glen.* But while in 1903 Clery was furious with Synge for besmirching the Irish peasantry with his foreign borrowings, O'Dempsey accused Harding, and indeed the Abbey playwrights, of inept imitation of Ibsen, whom he revered as a great master: 'It is discouraging to find the Ulstermen setting out, forsooth, to imitate Ibsen, forgetting that Ibsen's loneliness upon the heights was a reality, a terrible and none too pleasant reality to him.'[54]

A belief in the unsurpassed stature of Ibsen's plays is also notable in the reviews of Octavia Kenmore's productions of *A Doll's House, Hedda Gabler* and *The Master Builder* (11–18 May 1908). The *Irish Times* reviewer, for instance, while admitting his bafflement at the actions of their protagonists, praised the plays for their 'great beauty and originality of style and composition' and for being 'poems in prose' that, 'if somewhat unreal, are nevertheless very charming in their individuality'.[55] This critic's disinclination to justify his assertions makes the review read like a recital of second-hand opinions: respect for Ibsen did not stem from heart-felt admiration for his plays. Like earlier contempt for him, it was based on hearsay. Holloway claimed that the audience on each night of the Ibsen week consisted of 'the best class of Dublin playgoers', but 'unfortunately there [were] not enough of that class to fill the stalls'.[56]

The theatre critics of the nationalist weeklies did not usually review productions by touring English companies. A *Sinn Féin* article of 1906 on 'The Drama as a Nationalising Force' expresses a view of Ibsen that was steadily gaining popularity among the nationalist critics. Kathleen M. O'Brennan called on the Irish dramatists to employ the educative potential of drama to strengthen the national character: We are at a critical moment in Ireland, to-day. We are awakening as from a long sleep,' she wrote. 'Now the wide awake have a great responsibility before them for they have to teach the sleepy folk where they are, and what they have to do, while those who are still asleep have to be aroused and taught their duty to their country. This is the work for the dramatist, and it is no easy work.'[57] For O'Brennan, Ibsen was a 'nation-builder' who depicted the 'moral struggle' of characters taken '[f]rom every class of life':

> In all Ibsen's dramas, whether in *Peer Gynt, Hedda Gabler, Ghosts, The Enemy of the People*, &c., he studies this struggle, but with such sympathy, judgment, heart, that we follow him without knowing it. We do not feel that we climb or that the struggle is hard, so well does he exalt the beauty that we seek. He is one of those realists who place ugliness beside beauty to better enhance and idealise that beauty. When he asks us to make the toilsome ascent to the mountain, he repays us by showing us the light of day and letting us breathe the purer atmosphere after the weary journey.[58]

O'Brennan portrayed Ibsen as a moralist; yet while the moralising impulse is strong in Ibsen, it never takes over a play. Moreover, as Colum put it in 1948:

> Ibsen's mind was dialectical, opposing one theme to another: the necessity for truth in social relations which was the theme of *An Enemy of the People* is given its counter point in *The Wild Duck* where the danger of presenting the bill for absolute idealism is underscored.[59]

Ibsen's distrust of idealism, which Shaw has described as his quintessence, escaped O'Brennan. She considered him to be a 'great apostle of willpower [who] while teaching his public and solving for them the problems of existence, has had one great aim throughout all his work – character-building'.[60]

The Irish realists were thus expected to join the national effort by solving a few existential problems while educating their compatriots about their duty to their country – and in doing so they were supposed to follow Ibsen. One playwright who fell victim to this contradictory ideal of national, utilitarian and progressive Ibsenism was Colum.

Directed by Robinson, Colum's *Thomas Muskerry* was first produced on 5 May 1910. It is a tragedy of a workhouse master who, after lifelong dedication to his work and family, dies a pauper's death in his own workhouse, his plans for a peaceful retirement crushed by his money-grabbing relatives. The play is not a direct imitation of Ibsen, nor does it allude to any of Ibsen's plays. Colum shares Ibsen's longing for freedom and his distaste for social hypocrisy, but *Thomas Muskerry* is a work of a mature dramatist who was 'proud to say that [he] once disciplined [him]self in Ibsen's form'.[61]

Ibsen's name was first sounded by the *Evening Telegraph*. 'M. M. O'H' asserted that the play entitled Colum to join the 'company of playwrights of the very first class – to the company in which big names like those of Pinero and Shaw and Ibsen figure'.[62] This praise was countered by 'Firín' of the *Irish Nation*, who found *Thomas Muskerry* inaccurate in its treatment of Irish life and spoke of its author as suffering from an overdose of foreign literature: 'Padraic Colum has been influenced by the philosophy of Schopenhauer and Nietzsche,' he wrote. 'The gloom of Northern dramatists has entered into his soul.'[63] The controversy started in earnest when the poet Ella Young, writing in *Sinn Féin*, declared that the play was 'as good as the best work of Ibsen'.[64]

A *Sinn Féin* correspondent writing under the pseudonym of 'X' stepped up to answer the questions posed by the recurrence of Ibsen's name in the various responses to Colum's play. In an attack on *Thomas Muskerry*, 'X' tried to explain who Ibsen was, why he deserved the epithet of a great national writer and why, in spite of this distinction, his influence was not beneficial to Irish playwrights. Entitling his article 'Muskerryism', 'X' presented the following thesis: as a mere imitator of Ibsen, Colum did not only show himself an inferior playwright, he also failed to live up to his potential as a 'peasant-minded' writer.[65] 'The only literary man in Ireland,' lamented 'X', had 'set off after the gods of other peoples and his greatest praise now is to be compared with Ibsen.'[66] 'X' insisted that Colum's main mistake was his inability to understand Ibsen's true greatness – his patriotism, his respectful portrayal of Norwegian people and his dedication to the Norwegian language.

> If Ibsen had painted his countrymen as sexless creatures such as Thomas Muskerry ... if he had written his plays in the language of the country to which Norway was unwillingly bound, and produced them in Stockholm for the Norway-hating Swedes to judge of how true they were to the Norwegian character an analogy might be drawn.[67]

'X's' article testifies to the degree of popular ignorance of Ibsen's life and the reception of his plays in Norway. The discrepancy between the playwright's fame and the scarcity of productions of his plays in Dublin created a vacuum, and that vacuum was filled by myths. The idea that Ibsen was primarily a nationalist writer was one of them. This belief had been circulating ever since Yeats first postulated it in the 1899 campaign for the Irish Literary Theatre. Colum himself further contributed to it with his 1906 article 'Ibsen and the National Drama'. By 1910, as 'X's article indicates, the myth had become established as fact. It served an important purpose in resolving the dilemma between political and aesthetic appreciation of the theatre that was posed by the emergence of Irish realism.

As Hogan and Burnham observe, 'the mind of the ordinary theatregoer in the Abbey pit was in something of a schizophrenic state in 1910'.[68] The realistic plays of Colum, Robinson, Murray and Ray presented a view of the Irish peasantry and working classes that was offensive to nationalistic audiences. Their 'grasping, mean, malicious, treacherous, uncouth, and basically stupid'[69] characters seemed little better than that hated figure of the English theatre: the stage Irishman. However, Irish audiences could not ignore the new plays' dedication to the accurate representation of local speech, their tragic power and their modernity. Ibsen's figure loomed large over these new dramas. Their authors openly acknowledged their respect for his rarely seen and little known plays. Consequently, critics such as 'X' or O'Dempsey tried to establish Ibsen as an ideal beyond the reach of Irish playwrights. In their articles, Ibsen emerged as a realist who extolled his countrymen and a radical innovator who did not offend against established traditions, in other words, as a deeply desired impossibility.

Colum protested that his debt to Ibsen in *Thomas Muskerry* was as slight as Ibsen's to Eugène Scribe and Victorien Sardou. He disputed 'X''s claim that Ibsen 'wrote in language which is to Norway what Irish is to Ireland' by pointing out that Ibsen wrote in Bokmaal, a literary language close to Danish, rather than Landsmaal, a 'language peculiar to Norway'.[70] He noted that Ibsen was anxious for the good opinion of Danish critics and that his dramas were treated with contempt in Norway. He countered the charge that his portrayal of Irish people emasculated them by insisting that his characters 'are at least as masculine as Tesman in *Hedda Gabler* or Hyalmar [*sic*] in *The Wild Duck*'.[71] But his arguments were met with another eulogy to the supposedly patriotic Ibsen:

> When he was lashing Norway into consciousness, he smashed the plaster-of-paris Norwegian that no one believed in, but that all at home paid homage to and all abroad despised, and put in its place a real man ... He gently insinuated that not only was the Norwegian – schemer and liar in part though he painted him – as good a man as his neighbours, but, taking his circumstances into consideration, perhaps a trifle better. And that was what Ibsen did for his country. That is what the dramatists of the Abbey Theatre are not doing for Ireland.[72]

The *Thomas Muskerry* controversy rumbled on for several months. One of the most eloquent defenders of the play was Riobard Ua Floinn writing in *An tEireanach*. He argued against the practice of praising Ibsen and condemning Irish playwrights in the same breath and pointed out that nationalist literary criticism was becoming restrictive and self-negating. 'Is our national movement to be a movement for liberty or a movement of servitude?' he asked. 'If we vote for servitude, then we vote not only for the death of literature, but for the death of nationality, for these can only live in the sunny air of freedom or the desire for freedom.'[73] Ua Floinn's choice of words is markedly Ibsenite. His equation of servitude with death and freedom with the sun is reminiscent of Mrs Alving's speech in Act 2 of *Ghosts* in which she speaks of 'dead ideas and lifeless old beliefs'[74] and of her countrymen's pitiful fear of the light. Ua Flion's defence of *Thomas Muskerry* shows that Ibsen's ideas, the language of his plays and his metaphors had infiltrated Irish literary life, along with misconceptions of the kind expressed by 'X'. It also suggests that one of the main problems in the pre-1916 Irish reception of Ibsen was the discrepancy between the Ibsenian notion of freedom and that of the Irish nationalists.

In 1915, Padraic Pearse published an essay entitled 'Ghosts' which borrowed the title from, and revealed Pearse's misunderstanding of, Ibsen's play. 'Ghosts are troublesome things in a house or in a family, as we knew even before Ibsen taught us,' wrote Pearse. 'There is only one way to appease a ghost. You must do the thing it asks you. The ghosts of a nation sometimes ask very big things; and they must be appeased, whatever the cost.'[75] Ghosts are indeed troublesome in Ibsen's play – they are venereal diseases and incestuous relationships that lurk beneath the veneer of nineteenth-century respectability. They are outmoded ideals and stifling conventions that inhibit individual freedom. In his article Pearse inverted the metaphor. His ghosts are the voices of Wolfe Tone, John Mitchell, Thomas Davis, James Fintan Lalor and Parnell summoning Irishmen to arms. Ibsen's *Ghosts* is an exposure of the morbidity of idealism; Pearse's 'Ghosts' is a protest against the decay of ideals in his generation.

Pearse's article indicates that the Irish realists had to confront a more serious problem than the resentment of their countrymen. The new generation of Irish Ibsenites considered themselves national, indeed nationalist, writers and attempted to combine their nationalism with Ibsenism, two things which, as Pearse's misreading of *Ghosts* demonstrates, are not readily compatible.

Shaw defined the quintessence of Ibsenism in 1891 as an 'attack on ideals and idealism'.[76] Even though Ibsen's realist plays do not deal specifically with nationalism, his letters reveal a mistrust of this ideal: 'I do not believe,' Ibsen wrote in 1879, 'that it is our mission to be responsible for the freedom and independence of the State, but rather to awaken individuals to freedom and independence – and as many of them as possible.'[77] In 1884, Ibsen confessed to the Danish composer Niels Ravnkilde that while he was prepared to defend his native country from attack, he was no patriot. He considered his fatherland to be the entire world and humankind to be his nationality. He also believed that in time, the whole world would speak one language and constitute one nation.[78]

The difficulty in reconciling the Ibsenite attack on idealism with nationalist ardour is noticeable in Robinson's *Patriots*. When produced on 11 April 1912, *Patriots* was remarkably well received. The audience at the Abbey 'listened [to the play] with rapt attention like a class of well behaved children'.[79] *Patriots* was called 'a wonderfully balanced' play and a 'marvellous piece of characterisation'.[80] And, said one eyewitness, 'the funny part is that no one could be sure what [Robinson]'s politics [ar]e'.[81] Robinson's indebtedness to Ibsen was widely acknowledged, yet none of the reviews mentioned the play's obvious affinity with *John Gabriel Borkman.*

Like John Gabriel, the protagonist of Robinson's play is an ex-convict. After eighteen years in prison, James Nugent returns home hopeful of resuming his armed fight against the English occupation. He discovers that his past comrades in arms have sunk into drunken complacency, while his devoted wife Ann is an embittered miser. She has turned the shop that was once a safe place for rebels into a successful business. Parliamentarianism is predominant in the Ireland to which Nugent returns. In his attempts to rekindle the spirit of revolution, Nugent is followed only by the representatives of the younger generation: his disabled daughter Rose and her admirer Willie, the only son of his old friend. A confrontation with Ann occurs when Nugent tries to prevent her from evicting Willie's parents for not paying their rent. Ann confronts her husband by telling him how his arrest forced her to become the sole provider for their daughter; times were hard: she had no choice but to become harder. In the final scene, Ann tells Nugent that it was the shock of his arrest that caused her to go into premature labour, which left the child permanently disabled. On learning the truth Nugent seems to age instantly. He finds the strength only for these words:

> I've killed a man, I've crippled a child, I've got myself shut up for eighteen years – God knows what good came out of it all – but ... I meant – I tried ... I know I meant right – and in prison my cell used

> to be filled with the sad faces of men like me who had given everything for Ireland – they would not have come to me, would they? If I hadn't been of their company. They are here now – I see them all around me – there is Wolfe Tone, and there is ... oh quiet watching faces, I have tried – tried as you tried – and been broken ...[82]

A prisoner's return to freedom, lost chance wife, a squandered family fortune, an embittered happiness of an ideal for which unjust sacrifices have been made and which remains beyond the hero's reach – *Patriots* resembles a simplified version of *John Gabriel Borkman*. Like Ibsen's tragedy of an embezzler of Napoleonic ambitions, *Patriots* explores idealism through the juxtaposition of the impassioned hero and the spiritually impoverished people whose happiness he has destroyed. Both *John Gabriel Borkman* and *Patriots* lead their characters into a dead-end. Like Borkman's wife Gunhild and her sister Ella, the once passionate and loving Ann had given in to bitterness and hatred. Like the kindly Vilhelm Foldal, who alone believes in Borkman's ability to restore his name and make a fortune, Nugent's friends nurture their passive acceptance of foreign rule with feeble dreams of a better future and memories of their past battles.

A significant difference between the two plays is in the authors' choice of an occupation for their idealist-hero. In Ibsen's play the grandiose dreams of self-fulfilment, altruism and divine vocation are launched on the unlikely figure of a corrupt banker and would-be millionaire. Only through his powerful rhetoric does John Gabriel convince the audience that his monetary greed is nothing but a glorious, revolutionary ideal. Through his fantastic language, John Gabriel invests finances with the power and appeal of magic:

> I seem to touch them, the prisoned millions; I can see the veins of metal stretch out their winding, branching, luring arms to me. I saw them before my eyes like living shapes, that night when I stood in the strong-room with the candle in my hands. You begged to be liberated, and I tried to free you. But my strength failed me; and the treasure sank back into the deep again.[83]

As he recites this love song to his imagined riches, the audience loses sight of the swindler and sees a warrior of ancient splendour. Through his character's language, Ibsen demonstrates that the vitality and power of an ideal are independent of its immediate basis in reality. By contrast, Robinson chooses for his hero an ideal that would be immediately understood by his audiences and whose power has been developed in the real world, outside the bounds of his play. Consequently, Nugent's speeches do not need to be eloquent. It is enough that his wife remembers his ardent nationalist addresses, and the audience will recall the 'James Nugents of history'[84] and believe in the eloquence of Robinson's hero.

The play was interpreted as a homage to revolutionaries and as propaganda for the physical force movement, not only by some of the contemporary reviewers but also recently by Christopher Murray:

> Although it is clear that to Robinson Nugent is the real hero, violent though his republicanism is, it is equally clear from the ending of *Patriots* that the majority reject Nugent's dream. The play is thus a study of a social leader passed by and isolated by a change in public mood. The irony of the ending provides a sharp critique of this public mood, and adds as it were, a bold question mark to the play's title.[85]

Yet, while the Nugent is a more interesting and sympathetic character than his apathetic countrymen, it would be wrong to ignore his guilt for the fate of his daughter. The dreamy, patriotic Rose is an innocent victim, a casual sacrifice to Nugent's patriotism. Her name is important. In the tradition of *aisling* poetry, Rose stands for Ireland – an Ireland disfigured by the violence of her would-be saviours. Nor can one discount Ann's condemnation of patriotism in the following interchange with Nugent:

> JAMES I am thinking of my country. If patriotism demands –
> ANN Oh don't talk to me of patriotism – I am sick of it. It's made Sullivan a bankrupt; it's made Brennan a drunkard; you a murderer; it's destroyed my happiness; it's made Rose a cripple.[86]

The 'bold question mark' implicit in the play's title refers as much to the slovenly townspeople as to Nugent himself. The former are condemned for their lack of idealism and for their materialistic acceptance of foreign rule; the latter is condemned for disregarding the human consequences of his fight for freedom. Through the figure of the suffering child, Robinson reveals, like Ibsen in *Brand, Little Eyolf* and *The Wild Duck*, the horror at the heart of idealism, the inhumanity of a philosophy that believes in the supremacy of any cause, however righteous, over a single life.

This is not to discredit Murray's reading. Robinson himself invited this interpretation, dedicating the play to 'the James Nugents of history'. The dedication contradicts the play's conclusion. It is as if Ibsen had dedicated *The Wild Duck* to Gregers Werle. The dedication diverts the reader's attention from the play's Ibsenite condemnation of idealism and focuses it instead on the nationalist sympathies of its author.

Another interesting case is Thomas MacDonagh's *Pagans*, produced by the Irish Theatre on 19–24 April 1915, almost exactly a year before its author, one of the signatories of the Proclamation of Independence, was executed by a British firing squad. 'A Modern Play in Two Conversations', as it was subtitled, *Pagans* depicts three people for whom religion has no significance and who have no regard for the institution of marriage. Transposing the gender roles of *A Doll's House*, MacDonagh's play begins where Ibsen's ended. The husband has fled the doll's house in search of personal freedom, and the wife is left to meditate on the failure of their marriage. In a conversation with Helen Noble, an artist who admits to being in love with her husband, Frances Fitzmaurice analyses the reasons for John Fitzmaurice's leaving. Accustomed to high society life, she found her friends' condescension to John intolerable; she was even more disappointed by his failure to conform.

As in the case of the Helmers, idealism was partly to blame for the failure of this marriage. 'Can you not understand,' Frances says to Helen, 'that one may have an ideal – that one may want another – a husband, say – to be that ideal – that one may see that he could be so – that he is so at times? Is it wrong to wish him to have no other times – no other moods? He may spoil it by being lower than himself.'[87] A feminist and individualist, Helen believes that she would 'have accepted him as he was' while also being able to 'go her way': 'the thing that makes intercourse between people is the free play of individuality. We should let others be just what they are.'[88] This is why, in spite of her forebodings, she did nothing to prevent the Fitzmaurices' marriage. Helen tells Frances that she has recently seen John staring at the statue of the *Winged Victory of Samothrace* in the Louvre; when she saw him she fled in case John saw her. She returned three days later, saw him again and left Paris to return to Dublin.

The husband appears in Act 2. He had in fact noticed Helen at the Louvre. The shock of seeing his past love sent him back into the arms of his wife. Like the wild duck in Ibsen's play, the headless *Victory of Samothrace* becomes a symbol in which all the strands of the play coalesce. John had been reminded of the miniature reproduction of the statue in his wife's house. Then he saw Helen and realised that she might have loved him. Since it was too late to repair the damage done to Helen, he returned to Frances. Like Alfred and Rita Allmers at the end of *Little Eyolf*, the couple proceed to discuss the future of their relationship. In spite of her love for John, Frances realises that their life together would now be intolerable. And so the husband leaves once again, his conscience appeased and his freedom restored to him by his wife.

Pagans would have been no more than an imitation of Ibsen's plays and a reflection on Ibsenite ideas were it not for the final exchange between John and Helen, which, as Feeney observes, is foreshadowed 'only by a passing reference to his membership in revolutionary societies'.[89] The symbol of the Victory of Samothrace suddenly takes on a different meaning. As Levitas puts it, 'while ... gazing at the Victory of Samothrace [John Fitzmaurice] has been contemplating ... not adultery but the necessity of throwing himself into revolution'.[90] The ending of the play is worth quoting in full:

FRANCES Goodbye; you are right in all. I now feel quite free, too. For I, too, have been troubled often by a doubt as to the rightness of our separation. Now we know better. And I shall be glad to know that you can write your best work again.

JOHN Frances, I shall do better than write. A man who is a mere author is nothing. If there is anything good in anything I have written, it is the potentiality of adventure in me – the power to do something better than write. My writings have been only the prelude to my other work. Though I have been away from Ireland these three years, Frances, I know the progress of things here better than you do – and I know that the great opportunity is at hand. I have long regretted that I have not in my time had an opportunity of doing something worthwhile, and now it is here.

FRANCES Politics, John? What is the good of your leaving me, in order to free yourself, if you are going to mix yourself up in Irish politics? Half of our trouble was your political ideas.

JOHN I don't call them politics. Sooner than you think, Frances, politics will be dropped here, and something better will take their place. I am now free to do something to bring the better thing.

FRANCES John, you're a queer mixture. What had I to do with these things?

JOHN You were a hostage that I had given to the other cause – to this life that keeps you here. You are no longer my hostage.

FRANCES	John, what are you going to do?
JOHN	I am going to live the things that I have before imagined. It is well for a poet that he is double-lived. He has two stores of power. You will not know yourself in the Ireland that we shall make here – when I return to you. (*Exit John.*) [91]

In an instant, MacDonagh has transformed the play from a study of marriage that could be set anywhere in Europe into a play about the Ireland of 1915. The shock is considerable for the reader; it must have been even greater for the audience. The poet Michael Crevequer (who did not even like the play) recalled his state of mind on seeing it:

> Issuing forth into the lamplit April evening we felt impelled to run down the crowded length of O'Connell Street, talking as we ran, dodging round the pedestrians, and meeting again to continue our conversation, and finally reaching our rooms in a fever to prolong till morning the festive ecstasy *Pagans* aroused among our half-formulated theories of a thousand subjects.[92]

The ending reproduces the effect of unexpected elation that occurs at the end of Ibsen's plays. The wild landscape seen through the window in the settings of most of Ibsen's realistic dramas indicates, as D. E. S. Maxwell puts it 'the struggle between the wildness and closed life of the middle classes and the boundless life of the idealistic spirit'.[93] MacDonagh similarly created an atmosphere of a stifling doll's house. However, instead of gesturing towards the imaginary outside as the location of freedom, his ending points towards the auditorium as a source of that joy. It throws the doors open to the revolutionary spirit of the real Ireland.

But what of John's suggestion in the final words of the play that he will return to Helen? John here echoes Nora's parting words that should the greatest miracle occur, that is the transformation of their living together into marriage, she might regain her love for Torvald. But unlike Nora, who does not believe that 'a miracle of miracles'[94] may take place, John believes in the miraculous transformation of Ireland through which his union with Frances will become possible. The collapse of the old order, with its stifling social conventions, needs to occur before their life together can be resumed.

For all its emotional power, however, *Pagans*, as Michael Crevequer acknowledged in 1921, is not a good play; it is a 'philosophical statement rather than drama, an essay in dialogue'.[95] Moreover, what makes the ending of *Pagans* exciting is precisely the fact that it does not quite fit in with the rest of the play. Its final scene is a revolt against the constrictions of the writer's craft and a declaration of the author's allegiance to the adventure of real life. Like Robinson's dedication of *Patriots* or Pearse's misreading of *Ghosts*, MacDonagh's play demonstrates that Ibsenism did not work in the context of an idealistic struggle for independence. Like Pearse, who in his essay apologised 'to the shade of the Norwegian dramatist ... for a plagiaristic but inevitable title',[96] MacDonagh performed an exorcism of the spirit of Ibsen in preparation for the revolution.

Fourteen years after the Easter Rising, Shaw revisited his ideas on Ibsen's quintessence and reflected on the degree of public neglect of the social and political significance of Ibsen's plays to turn-of-the century Britain. Shaw contested, in the 1890s,

> that ... numerous body that may be called the Unintelligentsia was as unconscious of Ibsen as of any other political influence: a quarter of a century elapsed before an impatient heaven rained German bombs down on them to wake them to ... startling departures from the Victorian routine ... but they do not associate their advance in liberal morals with the great Norwegian. Even the Intelligentsia have forgotten that the lesson that might have saved the lives of ten million persons hideously slaughtered was offered to them by Ibsen.[97]

Writing primarily for English readers, Shaw does not include the Easter Rising in his consideration of idealism and war. Indeed, his position on the Rising was more complex than his pacifism might suggest.[98] Shaw's insight, however, is particularly relevant in the context of early twentieth-century Ireland. The Irish public knew even less than the English public did about Ibsen; and the Rising made the connection between idealism and death more immediately apparent to contemporaries than the First World War. Shaw's comment confesses the futility of such works as his own *The Quintessence of Ibsenism*; social changes may be predicted by artists and their explicators, but as the once radical ideas take root in society, the artists' influence is not acknowledged by the masses. The intelligentsia may overtly encourage artistic radicalism, yet this class too often proves to be blind or unwilling to grasp those facets of radical art that contradict current ideology.

Shaw has been largely discredited as a critic of Ibsen. Michael Meyer, for instance, pronounces Shaw's book on Ibsen as 'one of the most misleading books about a great writer that can ever have been written' and suggests *Ibsen Considered as a Socialist* or *The Quintessence of Shavianism* as more appropriate titles.[99] Yet Shaw's signalling to the attack on idealism as a key aspect of Ibsen's work is not only particularly important to his Irish reception, it also anticipates the work of modern literary critics in assessing Ibsen's position within the development of European modernism As Moi has recently argued, Ibsen's drama marks the beginning of modernism in its challenge to the idealist aesthetics. The late nineteenth–early twentieth-century belief that 'beauty, truth, and goodness were one', and that 'the task of art is to uplift us to point the way to the ideal', was reflected not only in romantic, but also in realist writing.[100] The plays of the early Irish realists discussed in this chapter and their reception are a case in point. Taking on board Moi's argument that modernism grew out of the disintegration of idealism,[101] the next chapter examines further Irish works from the 1910s. Plays by Murray and Martyn and a story by James Joyce are discussed alongside press responses to plays by Ibsen in which the modernist impulse appears particularly strong. These are plays that combine realism with symbolism or, to be more precise, in which the meticulous analysis of the life of the everyday exposes the disjointed state of reality. Superstition has replaced religious belief, and language has replaced logic.

4

Beyond Realism: the Reception of Ibsen's 'Symbolist' Plays

Ducks and anchors in the sitting room

George Moore tells the following anecdote about Edward Martyn's misadventures as a playwright:

> I went to see him one night, and he told me that the theme of the play he was writing was a man who had married a woman because he had lost faith in himself; the man did not know, however, that the woman had married him for the same reason, and the two of them were thinking – I have forgotten what they were thinking, but I remember Edward saying: I should like to suggest hopelessness. I urged many phrases, but he said: It isn't a phrase I want, but an actual thing. I was thinking of a broken anchor – that surely is a symbol of hopelessness. Yes, I said, no doubt, but how are you going to get a broken anchor into a drawing room? I don't write about drawing-rooms. Well, living rooms. It isn't likely that they would buy a broken anchor, and put it by the coal scuttle.
>
> There's that against it, he answered. If you could suggest anything better – What do you think of a library in which there is nothing but unacted plays? The characters could say, when there was nothing for them to do on the stage, that they were going to the library to read, and the library would have the advantage of reminding everybody of the garret in the *Wild Duck*.[1]

Moore's answer mocks Martyn's reliance on Ibsen. More than that – it uncovers a significant difficulty in contemporary reception of Ibsen's symbolism. In Ibsen's drama 'actual things', such as the bird or the artificial forest in the garret of *The Wild Duck*, the orphanage in *Ghosts*, the pistols in *Hedda Gabler* or the crutch in *Little Eyolf*, have the potential to be read as symbols standing for the central themes of the plays and the psychological tendencies of the characters. In the highly influential *The Ibsen Secret* (1907), Jeanette Lee proposed that uncovering such symbols was the key to understanding Ibsen's drama: 'An object or event is used as a central theme or motive of the play.'[2] The symbol always appears at the climax of the action, Lee insisted: 'Toward this symbol the ostensible action of the play moves, and from it, it recedes.'[3]

Indeed, this was the way Martyn used symbols in *The Heather Field* (1899), lauded by its co-author, Moore, as 'the first play written in English inspired by the examples of Ibsen'.[4] The heather field, which the protagonist Carden Tyrrell vainly attempts to cultivate, is, in Moore's reading, 'the symbol of his incurable nature: whatever its circumstances it will seek its destiny out and find it; and with the flowering of the Heather Field, Carden passes quietly over the border land'.[5] Martyn made it his business to highlight the connection between the central symbol of the play and its character in Act 1. Barry Usher explains that the sensitive and imaginative Carden should never have married the level-headed Grace. He then proceeds to speak of the field: 'Certain natures refuse domestication and if domesticated, something later breaks out with a vengeance.'[6]

The Heather Field is not a bad play. However, there is something jarring in Martyn's laboured use of the symbol. Moore's anecdote – written a decade after his praise for *The Heather Field* – derides the woodenness of Martyn's technique. The notion that a symbol could be introduced into a nearly finished play in order to secure its aesthetic integrity is ridiculed in the absurd image of the bored characters staring at a broken anchor in the middle of the living room. The statue of the *Victory at Samothrace* in MacDonagh's *Pagans* is just such a symbol. It was chosen, no doubt with some deliberation, for the richness of its revolutionary meaning and implanted in the play. The problem was that MacDonagh and Martyn's dedication to Ibsen was not accompanied by an in-depth understanding of the way symbolism is integrated into the language of his characters. Like Lee, Martyn regarded Ibsen's symbols as illustrations meant to facilitate the reader in uncovering the play's meaning. In Lee's words, the action in Ibsen's drama 'is not progressive, but static; and it is, thus, best revealed not by events, but by pictures; that is, by symbols'.[7]

Yet Ibsen was antagonistic to such readings of his plays. He was angered, for instance, by one critic's assertion that the Strange Passenger, who appears in Act 5 of *Peer Gynt*, 'is a symbol of terror and anxiety'. 'Even if I were on the verge of being executed,' Ibsen protested, 'and if all it would take to save my life would be an explanation like that, it would still not occur to me. I never thought of such a thing. I stuck in the scene as a mere caprice.'[8] When asked about the meaning of the Button Moulder in the same play, Ibsen suggested that he should be taken as a common fairy-tale figure,[9] not, that is, as a representation a philosophical idea. In 1897, when the majority of his so-called symbolist plays had been published, Ibsen was asked to comment on the Lugnë Poe's interpretations of his works in the Théâtre d'Oeuvre. Ibsen emphasised that the director had used too much symbolism and too much mysterious lighting. 'I am not looking for symbols,' he said. 'I depict people.'[10] Still, he was not averse to the term, describing *The Master Builder* to Maurice Bigeon as a 'symbolist play'.[11] In the same 1893 interview, Ibsen outlined the difference between his aesthetics and Zola's: 'The symbols Zola uses are the result of the events, a conclusion to the drama. My symbols are the beginning, the premises – are even the reason for the existence of things. They contain reality, while those of Zola are explained by reality.'[12]

What Ibsen rejects is any differentiation between the literal and the symbolic. This approach dominated late nineteenth- and early twentieth-century critiques of his plays (and has not quite disappeared in contemporary criticism). For Lee, Ibsen's drama appears realistic on first reading: its primary purpose is to represent life. The secondary meaning, conveyed through symbols whose meaning is developed through the course of the play, emerges on closer inspection. Ibsen's realism and his symbolism are thus separated in the critic's mind. The symbols merely represent the central facets of the characters and the themes of the play.[13] Similarly, Michael Meyer, in his analysis of *Peer Gynt*, applies the terms 'stand for' or 'represent' to such figures as the trolls, the Strange Passenger or the Button Moulder in order to explain what the play 'is really about'[14] as opposed to what it might seem to the naïve reader.

However symbols, fantastic figures and folkloric images are developed by Ibsen primarily not as metaphors for the abstract ideas explored in his plays. They should not be taken as belonging to a different semantic level from the plays' more realistic details. The existence of such 'unrealistic' elements, their validation and interpretation is couched in the language of the characters. It is the characters who allegorise their world[15] or seize on symbols as keys to understanding their predicament. Further, the belief in what Freud termed the 'omnipotence of thought'[16] permeates Ibsen's plays. His drama – at least from *Peer Gynt* on – explores the idea that reality may be altered through thought: tragic events can be caused by casually dropped phrases. Language in Ibsen has a power of its own, determining the action and outcome of the play. For Ibsen, as for the later modernist writers, language is the 'creating structure of the human world'.[17]

The Ibsen week, *The Master Builder*, T. C. Murray and *Ghosts*, 1908–10

From 11 May 1908, a 'special London company' headed by Octavia Kenmore and Leigh Lovell was engaged at the Gaiety Theatre to play *The Master Builder, Hedda Gabler* and *A Doll's House* for a week. They performed to almost empty houses. Holloway blamed the actors for making *Hedda Gabler* particularly tedious: 'there was a dreadfully dull monotony about the whole thing, and it was no wonder that a voice was heard to say "wake up!" during the second act.'[18] The acting style was unduly theatrical: 'None of the players looked their parts, and the undertone sing-song chant adopted by them wearied and was very difficult to follow no matter how much one liked to hear.'[19] 'The whole thing,' he concluded, 'was as stagey as a Queen's [Theatre] blood and thunder drama.'[20]

The Master Builder attracted the smallest audience and mystified most critics. The architect Holloway became deeply involved in the story of a fellow 'master-builder ... with little love for climbing scaffolding'.[21] However, he admitted that the 'play is full of strange fanciful ideas hard to rightly grasp the true inwardness of ... I candidly confess much of the doings on the stage puzzled me'.[22] J. H. Cox of the *Independent* was similarly baffled:

> The author presents a group of everyday characters in commonplace surroundings and preposterously improbable situations. It is allegory rather than reality and the key must be sought ... The difficulty with *The Master Builder* is that you don't know where the realism ends, and mysticism begins, the message is not clear.[23]

The 1908 production of *The Master Builder* was Dublin's first encounter with Ibsen's later drama, which relies on Norse folklore to a far greater extent than the prose plays pre-dating *The Wild Duck*.[24] The protagonist of the play, the middle-aged architect Halvard Solness, talks of trolls and demons, castles in the air and the distant kingdom of Orangia. This play, containing references to the legend of St Olaf and a troll church-builder,[25] is a supreme example of what Eric Bentley terms Ibsen's 'romanticism driven underground'. 'Ibsen's realistic tragedy,' writes Bentley, 'depends ... on non-realistic elements for its success. Inside the skins of those prim-looking women and beefy looking men lurk the trolls and devils of Norse folk tale, the trolls and devils of Ibsen's inner consciousness.'[26] Yet, the Irish public remained impervious to the folkloric resonances of the play, complaining merely how awkward Ibsen's use of symbolism was. The critic for the *Dublin Evening Mail* believed that a major flaw of the play (and not, he stressed, of the acting) was

> a staginess in the persons that we would find uncomfortable and bizarre in real life, while recognising its sincerity and truth, yet our verdict would be, 'It's not done.' There is a kind of exaltation, a mysticism, a symbolism in the play, in the people, and in the speeches, interwoven with an intense and exact realism, that turns the whole drama into a sermon, an exposition of life, an allegory and its persons, in some sort into types.[27]

The Master Builder confused not only Dublin theatre critics, but also the Trinity College professor Edward Dowden. 'Both the action and the dialogue of *The Master Builder*, which may serve as an example of his latest group of plays,' he wrote, 'are denaturalized by the symbolic intentions.'[28]

As Grene demonstrates in his analysis of the public's antagonism to *The Playboy*, turn-of-the-century Dublin audiences demanded clear distinctions between symbolism and realism, social critique and extravaganza.[29] The popular approaches to the rarely staged Ibsen encapsulated this need for such distinctions. Ibsen was regarded primarily as a social realist and on some occasions as a patriotic revivalist. The idea that Ibsen's plays merged folklore and realism had not yet been advanced in Dublin press. Moreover, in their analyses of *The Master Builder*, Dublin critics missed a significant point – a passage central to the understanding of the protagonist's dilemma and the play's thematic and stylistic novelty.

J. H. Cox explained that the play concerns Halvard Solness, a 'foremost architect afflicted with a dread that some man of the rising generation will snatch his laurels'.[30] He is also, Cox said, tormented by guilt:

> He broods on the conviction that the fathomless melancholy of his childless wife is traceable to the loss, years before, of their twin infants, whose death resulted from the burning of their first house. Conscious of supreme will power, he feels an inward guilt that the fire was induced by his yearning to win a name by the buildings he would raise on the vacant site. And he believes that he thus sacrificed domestic joy to worldly fame.[31]

This summary of Solness's confession to Hilda Wangel imposes a causal link between the fire and Solness's guilt. Yet this is not the case in Ibsen's play.

Solness's children did not die in the fire. Rather, their death was an indirect result of the accident: Solness's wife, Aline, sank into depression following the destruction of her home. Her milk became poisonous, yet, out of a sense of duty, she insisted on nursing the twins until they were beyond saving. And Solness's guilt does not originate solely from his confidence in the power of his will: it is rooted in the selfish behaviour which preceded but did not cause the outbreak of the fire. 'Just sit down again, Hilda, and I'll tell you something funny, he says and proceeds to explain how he noticed a 'crack in the chimney'.[32] He did not repair it or inform anyone about the flaw because, he says, 'I was revolving something in my mind. Through that little black crack in the chimney, I might, perhaps, force my way upwards – as a builder.'[33] Solness then proceeds to tell Hilda his dream-turned-nightmare about a fire, which, harming no one, would enable him to gain fame.

Up to this moment, writes Robert Brustein, 'the passage looks like a perfectly conventional piece of exposition, with the playwright demonstrating how the past influences the present – how Solness began his career and developed his guilty conscience ... . But then something extraordinary happens in the scene, as Ibsen proceeds to annihilate his own very carefully fashioned casual construction':[34]

HILDA Well, but now listen, Mr. Solness. Are you perfectly certain that the fire was caused by that little crack in the chimney!

SOLNESS No, on the contrary – I am perfectly certain that the crack in the chimney had nothing whatever to do with the fire.

HILDA What!

SOLNESS It has been clearly ascertained that the fire broke out in a clothes cupboard – in a totally different part of the house.

HILDA Then what is all this nonsense you are talking about the crack in the chimney![35]

The dialogue contrasts the rational view of the world, in which one can only be guilty for the direct results of one's actions to Solness's magical worldview. Solness cannot shed off his guilt even though he knows that his actions did not physically cause the fire. In fact, he becomes almost certain of his implication in the tragedy precisely *because* there is no link between his actions and the accident.[36] The play's power lies in convincing the reader of the plausibility of Solness's fantastic interpretation of events.

Confronted with the text of *The Master Builder*, the reader (or spectator) seeks to impose order on the chaos. Discovering a connection between the disjointed events of the house fire, the twins' death and their father's obsession with the crack in the chimney seems necessary for solving one of the main problems of the play: the extent of Solness's guilt. Had Ibsen made the broken chimney the cause of the fire, then Solness would be guilty. Had Ibsen neglected to mention Solness's failure to repair it, then Solness would be innocent: the connection between his fantasies and the actual fire would be a mere coincidence. As the play stands, Solness appears to be guilty of a coincidence. Solness believes that the incident with the crack in the chimney is proof of his unconscious ability to summon 'the helpers and the servers'[37] – figures of his private mythology. This idea might well be the product of obsessive-compulsive disorder, but the reader becomes convinced that Solness is right. The play exploits the desire for events to have a cause, at least events in plays. Solness's belief in the 'helpers and servers' provides the necessary logical connection between the tragedy and its confessed culprit. It is through logic and rationality that the play whispers to the reader its dark tale of the malignant power of dreams and desires.

Brustein contends that in this passage Ibsen anticipates modernism by 'undermin[ing] a basic assumption of the naturalist universe'.[38] In the post-Einsteinian age, he suggests, there are no clear connections between causes and their consequences: 'Isn't it possible that events are so multiple and complex that human intelligence may never be able to comprehend the full set of causes preceding any situation, consequence, or feeling?'[39] Moreover, what constitutes Ibsen's modernism, as revealed in *The Master Builder*, is not merely the replacement of the nineteenth-century view of the universe with the admission of the ineptitude of rationalism in the face of the world's complexity. The play is Ibsen's test-case revealing the degree to which myth permeates modern psychology.

For Solness, the mysterious 'helpers and servers' and the troll that he thinks may hide within him are not metaphors or symbols, but threatening creatures of his private mythology. The power that Solness ascribes to his thoughts is akin to what anthropologists term 'mana'.[40] Like a tribal chief, Solness believes in luck as an external and sometimes malevolent force that accompanies his life. James Frazer, coming after

Ibsen, would insist on a distinction between the primitive and the civilised worldview. Ibsen, however, anticipating later developments in anthropology,[41] admits a difficulty in such a separation. Solness develops his mythical view of the universe out of the Christian belief in sin, whereas 'rational' readers accept the myth because of its internal logic.

Dublin audiences, puzzled by *The Master Builder*, dismissed its nuanced analysis of mythical thinking as poorly developed symbolism. Indeed, Ibsen's Irish disciples, the Cork Realists, were similarly oblivious to this aspect of their master's art. Lennox Robinson's *Patriots*, for instance, traces a causal relationship between the protagonist's guilt and the events that led to his child's disability. This guilt, in turn, implicates his understanding of himself as a failed patriot. T. C. Murray's *Maurice Harte* (1912) is another work that simplifies the Ibsen play which it self-consciously follows.

Maurice Harte (premièred in Dublin on 12 September 1912) is the tragedy of a seminarian who has not experienced a vocation. Maurice suffers a mental breakdown after succumbing to his family's demand that he become a priest. At the core of the play is the Ibsenite conflict between duty to oneself and social and family responsibilities. For Maurice, becoming a priest amounts to sacrilege. However, his mother tells him that the family has put themselves in debt to pay for his education. Both the family's good name and his brother's marriage prospects depend on his ordination. Maurice fails to communicate the depth of his mental anguish to his family or the local priest. He decides to return to the seminary, only to suffer a complete mental breakdown two weeks before his ordination. In the final scene, the family listen helplessly to Maurice's insane ravings. The young seminarian falls victim to the society in which hypocrisy has become a means of survival and which is constrained by the overt structures of Catholicism, not its moral tenets.

The play also contains one of Ibsen's favourite tropes – the parents' unwitting or misguided destruction of their children (which occurs in nearly all the plays from *Lady Inger of Ostrat* to *When We Dead Awaken*). It is written concisely, with no monologues or asides. Exposition of past events is artfully conveyed through the characters' recollections. However, as Albert J. DeGiacomo observes, Murray was not able to see beyond the formal structure of Ibsen's plays.[42] A comparison to *Ghosts* reinforces the point.

The endings of the plays are markedly similar. In Murray's play Maurice 'gaz[es] intently into the heart of the fire'. 'In his profound absorption', he 'seems dead to externals'.[43] This recalls Ibsen's Oswald's sudden descent into madness, the moment when he 'seems to shrink together to the chair; all his muscles relax; his face is expressionless, his eyes have a glassy stare'.[44] Maurice's 'speaking to himself in a voice and manner startling in their indefinable strangeness'[45] reflects the 'dull, toneless voice' in which Oswald repeats the phrase: 'The sun – The sun'.[46] Mrs Alving's final utterance of horror and helplessness – 'No. no; no! – Yes! – No; no!' is echoed in the in the closing lines of *Maurice Harte*:

> MRS HARTE (*tottering towards a seat*). My God! My God! My God! (*The* priest looks at her with a pained sense of his own helplessness. The *curtain falls very slowly*)

Yet, in thus transposing *Ghosts* into an Irish setting, Murray simplified Ibsen's play. Consider the differences between what causes Oswald's breakdown and Maurice's. In both cases, the son's insanity is retribution for the mother's prioritising social conventions over individual truths. In Murray, there is a direct connection of cause with effect between the mother's behaviour and the son's demise. In Ibsen's play, the connection is indirect.

Oswald does not go insane because Mrs Alving reveals to him her past hypocrisy. He does not inherit syphilis because she had sent him away from home in an attempt to shield him from his father's depravity. He could not have been saved had Mrs Alving followed the dictates of her heart and abandoned her husband for her beloved Pastor Manders. Yet all these factors have a bearing on the final catastrophe of the play. For the reader, as well as for Mrs Alving, Oswald's madness is the ultimate revenge of the ghosts of 'dead ideals, and lifeless old beliefs'.[47] Seen from a purely naturalistic point of view, Mrs Alving is guilty only of conceiving a child with a man who, as she might not have known at the time, had syphilis. Yet (in ways similar to *The Master Builder*) *Ghosts* develops a deeper sense of Mrs Alving's implication in Oswald's fate.

This connection is established through the development of the motif of 'ghosts', a word originally used by Mrs Alving in Act 1, in reference to her recently acquired liberalism. She confesses to Pastor Manders her fear of 'the ghosts that hang about [her]', suggesting that 'we are all ghosts':

> It is not only what we have inherited from our father and mother that 'walks' in us. It is all sorts of dead ideas and lifeless old beliefs, and so forth. They have no vitality, but they cling to us all the same, and we cannot shake them off. Whenever I take up a newspaper,

> I seem to see ghosts gliding between the lines. There must be ghosts all the country over, as thick as the sands of the sea. And then we are, one and all, so pitifully afraid of the light.[48]

This language has the power to conjure visual images, all the more forceful because they are not depicted on the stage. Some readers may consider the word 'ghosts' an arbitrary metaphor used ornamentally by Mrs Alving and the author. Yet the term's recurrence in varying and conflicting contexts makes it difficult to dismiss it as a mere code-word. What one imagines when listening to Mrs Alving are malevolent creatures of European folklore and childhood nightmares.

The ensuing events of the play are, on one level, the workings of the magical undercurrent within Mrs Alving's seemingly predictable, rational and realistic world. Jorge Luis Borges has suggested a link between the belief in sympathetic magic, common to most 'primitive' cultures, and the structure of the novel. Catastrophes are foreshadowed in the fiction of Chesterton, Poe and Joyce through linguistic echoes. 'Every episode in a careful narrative is premonition';[49] casual conversations and trivial incidents may hint at the eventual tragedy. Ibsen's plays are also governed by this 'different order, both lucid and primitive: the primeval clarity of magic'.[50]

Mrs Alving summons up ghosts through her rhetoric, and the reader and audience long to see tangible proof of her ideas. They await a resolution that would confirm the fantastic notion that inherited ideals have a malevolent life of their own, that 'lifeless beliefs' have the power to destroy. The audience's trust in Mrs Alving's language is validated by the play's conclusion. Her metaphors are materialised when Oswald reveals that he has indeed inherited a mind-crippling disease, when, in the final scene, he gropes for the light and asks to be given the sun. The audience are thus manipulated into seeing a connection between language and action, between inner thoughts and external events, and between their own desire for a tragic resolution and the play's conclusion.

John Northam points out how Oswald, in describing his disease, echoes Mrs Alving. He speaks of his disease as his 'inheritance' 'lurking' (or waiting, as Archer translates *lurer*) within him, employing the words 'Mrs Alving herself used to describe what she meant by "ghosts"':[51] 'Yes, mother, it is seated here waiting. And it may break out any day – at any moment' (*den sidder herinde og lurer. Og den kan bryde løs hvad tid og time det skal være*).[52] His words echo Mrs Alving's earlier words, spoken of ghosts: '*Det er ikke levende i os; men det sidder i alligevel og vi kan ikke bli' det kvit.*'[53] Archer's translation of these words loses the syntactic echo.

Oswald and Mrs Alving refer to the disease and ghosts, respectively, in third-person singular. Oswald's 'it is seated inside' echoes Mrs Alving's 'it is not alive in us, but is seated there all the same'.

These are only a few out of the complex web of echoes and allusions through which Oswald's disease is linked to Mrs Alving's speech. As Northam points out, in Act 2, Oswald 'gives a wider reference to his disease; it is no longer a single, individual fact, but a fact related to, produced by, those ghosts of dead ideas by which society, and, as has been abundantly revealed, even Mrs Alving have always been haunted'.[54] The development of the motif of ghosts with all its attendant meanings establishes Mrs Alving's guilt. Her past conservatism, her surrender to a sense of duty, even her lack of love for her husband are all reflected in Oswald's fate. He becomes proof that malignant ideals can do physical harm.

Such mind-games are alien to Murray. The protagonist of his play goes mad simply because of his inability to resolve a conflict between the duty to his parents and the duty to his conscience. His parents are clearly to blame for his tragedy, as are the social and economic conditions of peasant Catholic Ireland. Oswald's insanity is related to his mother's thoughts; Maurice's insanity is the result of his mother's actions. Both *Ghosts* and *Maurice Harte* expose the horror of social conventions. But while in Ibsen social conventions become mythical forces, in Murray they are merely obstacles to individual fulfilment.

That Cork Realists, in spite of their admiration of Ibsen, ignored the complexity of his dramatic technique should not surprise us. Writing in 1980, Brustein deplored a similar problem in the development of American realistic drama: 'The fires that burn through most American plays have been caused by that crack in the chimney, and the guilty conscience of our theatrical characters can usually be traced to a single recognizable event.'[55] In other words, the Cork Realists' neglect of the problem of causality in Ibsen's plays and its relation to myth was a common phenomenon affecting Ibsen's reception throughout in the English-speaking world.

The Metropolitan Players and Edward Martyn as interpreters of Ibsen, 1913–16

From 1913 to 1916, the Metropolitan Players produced several Ibsen plays: *Little Eyolf* (premièred 17 May 1912, and staged again on 10 December the same year), *The Lady from the Sea* (9 and 11 December 1912), *Rosmersholm* (8 December 1913) and *The Master Builder*

(11–12 February 1916). According to one source, the company also produced *Ghosts* between 1914 and 1915.[56]

The Metropolitan Players evolved from the Dublin Players' Club. Both companies were supported by Martyn. He attended rehearsals and publicised the performances. George Nesbitt, who had performed in the earliest Dublin productions of Ibsen's plays, was the male lead for both companies. However, Flora MacDonnell, who had starred for the Dublin Players' Club, was succeeded by Elizabeth Young. Martyn was of the opinion that Nesbitt was 'the best Ibsen actor he ever saw'[57] and that Young was 'a born Ibsen actress'.[58] We get a glimpse of Young from the following recollection by Shelah Richards:

> Elizabeth Young ... was enormously conscious, and wanted you to be conscious, that she was a great actress of an era that had just passed ... She wore impressive hats and had veils dripping around her, and chains, and necklaces ... Elizabeth Young was the amateur actress supreme, and she talked in an ethereal whisper ... An incredible lady of a kind which every small capital has somewhere, but ... one was inclined to giggle at her. Still she ... had something ... She was terribly thin and had this wonderful, slightly foggy, ghostlike voice emerging from her pre-Raphaelite veils.[59]

Even taking into account Richards' habit of comic exaggeration, it is possible that Young, who played Ellida Wangel, Rita Allmers, Rebecca West and Hilda Wangel, invested these roles with mysticism and reinforced the supernatural element common to all the plays.

There is a discrepancy between the apparent coherence of this company's approach to Ibsen and the publicity of their productions. The plays were presented in aid of the Irish Women's Reform League (the Dublin branch of the Irish Women's Suffrage Federation established in October 1912).[60] The first Ibsen production by the Metropolitan Players was advertised in the suffragist newspaper *Irish Citizen* (established in 1912 by James Cousins and Francis Sheehy-Skeffington). Yet this article, entitled 'Henrik Ibsen: Feminist', testified more to popular ignorance about Ibsen (even among the feminist readers of the newspaper) than to any depth of engagement of the movement with his plays. 'It is not often enough recognised', wrote the anonymous author of the article, 'that [Ibsen] was a prophet and an apostle of the cause of woman: few modern writers have shown so keen and yet so sympathetic a comprehension of her nature and her latent powers.'[61] Evidently four productions of *A Doll's House* (the last, by Ben Iden Payne's company, performed on 7–11 March 1911) had not been enough to convince the public of Ibsen's feminism. Moreover, the *Irish Citizen* article did not provide any details of *The Lady from the Sea* and *Little Eyolf*, suggesting baldly that the performance should be welcomed by those 'interested in the woman movement'.[62]

Ibsen's belief that the sexes are equal in their needs and aspirations can be found in all his plays. However, unlike *A Doll's House*, these plays, as well as *Rosmersholm*, performed during Suffrage Week organised by the IWFL in 1913, cannot be easily interpreted as feminist manifestoes. Ellida in *The Lady from the Sea* chooses her wifely duties over passion; *Little Eyolf* explores female sexuality as a destructive force; *Rosmersholm* is a critique of the liberalist ideals, including that of emancipated womanhood. That these plays were performed in Dublin in aid of the Irish Women's Reform League and publicised in the suffragist paper is a puzzle. One solution is proposed by Paige Reynolds. She demonstrates how the rhetoric of self-sacrifice in *Rosmersholm* allowed the suffragist beneficiaries of the production to underline the similarities between their cause and nationalism.[63] Yet, it would be difficult to advance a similar argument in relation to the other two Ibsen plays presented by the Metropolitan Players in aid of the suffragists. Indeed, the *Irish Citizen* abstained from elaborating on Ibsen's feminism in its notice on *Rosmersholm* (the only play of the three to be reviewed in the paper). 'Miss Young', this critic argued, is 'almost too good for the play. For stage-presentation, it is not among Ibsen's best: its subtleties are too fine, its dialogue too long drawn out, its lack of incident – till the final catastrophe – too marked to make it really an effective drama.'[64] It is more likely that the suffragists did not have a part in selecting the plays from whose performances they benefited.

Sinn Féin, the *Irish Times* and the *Irish Review* published enthusiastic reviews, but they were all written by Edward Martyn. Most other critics abstained from any discussion of the plays. The press notices of *Little Eyolf*, *The Lady from the Sea* and *Rosmersholm* were confined to plot summaries and qualified praise for some of the actors, in particular Young. The *Irish Times* review of *Little Eyolf*, for instance, starts as follows: 'Without expressing about the play itself any opinions which might take too much space in justifying ...'[65]

One notable exception is an article by Evelyn Gleeson (a friend of Lily Yeats and a co-founder of the Dun Emer Guild) which appeared in *Sinn Féin* shortly before the December productions of *The Lady from the Sea* and *Little Eyolf*. 'Ibsen needs to be known,' Gleeson contended. 'Men think of Ibsen as dull and bald and dismal. Because he is plain spoken and fearless, they deny his lofty teaching. If he has held up the Norwegians in the pillory and pelted their faults with satire and contempt, he has taught the world to understand them.'[66] Noting Ibsen's greatness as a critic of social problems, Gleeson emphasised the importance of folklore in his writings: 'Sent by his Government early in the 'sixties to collect folk-lore and fairy tales, the old stories took strong hold of Ibsen's imagination.' 'All his poetry is tinged with the mystery of "the peaks and the stars and the great silence",' she observed, quoting from *Little Eyolf*, 'and his fancy recreates the weird and freakish beings of the Norse underworld.'[67]

This appears to be the first time that someone had pointed out in the Irish press the significance of folklore to Ibsen's later drama. The 'supernatural' and poetic facets of Ibsen's work had usually been ignored. The debate about the future of Irish drama, while it focused on whether romantic revivalism or realism was the best course for its development, had not explored a third possibility evidenced in the psychological drama of Ibsen – the marriage between realism and romanticism. In *The Lady from the Sea, Rosmersholm, Little Eyolf* and *The Master Builder*, Ibsen used folklore to reveal the haunted condition of the modern world. The irrational world of folk legends, myths and fairy-tales exists in the subconscious desires and fears of the realistically conceived characters. In 1912 Dublin, such an approach to folklore was a novelty. One playwright who attempted to imitate Ibsen's method was the person most responsible for the Metropolitan Players' productions of Ibsen's plays: Edward Martyn.

Martyn's *The Heather Field* (1899), *An Enchanted Sea* (1904) and *Grangecolman* (1912) are not merely influenced by Ibsen. Martyn went further. Unburdened by any anxiety to conceal his influences, Martyn alludes to Ibsen's characters, dialogues and themes. Echoes of *Ghosts, The Wild Duck, The Master Builder* and *Little Eyolf* are found in *The Heather Field.*[68] *An Enchanted Sea* recalls *The Lady from the Sea, Rosmersholm* and *Little Eyolf. Grangecolman* brings together *Hedda Gabler* and *Rosmersholm.* Gun-handling Hedda is recalled in the first scene of the play. Clare Farquhar, who is admonished for a similar habit, is a secretary to Michael Colman; their relationship is like Thea and Lovborg's, or indeed Rebecca West and Rosmer's: its passion emerges from a joint devotion to an intellectual cause (through which it is also temporarily sublimated). Yet the owner of an ancient Irish estate (whose name, Grangecolman, replicates Rosmersholm), Michael Colman, is not only Rosmer, he is also the late Dr West, Rebecca's adoptive father and (as it crucially emerges in the play) her biological father. Clare Farquhar mirrors Rebecca's feelings for Dr West: she adores Michael Colman as one who enlightened her and helped her discover her academic acumen. Rosmersholm is said to be haunted by a white horse portending death. A parallel belief in a ghostly white lady is found in Grangecolman. In both plays a servant impresses on the heroine the importance of the superstition for the master of the estate.

Martyn's ideology was radically different from Ibsen's. As W. J. Lawrence noted, with *Grangecolman* Martyn threw a 'bombshell into the camp of the Suffragists'.[69] Through the figure of Colman's daughter, who stages her suicide to prevent her father's marriage to Clare, Martyn attacked the suffragists' supposed self-indulgent denial of reality. His lack of interest in Ibsen's liberalism singles Martyn out among the contemporary Irish followers of the Norwegian playwright. Martyn's Ibsenism was aesthetic, not political. He admired Ibsen's psychological subtlety and classicism, comparing his work to the tragedies of Racine.[70] The inadequacy of Martyn's engagement with Ibsen is not, however, in the ideological disagreement of this conservative Catholic with the iconoclastic rebel against religious morality. Martyn's limited understanding of Ibsen's plays emerges in his attempts to imitate Ibsen's use of folklore.

When we consider the functions of the apparition of the white horse in *Rosmersholm*, it is useful to take on board Freud's convincing argument that Rebecca's suicide is promoted by the discovery that her relationship with Dr West was incestuous.[71] In referring to this essay, I do not propose to advance a Freudian reading of *Rosmersholm*. Rather, Freud's insight allows one to see how sexual anxieties and folkloric images are interwoven in Ibsen's play. Further, Freud's essay does not address folklore in *Rosmersholm*. Yet if for the modern reader the connection between the language of folklore and that of the subconscious, as it emerges in *Rosmersholm*, appears plausible – more readily accessible, that is, than it was for most turn-of-the-twentieth century readers of the play – this is due to our culture's gradual and prolonged exposure to Freud's theories on the proximity of dreams and folklore.

The white horse of Rosmersholm is simultaneously a folkloric being and an expression of Rebecca's thoughts and associations; and in this latter sense, the white horse is connected with her sexual desires and fears. These three meanings of the white horse, the folkloric, the sexual, and the one developed by Rebecca (and the reader) are unified in the play, though initially, they were discrete. The white horse is a legend preserved by Madam Helseth. '[I]t's the dead that clings to Rosmersholm,' she tells Rebecca, 'if it wasn't for that, there would be no White Horse.'[72] For the sceptical Rebecca, it is a metaphor for the tenacity of conservative ideas. She first uses it in relation to Kroll, Rosmer's former friend and brother-in-law. 'Let us hope he mayn't meet the White Horse! I am afraid we shall soon be hearing something from the bogies' (48), she says, as Kroll leaves the house furious at Rosmer's religious apostasy and newly discovered liberalism. The white horse was also an obsession of the allegedly mentally ill Beata, Rosmer's late wife. She alluded to the white horse, as she hinted to Kroll that her suicide was imminent. She also told him that she believed Rebecca was pregnant with Rosmer's child. Kroll did not confide Beata's accusations to Rosmer, believing his sister to be deranged. He saw the white horse and Rosmer's love affair as equally preposterous delusions of a diseased brain.

Rosmer and Rebecca have discovered the ideal of free thought and are set to liberate society from the crippling influences of guilt-ridden morality and religion. As this vision comes under attack from psychological and social forces, the separate meanings of the white horse gather into a single cluster of meanings. Once he hears of Rosmer's apostasy, which he associates with a moral lapse, Kroll starts to believe in Beata's suspicions and discloses them to Rosmer. Rosmer's newfound guilt causes him to doubt his vocation as an apostle of liberalism. For a while Rebecca clings to rationalism, presenting his guilty conscience as a form of superstition:

> ROSMER ... no cause ever triumphs that has its origin in sin.
>
> REBECCA (*vehemently*) Oh, these are only ancestral doubts – ancestral fears – ancestral scruples. They say the dead come back to Rosmersholm in the shape of rushing white horses. I think this shows that it is true.
>
> (109)

But Kroll deals an underhand blow when he tells Rebecca that his sources confirm that Dr West was her biological father. It is this that propels Rebecca down a suicidal path, beginning with her confession of a crime. She admits that she planted the idea of her pregnancy in Beata's mind. Through hints and suggestions she gradually pushed Beata towards suicide. Rebecca loved Rosmer and wished his wife would go; but these thoughts were never fully articulated. 'Surely you do not think I acted with cold and calculating composure,' she insists:

> I wanted Beata away, by one means or another; but I never really believed that it would come to pass. As I felt my way forward, at each step I ventured, I seemed to hear something within me cry out: No farther! Not a step farther!' And yet I **could** not stop.
>
> (130; original emphasis)

What Rebecca uncovers, through her confession, is the impossibility of seeing liberalism as a force of enlightenment opposed to conservative darkness. Through her manipulation of Beata, Rebecca has allied herself with precisely those 'prejudices and scruples' that she ridiculed as the 'white horses' of the modern world. She exploited the deep-rooted shame of the barren woman and exploited the common suspicions of her class, that friendship between an aristocrat and a servant is rarely platonic. The white horse can no longer be seen as a mere delusion or an amusing folk belief. For Rebecca, it loses its power as a metaphor for the limited worldview prevalent in Rosmersholm, becoming instead an expression of her inability to separate rationalism and superstition, liberalist idealism and conservatism, her plans for the emancipation of the masses and her incestuous past.

As she tries to leave Rosmersholm following her confession, she tells Madam Helseth that she has seen 'a glimpse of white horses' (133). These words acquire a power of their own, being an unconscious premonition of her death. At the end of the play, Madam Helseth thinks she sees something white glimmering in the dark park. The white form may simply be Rebecca's white shawl. Yet when Madam Helseth sees Rosmer and Rebecca plunge into the mill race, she sees their death as the work of a family ghost: 'The dead wife has taken them' (104). These last words serve to bring together the conflicting forces at work within *Rosmersholm*. The supernatural explanation of Rebecca and Rosmer's death given by Madam Helseth, has in this final scene the same hierarchical status as the explanation that sees Rebecca's troubled sexuality as what drives her to suicide, or indeed the approach which sees her death as atonement for Beata's. All these explanations are equated through the development of the motif of the white horse to its final destructive potential.

Through his use of the 'white lady' in *Grangecolman* as central to the family tragedy, Martyn attempted to mimic *Rosmersholm*. The white lady is mentioned twice in *Grangecolman* – in the opening scene, and again in Act 2, when the butler mistakes the white-clad Clare for the ghost. Like Rebecca, Clare sneers at the superstition. She declares that she would gladly shoot the apparition. True to her word she fires out the window at a white shape, only to discover that she has unwittingly killed Catherine, her fiancé's daughter. Catherine has sacrificed herself to prevent her father's marriage. Martyn was appreciative of Ibsen's ironic use of the white horse in *Rosmersholm*. In Martyn's play, as in Ibsen's, bright visions of the future contain signs of the impending tragedy. Clare is determined to shoot the ghost. She is happy to withstand all attempts at her master's liberty and peace of mind, including the demands of his daughter. Yet she is manipulated by Catherine to kill her, and in killing her make permanent Colman's guilt and superstitious dread.

Two things are missing from this construction. First, there is no sense in *Grangecolman* that the white lady may be real. Second, Martyn is blind to the nature of the relationship between Rebecca and Dr West. Or rather, in Colman and Clare, he presents a different version of their relationship, one that does not transgress sexual taboos. Clare thinks of Colman as her 'dear master', one who liberated her mind. She agrees to marry him because she is loath to leave him. Sexual passion is not articulated in Martyn's play, let alone sexual transgression. Yet the complex role of the motif of 'white horse' in Ibsen's play rests on the interplay between the power that her guilty secret has over Rebecca and Madam Helseth's belief in the local legend. Martyn, however, treats the supernatural only as an arbitrary structural device.

Nor does Martyn's 'white lady' reflect any specifically Irish legend: it is instead a generic ghost. By contrast, Ibsen's white horse reflects a number of Norse beliefs in shape-shifting horses and horses portending death. Folklore in *Rosmersholm* (and indeed in all later plays) is used in ways that anticipate Claude Lévi-Strauss, who 'recognizes the psychological component of myth, and even treats myth and neurosis as homologous manifestations of psychic trauma'.[73] Such an approach to folklore was unavailable to Martyn precisely because it involved addressing sexuality.

Martyn's difficulties with the subject emerge in *An Enchanted Sea*. In this play, as in *Rosmersholm*, the death of the aristocratic protagonist seems to fulfil a peasant superstition. Lord Mask returns to Ireland from Oxford in the hope of furthering the cultural revival through the study of folklore. He is believed to be descended from a sea fairie – a 'white lady' whose recent appearance on the shore is said to portend the end of the Mask line. The fairie has been sighted by some peasants and by Guy Font, the fifteen-year-old owner of an Irish estate run by his aunt. Reared by the tenants, Guy is a child of nature: '[h]is school is with those old world personifications of nature's forces'.[74] He is said to possess 'extraordinary powers' (134), 'a kind of second sight' (138). Lord Mask's hopes of Ireland and his passion for the ocean find answers in his friendship with Guy. The boy takes Lord Mask to a cave overlooking the sea where the two share a vision of the Irish sea-god Mananaan MacLir, surrounded by a host of chanting youths. Inspired by the sight, which reminds him of classical Greece, Lord Mask proposes a scheme of cultural revival for Ireland: 'Here in the Insula Sacra – the Ogygia of

Homer and our Hellenic ancestors – the genius is here and will soon awaken, and he will revive arts and trades and letters in our ancient tongue which all will speak again' (161). Guy's role will be the 'kindl[ing of] a nation's imagination'; Guy's cousin Agnes, who is in love with Mask, will 'attend a stall for Irish industries' and Mask himself will 'be prophet of all' (161). This plan is frustrated by Guy's aunt, Mrs Font. When she hears that Mask will not marry Agnes, she kills Guy in the cave. Lord Mask wanders off into the sea in the belief that he can see Guy's spirit and drowns.

An Enchanted Sea was performed once by the Players Club in 1904 in the same week as *Hedda Gabler*. It was a failure. Thomas MacDonagh proposed that the Irish Theatre revive it in 1914–15, but 'Edward would not hear of it and confided to him that Moore had suggested a disgusting connection between two characters which made Edward want to burn every copy of the play'.[75] What Moore was probably hinting at is that the relationship between Lord Mask and Guy is sexual. Indeed, it is hard to escape the feeling that Mask is in love with Guy and that it is this love that makes him reject Agnes. Mask associates Guy with his erotic dream of Greece:

MASK But your life of vision – it has awakened for me the genius of the Antique!
GUY What is the genius of the Antique?
MASK (*with abstracted exaltation*) Youth and form – pale marble form – !
GUY (*as if remembering.*) Like the boys in the court of Mananaan –
MASK I have dreamed it all in solitary days at Eton and Oxford; and now your genius has made me see in Ireland my dream of old Greece. How wonderful you are! You do not know how wonderful you are!

(158)

The sexual dimension is also detectable in Mask's body language. In one scene he playfully 'rushes at Guy, catches him and pretends to beat him', saying: 'Will you be good now?' (147). Although Jerry Nolan denies the 'primacy of a sexual dimension' in Martyn's early plays,[76] the homoerotic subtext of *An Enchanted Sea* is not only undeniably present, it also makes it a better play.

In *An Enchanted Sea*, as in *Rosmersholm*, and indeed *The Lady from the Sea* and *Little Eyolf* (linked through the motif of drowning), tabooed sexual yearnings and death wishes are interwoven through the author's use of the supernatural. Consider Mrs Font's hatred of Guy. It is said to originate from her fear that the boy will somehow endanger Lord Mask and thus prevent the marriage between him and her daughter, Agnes. She becomes convinced that the boy is 'an evil spirit changed in place of the real Guy, whom the fairies have taken' (153). She is supported in that by a report that Guy has drowned a boy at his boarding school. Mrs Font's superstitious hatred of Guy seems at odds with her character for she is a strong-willed, shrewish and materialistic person. But her feelings for Guy become more consistent with her character if we take the host of superstitions that surround Guy – his 'otherness', the strange powers that he seems to possess – as a code for his sexual deviance. The story of Guy's killing another boy at school also makes more sense as a coded reference to homosexuality. It is hard to reconcile the idea of homicide with Guy's kind and open-hearted nature. He is the kind of person who is more likely to be expelled from school for committing homosexual acts than for murder. The motifs of drowning and of the supernatural, which seem to be related to the play's allusions to homosexuality, coalesce in the ending. As Mask wades into the sea in an attempt to follow the spirit of the now dead Guy, the two men are finally united on the supernatural plane.

That said, the sexual subtext of *An Enchanted Sea* may have been unintentional. Until Moore embarrassed him by pointing out the nature of the relationship between Mask and Guy, Martyn seems to have been as unaware of the deeper meaning of his own work as he was of the intricacies of Ibsen's plays. For all their lavish praise for Ibsen and the actors, Martyn's articles on the Metropolitan Players Ibsenite productions contain very few interpretive comments. His review of *The Lady from the Sea* is really covert praise for *An Enchanted Sea*:

> *The Lady from the Sea* gives expression to that yearning and enchantment which the ocean has for certain natures. An enchanted sea! How can I tell the feelings that rise in the heart when we look afar to sea from the barren coast in West of Ireland? The illimitable Atlantic with all its mystery and beauty calls for us.[77]

Martyn's most detailed comment on *Little Eyolf* was that 'in those scenes between the husband and wife, especially in the third act, there is the same symphonic beauty [as in *The Master Builder*] that lingers haunting our souls'.[78] This is a rather tame introduction to a play in which a child's death is shown to be related to his parents' sexual lives and which explores such themes as incest and repressed homosexuality. Shaw called the play a 'clinical lecture on morbid psychology'[79] and a 'terror'[80]. A. F. Spender, whose 1897 article '*Little Eyolf* – A Plea for Reticence' was one of the earliest Irish articles on Ibsen, protested that the play 'pander[s] to the modern craving for what is morbid and unwholesome'.[81] For Martyn, however, *Little Eyolf* was an expression of beautiful longing.

He did not fully understand the dramas that he loved and imitated. *An Enchanted Sea* cannot be regarded as a fully conscious experiment in the psychological merging of folklore and realism. In this respect, Edward Martyn is a contrast with the younger devotee of Ibsen in Ireland, one who declared to the Irish Revivalists in 1904: 'that they may dream their dreamy dreams I carry off their filthy streams'.[82]

Ibsen in James Joyce's early fiction: *Little Eyolf* and 'An Encounter'

Among the literary works of pre-1916 Ireland, the closest approximation to Ibsen's use of myth is found in the early fiction of Joyce. Bjørn Tysdahl, while emphasising the primary importance of Ibsen's realism for Joyce, notes that the young Irish author found in his reading of Ibsen more than merely 'crude naturalism'.[83] As his notes to *Exiles* suggest, writes Tysdahl, 'Joyce had noticed Ibsen's attempt to combine the realistic and the symbolic, and that he himself tried to do the same thing'.[84] This method, perfected in *Ulysses*, had already been used in *Dubliners*. These stories rely on folkloric and archetypal motifs and plot structures in a way that allows for the simultaneous perception of the fictional world as both 'realistic' and 'magical'.[85]

In 1912, Joyce visited Ireland in a last-ditch attempt to ensure the publication of *Dubliners*. Coming to Dublin in July and leaving in September, he missed the productions of *Little Eyolf* by the Metropolitan Players. However, several elements of this play – the relationship between sexuality and death, the motifs of drowning and of gazing, and the use of folkloric structures – are explored in 'An Encounter', the second story in *Dubliners*.

Both *Little Eyolf* and 'An Encounter' deliberately frustrate the reader by the seeming clumsiness of their structure. In *Little Eyolf*, the eponymous character, a disabled boy, drowns at the end of Act 1: the play seems to end before it begins. The other two Acts record a series of conversations between his parents, aunt and the aunt's admirer. As Archer puts it, 'after the death of Eyolf ... there is practically no external action whatsoever.

Nothing happens save in the souls of the characters.'[86] The wife's unrequited passion for the husband is mentioned and his attachment to his half-sister is discussed, along with his atheism and the cause of the boy's disability. The play's analysis of the events that led to the drowning seems to move away from the tragedy itself; its exploration of the parents' grief and guilt uncovers aspects of their psychology that are only covertly related to their loss.

'An Encounter' is similarly 'uneventful'. Moreover, like Ibsen's play, it contains false starts and false leads. The story begins with the words: 'It was Joe Dillon who introduced the Wild West to us.'[87] The first paragraph gives a detailed portrayal of Joe Dillon, his wild childhood and surprising vocation; yet Dillon does not reappear in the story. The last words of 'An Encounter' reflect the narrator's attitude to his friend Mahony: 'He ran as if to bring me aid, and I felt penitent, because I always despised him a little' (184). However, there is very little in the story to prepare the reader for this conclusion. References to the relationship between the narrator and Mahony are scant; the real interest seems to lie elsewhere.[88]

The sense of unease that both texts awaken is partly suggested by their use of fairy-tale tropes. Both works relate an encounter of an imaginative child with a strange figure: half realistic vagabond, half fantastic monster. Eyolf drowns because of his curiosity about the Rat-Wife, an old woman who tramps the country roads making a living by luring rats into the sea. In 'An Encounter', the narrator meets on his day 'mitching' school, not the adventures that he had hoped for, but an old man whom he does not identify as a paedophile, but who nevertheless arouses in him, first a desire to confide, then inexplicable terror and guilt. Like the Rat-Wife, the old man in 'An Encounter' is presented in a way that suggests his otherworldly character. Act 4 of *Little Eyolf* and 'An Encounter' are fairy-tales gone wrong.

In a classic fairy-tale, the meeting with a monster is conducive to the hero's fulfilment of his quest and his achievement of maturity. In *Little Eyolf* and 'An Encounter' this quest is doomed. Eyolf drowns and his parents' ruthless analysis of his death leads them to uncover secrets of their sexual life. Joyce's narrator is left stranded with his uncanny sense of penitence as the story ends, leaving the reader regretful at the loss of the boyish vision of the world. By the end of the story, words one commonly associates with childhood and wonder have been contaminated by the encounter. An 'adventure' is now seeing a paedophile masturbate at the side of a field. And the 'elaborate mystery' is now the description of this man's confusing talk about 'whipping young boys'.

Archer's comment on the Rat-Wife is representative of the early critical reactions to this character:

> The story he tells is not really, or rather not inevitably, supernatural. Everything is explicable within the limits of nature; but supernatural agency is also vaguely suggested, and the reader's imagination is stimulated, without any absolute violence to his sense of reality. On the plane of everyday life, then, the Rat-Wife is a crazy and uncanny old woman, fabled by the peasants to be a were-wolf in her leisure ... At the same time, there cannot be the least doubt, I think, that in the, poet's mind the Rat-Wife is the symbol of Death, of the 'still, soft darkness' that is at once so fearful and so fascinating to humanity.[89]

Similar things have been said of 'An Encounter' by critics who, while acknowledging the story's realism and even naturalism, emphasise the symbolic functions of the old man. Thus Sydney Feshbach, pointing out the parallels between this story and the late medieval elegiac tradition, argues that the old man is a personification of Death, 'a typical character with ancestors in English literature at least as early as Chaucer's "Pardoner's Tale"'.[90] Similarly, A. M. Leatherwood, while noting Joyce's insistence that 'An Encounter' was based on actual experience, speaks of the man as a mythical figure: he 'absorbs the myth [of the initiation quest] he represents to become an embodiment of evil with the power to convert a symbol of life and rejuvenation into a symbol of death and decay'.[91]

These readings of *Little Eyolf* and 'An Encounter', in which 'symbols' and 'reality' belong to different levels of interpretation, gloss over the source of this duality in the texts. Yet the reason that some critics construe the figures of the Rat-Wife and the old man as symbols is imbedded in the texts – in their peculiar description, their language and in the other characters' responses to them. A comparison of Ibsen's play and Joyce's story should be guided by those approaches that set aside the question of what the Rat-Wife may represent, asking instead what function she has in the text, why, that is, she should appear to have this dual significance.[92]

Before the Rat-Wife arrives, she is already established as a half-mythical creature by Eyolf. A bookish nine-year-old, he is fascinated by the legend of the Rat-Wife: 'perhaps it may be true after all,' he says, 'that she is a were-wolf at night.'[93] His father, Allmers, is not inclined to believe this; yet the idea that the Rat-Wife may be a supernatural creature has been implanted in his mind and in the audience's. When she enters the scene, 'softly and noiselessly', it is not merely her appearance, her 'shrunken figure', 'piercing eyes' , her 'old-fashioned flowered gown, with a black hood and cloak' or the large umbrella and black bag that she carries that set her apart from other characters (19). The doubt expressed, a few moments earlier, about her supernatural essence makes one want to inspect all these items for signs of magical significance. During the momentary hush at her entry, all eyes are turned to her. For a moment, all interpretive energy is focused on the Rat-Wife. Are we in a dream play or is this reality reflected on stage?

The appearance of the old man in 'An Encounter' produces an effect similar to that of the Rat-Wife. In this story, whose very title creates suspense, every trivial event – looking for green-eyed Norwegian sailors at Liffey pier, buying currant buns or looking at biscuits in a shop window – has, for the narrator, the potential of adventure. Every recorded action of the boys appears, on first reading, as a portent of the promised encounter. The old man 'comes along the bank slowly', walking 'with one hand upon his hip and in the other hand he held a stick with which he tapped the turf lightly' (180).

The passage describing the man's slow passage across the field and his slow retreat towards the boys creates tension. It is written in what Erich Auerbach has identified as the style peculiar to the Old Testament, which builds up suspense and convinces the reader of the truth of the narrative through deliberate scarcity of information.[94] Certain details are highlighted: we are told that the narrator is chewing 'one of those green stems on which girls tell fortunes' (180) and that the man is wearing a 'suit of greenish-black and wore what we used to call a jerry hat with a high crown' (180). We know that the boys 'followed him with [their] eyes' (180) as he passed, and that 'when he had gone on for perhaps fifty paces he turned about and began to retrace his steps' (180). But we are not privy to the narrator's feelings. Like the story of Abraham's sacrifice of Isaac, which Auerbach uses to highlight key aspects of the Old Testament style, 'An Encounter' uses narrative silences to manipulate the reader. We want to know what the boy is feeling, and as a result we read our own discomfort and fear into the story.

The short sentences, describing the slow passage of the old man through the field, each beginning with the third-person pronoun, draw attention to the importance of the events described. But their actual significance remains hidden. These are sentences 'fraught with background',[95] prompting the reader to search for something that would explain the meaning of the old man. It is the style of the passage that prompts such critics as Feshbach and Leatherwood to adopt an exegetic approach to the story and look for its embedded secrets. The green stem which is said to possess magical properties, the green eyes that he expected to find among the Norwegian sailors at Liffey pier, are thus reinterpreted with the arrival of the man in his 'greenish-black suit' (180), acquiring a new and symbolic significance.

The Rat-Wife and the old man thus plunge the characters and the readers into a state of doubt, the kind of hesitation as to the correct interpretation of possibly supernatural events that Tzvetan Todorov describes as the primal condition of the fantastic.[96] This doubt grows stronger as they begin to speak. At the very beginning of the conversation with the old man, Joyce's narrator notes the discordance between his approval of the man's opinions and the odiousness of the words he uses: 'Every boy,' he said, 'has a little sweetheart ... In my heart I thought that what he said about boys and sweethearts was reasonable. But I disliked the words in his mouth and I wondered why he shivered once or twice as if he feared something or felt a sudden chill' (181–2).

The man's monologue becomes ominous for reasons that seem, for the narrator, to lie outside its content, having to do more with the form in which his ideas are couched:

> He gave me the impression that he was repeating something which he had learned by heart or that, magnetised by some words of his own speech, his mind was slowly circling round and round in the same orbit. At times he spoke as if he were simply alluding to some fact that everybody knew, and at times he lowered his voice and spoke mysteriously as if he were telling us something secret which he did not wish others to overhear.
>
> (182)

This description fits the peculiar speech of the Rat-Wife. She inquires whether Rita and Alfred Allmers 'are troubled with any gnawing things in the house', and proceeds to explain how tired she is:

THE RAT-WIFE	I have been out all night at my work.
ALLMERS	Have you indeed?
THE RAT-WIFE	Yes, over on the islands. (*with a chuckling laugh*) The people sent for me, I can assure you. They didn't like it a bit; but there was nothing else to be done. They had to put a good face on it, and bite the sour apple. (*Looks at EYOLF, and nods*) The sour apple, little master, the sour apple.[97]

She talks 'as if alluding to the fact that everybody knows'. 'The islands', 'the people', 'they [who] had to put a good face on it' – all these phrases refer to what neither the Allmers nor the audience have heard of. Yet the Rat-Wife creates the illusion of mutual understanding where none is to be found. As she turns to the mystified child and nods, she repeats the phrase 'sour apple', as if to imply that he ought to understand the obscure reference. She forces him to take seriously both the phrase and the process of its interpretation. Through the repetition of mystifying phrases and trivial expression, she acts as if she 'unfolds an elaborate mystery'.

Like the old man, the Rat-Wife is 'magnetised by some words of [her] own speech':

THE RAT-WIFE	Why, because they couldn't keep body and soul together on account of the rats and all the little rat-children, you see, young master.
RITA	Ugh! Poor people! Have they so many of them?
THE RAT-WIFE	Yes, it was all alive and swarming with them. (*Laughs with quiet glee*) They came creepy-crawly up into the beds all night long. They plumped into the milk-cans, and they went pittering and pattering all over the floor, backwards and forwards, and up and down.

Her repetitive verbosity, whereby each word is supplemented by its synonym, and which seems itself to creep 'backwards and forwards and up and down', never reaches the 'centre' or the precise meaning of her story. Her mind, like that of the man in Joyce's story, merely 'circles round and round in the same orbit'. Sparking associations and rooting up memories, her speech is self-referential, each movement forward being a throwback to the previously uttered phrase.

The Rat-Wife calls the rats she kills 'sweet-little creatures' and describes her work as doing good to 'the poor little things that are hated and persecuted so cruelly'.[98] This ambivalence, whereby abhorrence and attachment, the act of love and that of violence become interchangeable, is also present in the speech of the old man: 'He began to speak to us about girls, saying what nice soft hair they had and how soft their hands were and how all girls were not so good as they seemed to be if one only knew' (182). The word 'nice' here becomes sinister. Further into the conversation (and after he withdraws to the side of the road to perform what the other boy in the story, Mahony, calls the act of 'a queer old josser'), the man seems to 'forget his recent liberalism' and begins to speak of whipping boys. He explains that he would gladly whip a boy if he found out he had 'a sweetheart and told lies abut it':

> He said that there was nothing in this world he would like so well as that. He described to me how he would whip such a boy as if he were unfolding some elaborate mystery. He would love that, he said, better than anything in this world; and his voice, as he led me monotonously through the mystery, grew almost affectionate and seemed to plead with me that I should understand him.
>
> (183–4)

It is at this stage that Joyce's narrator becomes frightened and stands up determined to escape the maelstrom of words. What he is afraid of is not the actual sexual threat that the paedophile poses to him and his companion; he does not quite understand what the man has been doing at the side of the field. Yet at the core of his fear is the dimly imagined idea of the sexual act, conveyed through the invasive language of the man.

In *Little Eyolf*, the Rat-Wife similarly begins her speech with talk of rats and ends it with disturbing equations between these ambivalently conceived creatures and men:

THE RAT-WIFE	... In the old days, I can tell you, I didn't need any Mopsëman [*her dog*]. Then I did the luring myself – I alone.
EYOLF	And what did you lure then?
THE RAT-WIFE	Men. One most of all.
EYOLF	(*With eagerness*) Oh, who was that one? Tell me!
THE RAT-WIFE	(*Laughing*) It was my own sweetheart, it was, little heart-breaker!
EYOLF	And where is he now, then?
THE RAT-WIFE	(*Harshly*) Down where all the rats are. (*Resuming her milder tone.*) But now I must be off and get to business again. Always on the move. (*To RITA*) So your ladyship has no sort of use for me to-day? I could finish it all off while I am about it.[99]

Her language links not only the image of the rats with that of 'her own sweetheart', but also love with death. In a foreshadowing of his own death, Eyolf becomes equated with her victim: the 'little heart-breaker' may be an address to Eyolf or a phrase used of her past lover (syntactically in opposition to 'my own sweetheart'). All the while she is addressing Eyolf, the Rat-Wife is talking to his parents. Her speech reminds them of their own problematic relationship. The words that she uses – 'lure' (*lokke*), and 'gnaw' (alternatively *gnage* and *nage*) – are found in the speeches of Allmers and Rita in relation to their sexual relationship and their son.[100]

There is a sense in *Little Eyolf* that the Rat-Wife, through her language, unleashes hidden forces of the adult world that consume Eyolf. As we find out later, Rita Allmers once 'lured' her husband, who was supposed to be in charge of minding their baby son. In her embrace, Allmers forgot about baby Eyolf asleep on a table. Allmers did not love his wife. Having married her for her money, he longed for his childhood and the beloved image of his pubescent half-sister Asta dressed in boy's clothes. During their love-making, Allmers told Rita the nickname that Asta adopted when she was cross-dressing: Eyolf. This was the moment, Rita explains, when the other Eyolf – their son – fell off the table and was disabled. Emotional betrayal (by Allmers of Rita), sexual enslavement (by Rita of Allmers) and imaginary incest (between Allmers and Asta) emerge as causes not only of Eyolf's disability, but of his eventual drowning (his disability meant he could not swim).

In 'An Encounter', the malignancy of the adult world – its perversion-riddled conservatism, its life-denying piety (as in the open vignette in which the boisterous Dillon discovers he has a vocation and disappears from the story into the sepulchral world of his mass-going parents), its snobbery and violence – is concentrated in the figure of the old man. With his talk of whipping boys he is less a reminder than a dark image of the narrator's teacher, Father Butler, who makes a similar threat at the beginning of the story. On some level the narrator escapes. Yet his use of the word 'penitent' suggests that religious conservatism triumphs over the spirit of adventure.[101]

The similarities between Ibsen's complex play and Joyce's short story amount to more than an accidental affinity. There is a phrase at the start of 'An Encounter' that suggests that Ibsen's plays were at the back of Joyce's mind when he was writing the story. As the narrator observes the ships at Liffey pier, he is told one of them is Norwegian. He proceeds to 'examine foreign sailors to see had any of them green eyes', because, he explains, 'I had some confused notion' (179). Tysdahl believes this to be an allusion it to *The Lady from the Sea*. In this play, the Stranger, a sailor, has greenish eyes, the colour of the sea. Norway is usually mentioned in Joyce's works in connection with Ibsen; for him, as for his fellow Dubliners, the country was almost synonymous with the name of its most famous author. Tysdahl explains that this is an authorial 'intimate greeting' to Ibsen: while the narrator could not have read *The Lady from the Sea*, Joyce declares that he has.[102] Thus he establishes a connection between the two literary works which exists exterior to the characters.

To answer the question whether such an 'intimate greeting' has a thematic function in the story, one should note that the interwoven motifs of 'eyes' and 'the sea' are used by Ibsen in both *The Lady from the Sea* and *Little Eyolf*. In *The Lady from the Sea*, Ellida Wangel is simultaneously threatened and fascinated by the idea that her real place is not with her husband but with the Stranger to whom she once pledged her love. She believes that her baby son, conceived after her marriage to Dr Wangel, has inherited the Stranger's eyes – their colour mirroring the waters of the fjord. This child is dead when the play begins. Most of the action is preoccupied with Ellida's warring feelings for the Stranger: her longing for the freedom and passion he had promised her, and her terror of his revenge. (This is also expressed through the 'eye' obsession: 'I see most distinctly his scarf-pin most of all, with a large bluish-white pearl in it,' Ellida confesses. 'The pearl is like a dead fish's eye, and it seems to glare at me').[103] Her feelings about her child are not fully articulated by Ellida or her husband, even though the play at times resembles the determined inquiry of a clinical analysis. Yet her grief, guilt and terror, which she associates with the Stranger, are directly related to the death of her son.

Like Solness, Ellida views the world magically. Deed originates in thought; sexual longings beget children; betrayal of love results in retribution. Her son had the eyes of the Stranger because the son should have been his. The child died because Ellida has betrayed the Stranger. This line of thought is not fully articulated in the play; it has to be deduced by the reader alone. For Ellida it is 'the unspeakable':[104] to say it out loud means fully accepting the magical view of the world. It would mean beyond doubt that she is guilty of her son's death.

Parental guilt is expressed in a similar way in Ibsen's later play. In *Little Eyolf*, sea and eye imagery are interwoven in Rita's terror of Eyolf's 'great open eyes' staring at her from the fjord's depth. Alfred diagnoses this obsession as evidence of Rita's direct implication in their son's death. She was frustrated at her husband's sexual remoteness and angered by his sudden decision to dedicate his life to Eyolf. For a moment she saw the child as an obstacle to marital happiness: 'I have begun to believe in

the evil eye. Especially in a child's evil eye.'[105] Eyolf drowned moments after this and Allmers' verdict is resolute:

RITA	(*Wailing*) I shall see him [Eyolf] day and night, as he lay down there.
ALLMERS	With great, open eyes.
RITA	(*Shuddering*) Yes, with great, open eyes. I see them! I see them now!
ALLMERS	(*Rises slowly and looks with quiet menace at her*) Were they evil, those eyes, Rita?[106] …
ALLMERS	Now things have come about – just as you wished, Rita.
RITA	I! What did I wish?
ALLMERS	That Eyolf were not here.
RITA	Never for a moment have I wished that! That Eyolf should not stand between us – that was what I wished.
ALLMERS	Well, well – he does not stand between us any more.
RITA	(*Softly, gazing straight before her*) Perhaps now more than ever. (*With a sudden shudder*) Oh, that horrible sight!
ALLMERS	(*Nods*) The child's evil.[107]

For Solness, Ellida and Allmers – as well as most other Ibsen protagonists from Peer Gynt to Rubek) – their private mythology is paramount, replacing religious belief as well as rationalist materialism. Guilt is always the source of such a magical worldview. Indeed, the belief in the magic inherent in words and thought serves as an unconscious strategy in dealing with the realistic possibility of guilt. Little Eyolf died because his parents did not look after him; Solness's twin boys died because neither he nor Aline was quick enough to respond to the threat to their lives posed by Aline's condition.[108] Yet, the parents refuse to think along these lines. The magical explanation is easier because it allows them to admit their guilt, while also creating a hope for its absence. In other words, the magical worldview is readily embraced by Ibsen's characters because, as inhabitants of a supposedly rational society, they hope it can be as readily discarded.

In 'An Encounter' a similar displacement of guilt and fear occurs. The narrator's fear of the man seems to reach its peak when he 'involuntary glance[s] up at his face' (183). The text then subverts the earlier association of adventure with green-eyed Norwegians: 'As I did so I met the gaze of a pair of bottle-green eyes peering at me from under a twitching forehead. I turned my eyes away again' (183). This image of the eyes gazing from beneath is reminiscent of Rita's fear of the 'great, open eyes' staring at her from the depth of the sea. Moments after that the narrator stands up, walks away and shouts for Mahony, at whose appearance he feels penitence.

There is a similarity in Ibsen's and Joyce's approach to myth and their presentation of displaced guilt as both the cause and the result of magical thinking. The Rat-Wife's arrival appears to be a literal manifestation of their marital disharmony. Both Rita and (more strongly) Allmers regard the drowning of their child as a magical action carried out by the Rat-Wife – retribution for a sin committed. Throughout the play, through mutual accusations and demands for sympathy from Asta, they scour their past lives for this sin. Among the possibilities are Rita's partial neglect of the child, Allmers' confused sexuality and finally, and rather disturbingly, their lack of social responsibility.

The old man also appears as if summoned by magic, a creature personifying the vague threats of schoolboy life and its unknown dangers. His fantastic essence is rooted in the language of the story: the reader becomes involved in regarding the story of the two boys and a paedophile as a mythical quest. By the end of the story something seems wrong. Something is lost, whether it is the sense of wonder, the promise of excitement or even, as Leatherwood, has pointed out, the sense of identification with the narrator, suddenly denied to the reader in the last sentence. The displaced guilt that the narrator feels at the end, the strange feeling of loss that is the reader's, are connected to the myth thus created.

Looking at Dublin theatre critics, Edward Martyn and James Joyce as interpreters of Ibsen places one at the beginnings of Irish literary modernism. Ibsen's approach to myth was unique in that it challenged the commonly held distinctions between the real and the mythical and, indeed, between the literal and the symbolic. Brian Johnston, who identifies Ibsen as the forefather of Joyce, as well as Ezra Pound, T. S. Eliot, Thomas Mann and Samuel Beckett, explains that these modernist writers share with Ibsen the innovative approach to archetypal and mythical allusions: they 'do not just smuggle [them] into their modern texts' in Ibsen's Cycle and in *Ulysses* 'the mythopoetic and cultural layers are structurally and textually built into the substance of modern reality. ... They represent what is perceived as the more adequate truth of that reality.'[109]

Early twentieth-century approaches to aesthetic symbolism were dominated by a belief in clear distinctions between dream and reality, an artist's symbolic riddle and its critical solution. Interpretations were thus sought outside the text, in the elusive idea of the 'poetic mind', for instance. Authors were quizzed as to the meaning of their symbols; and frustration often followed when the symbol appeared too obtuse (as in the case of Ibsen's *The Wild Duck*, which exasperated audiences in France and England). In 1912–14, while the Metropolitan Players were performing Ibsen's badly understood 'symbolist' plays to Dublin's sceptical audiences, Joyce's short story remained unpublished. Ibsen's innovative approach to myth as inseparable from modern life was not widely understood. In the culture informed by contemporary anthropologists' claim of a radical difference between the primitive mind and the civilised mind,[110] it was not apparent how mythical thinking could be part of the psychological make-up of the modern man.

The Irish Revivalist initial approach to myth was ornamental and instrumental: bringing ancient legends to life would invigorate Irish poetry and drama while stimulating the national consciousness of the readers and audiences. Demonstrating that ancient myths were revived in the creation of (sometimes damaging) private mythologies, that civilised culture and primitive culture were thus closely related, was not part of the Revival's ostensible agenda. Indeed, Synge's *Playboy*, which explores this possibility, was repudiated by the audiences. Yet, the most significant developments of Irish Literary Revival are anticipated by Ibsen. His late plays develop the interplay between language and reality seen in earlier works while also using Norse folklore. They present a world whose outward realism is as fictive as the supernatural undercurrent informing the thinking of its characters. This mode, whose influence on Irish writing was barely perceptible in the first decade of the twentieth century, became more apparent in later years.[111]

5
Ibsen out of Date?

A Doll's House and the Irish suffragists

On 10 March 1911, Ben Iden Payne's company came to Dublin with Shaw's *The Philanderer* (1893). Shaw later noted that the play suffered from a 'disease to which plays as well as men become liable with advancing years'.[1] *The Philanderer* is a satirical reaction to the London Ibsen wrangle of the 1890s; much of the action takes place in the imaginary Ibsen club, whose membership is restricted to 'unwomanly women and unmanly men'.[2] It was obviously out of date. The *Irish Times* commented that it belonged to the days 'when Ibsenism, like Wagnerism and impressionism was "advanced" and when the feminist movement was a crude and unlovely thing'.[3] The critic suggested that '[n]ow that Post Impressionism has arrived, and, despite all affectation of sprightliness, is being regarded as passé the "topical" elements in *The Philanderer* appear almost mid-Victorian'.[4]

How could Shaw's play appear dated in Ireland without ever having been topical? How could the critic, moreover, speak of feminism as a thing of the past? The Irish suffragist movement was strong. The Irish Women's Franchise League was founded by Hannah Sheehy-Skeffington and Gretta Cousins in November 1908.[5] By 1910 suffragettes were coming under fire in the nationalist press – many believed that their fight for the right of vote in the British Parliament was inconsistent with Irish nationalism. Demonstrations, smashed windows, arrests and hunger strikes were soon to follow. If the feminist movement could once have been described as a 'crude, unlovely thing', surely it had not improved its looks.

Two other plays produced by Payne's company were Shaw's *Man and Superman* and Ibsen's *A Doll's House*. The *Irish Times* declared that the earlier generation of critics had not appreciated Ibsen's genius and praised Mona Limerick for her interpretation of Nora:

> She was the thorough doll at first; and her irresponsible babbling and her cajoling graces gave full point to the section. Later she was the doll-child in trouble, pettish, wilful and hysterical when she found herself at the mercy of currents she could not control by mere pretty graces. Then at last she found her womanhood.[6]

The ability to see the play from Nora's point of view rather than as a tragedy of a household torn apart by a woman's madness – the most common critical reaction to the play when it was produced in 1903 and 1908 – might suggest that Ibsen's feminism had finally been acknowledged by the press. Yet, barely a week after the performance, the *Irish Times* ridiculed two leading English suffragists, Lady Selbourne and Lady Constance Lytton, for regarding forgery as an offence excusable by the justice of their common cause.

It will be remembered that Ibsen's Nora Helmer forges her father's signature in order to secure a loan to save her husband's life. When the forgery is discovered, Torvald Helmer repudiates Nora for bringing the family into disrepute, quite oblivious to the reason behind her act. When the threat of scandal is removed, Torvald construes Nora's alleged irresponsibility as evidence of her 'womanly helplessness' and proposes to act as her teacher and protector.

Lady Selbourne wrote a letter to the London *Times*, supposedly penned by Lady Constance Lytton. The letter argued that throwing a 'stone at the Prime Minister's carriage' was far more likely to direct 'people's attention' to the demands of the suffragists than peaceful meetings.[7] In subsequent correspondence with the paper, Lady Selbourne explained that she had written the letter herself in order to make the public 'understand how hard it is for women ... who have no inclination to adopt militant methods, to get [their] views reasonably set forth before [their] fellow country-men'.[8] Lady Constance Lytton then responded by accepting full responsibility for the letter. The press reaction to this 'comedy of manners',[9] as the *New York Times* reporter called it, reflected Ibsen's play. The whole suffragist movement was made appear ridiculous by the reckless behaviour of the two women. According to *The Times* the

> serious friends of woman suffrage ... [were] to be commiserated. Theirs is an uphill task, and the ladies they are trying to help seem

> determined to make it impossible by supplying the public with convincing reasons for not granting their demands.[10]

The writer further suggested that the story should be taken seriously 'unless we are to regard the entire suffragist movement as an elaborate practical joke ... and if the ladies cannot see it for themselves, some of the men who are assisting their campaign will, no doubt enlighten them'.[11] The editor of *The Times* echoed Torvald's belief in Nora's inability to act responsibly, her 'inexperience' and the need for his 'guidance'.[12]

In 1911 the *Irish Times* could easily condemn the English suffragists while praising Ibsen's heroine. Ben Iden Payne's production, coinciding with an increase in suffragist activities in Dublin, did not appear to have absorbed the political energies of the capital. This is also true of previous and subsequent productions of *A Doll's House*. The play that made all 'Scandinavia r[i]ng with Nora's "declaration of independence"'[13] appears to have stimulated no political debate in Ireland. Yet, the readers of the *Irish Times* would have been aware of its political significance and some aspects of its international reception. In 1912 there were reports of Ibsen's influence on the Japanese female suffrage movement. According to the *Irish Times*, Japanese women were less interested in the 'the whole duty of woman' than in 'seeing and discussing a translation of Ibsen's *Doll's House*, and anti-suffragists are cursing the day when an enlightened and progressive Government allowed the play, and others like it to be produced'.[14] The article went on to argue that there was 'some connection between the presentation of the play, and its effect' and the Japanese Diet's rejection of the 1912 Bill proposing that women be allowed to take part in political meetings.[15] Rumours of Ibsen's detrimental effect on family life had been circulating since the start of the London controversy. Dubliners would not have thought it odd that a Scottish woman should leave her husband because she 'filled her mind ... with the writings of Ibsen and others of that sort, and had been living in touch with the theatre, which gave her a distaste for ordinary domestic life'.[16]

We do not find direct engagement with Ibsen's politics in the Irish press. However, we get glimpses of the suffragist interest in the Norwegian playwright. At the 1908 production of *A Doll's House*, Holloway spotted Thomas and Anna Haslam, 'the former looking like the photos of Ibsen'.[17] The Haslams had founded the Dublin Woman's Suffrage Association in 1876 (the first such organisation in Ireland) and were still active suffragists in the early 1900s. Another suffragist often present at

Ibsen productions was Francis Sheehy-Skeffington. His admiration of Ibsen went to his University College Dublin days, before his marriage to Hannah and the founding of the Irish Women's Franchise League and its journal, the *Irish Citizen*. The League's involvement with the Metropolitan Players' in 1912–16 has already been noted. Productions of *The Lady from the Sea*, *Little Eyolf* and *The Master Builder* were in aid of the League, while *Rosmersholm* was included in the 1914 suffragist festival. *The Master Builder* was discussed in a lecture given by Maud Joynt (later to become a scholar of medieval literature) on 4 April 1916 at the offices of the League, two months after the 11–12 February production of that play.[18] As they enacted *A Doll's House* on the Irish political scene, the suffragists showed an interest in Ibsen's other plays, even though the precise nature of this engagement is unclear.

For one contributor to *Sinn Féin*, Inghean Dubh, suffragist politics amounted to the abandonment of the nation, metaphorically described as the homestead. The Irish suffragette was

> [l]eaving her country – a far city to roam – her desperate country – while sadly we wonder. Were Ireland her home? Were Ireland her father? Were Ireland her mother? Were Ireland her sister? Were Ireland her brother? Or was England a dearer thing still and nearer thing yet than all other?[19]

This kind of criticism allows us see the Irish suffragists' activities as *A Doll's House* of the 'real world' and points to a greater sphere of resemblances between their reception by the nationalists and the opposition to Irish Ibsenite plays. Nationalist objections to the suffragists peaked in the early 1910s. The Franchise League campaigned for the inclusion of women in the Home Rule Bill, even though Prime Minister Asquith and the leader of the Irish Party, John Redmond, opposed female suffrage.[20] The Irish suffragists' campaign was seen as a threat to Home Rule. Their methods, moreover, seemed to go against public morality. Suffragist demonstrations, window-breaking and violent arrests were, for one female opponent of the movement, 'scenes that would disgrace the lowest our sexes'.[21] How could women who took part in these scenes rear their sons 'to love God and revere women?'[22]

The charges levelled against the suffragists resemble those raised in 1903 against Synge's *In the Shadow of the Glen*. The piece of 'Irish Ibsenite propaganda', as it was called by Moran, allegedly threatened the cause of Irish nationalism. It was the brainchild of a Protestant: contaminated by foreign influence, vulgar and indecent. These complaints were levelled against the suffragists, many of whom, like Synge, were non-Catholic members of the upper middle class.

Moran, who in 1903 described Synge's play as a gross misrepresentation of Irish life, remarked in 1910 that the female suffrage 'movement in Ireland smacks rather of imitation of the English, and we do not regard it as a native or spontaneous growth'.[23] Maud Gonne presented her 1903 withdrawal from the Irish National Theatre in terms of allegiance to a grander cause than freedom for the theatre from politics. She demanded 'freedom for it from ... the insidious and destructive tyranny of foreign influence'.[24] In 1909, *Bean na-h-Éireann*, the journal of Gonne's feminist organisation, expressed a similar idea in relation to the Irish Women's Franchise League, berating them for 'cooperating with British suffragist organisations'.[25] The leader of Inghinidhe na hEireann believed that feminism was of secondary importance to the ideal of Irish independence. Unlike Ibsen's Nora, who declared herself to be 'before all else ... a human being',[26] Maud Gonne prioritised nationalism in the construction of her identity.

During the 1903 press debate in the *United Irishman* between Yeats and Griffith, the central issue was whether art should be above politics. Griffith believed in the superiority of propagandist plays over works that stood apart from or queried nationalist ideals. 'This talk of "politics"', he declared, ' – this assurance that a Theatre intended to be a free and National Theatre has no propaganda save for that of good art – savours to us of consideration for the feelings of the servants of the Englishmen who are among us.'[27] Griffith's views on the political duties of national artists are paralleled in Francis Cruise O'Brien's criticism of the suffragists. Cruise O'Brien admonished his sister-in-law, Hannah Sheehy-Skeffington, for declaring that until 'women achieve the rights of citizens ... [they] can serve no party'.[28] Cruise O'Brien urged her to consider the conflict between unionism and nationalism as a question of Ireland's political independence, not a 'mere conflict between parties'. 'One would really imagine that the National cause in Ireland was a mere conspiracy of men to get power into their hands,'[29] he declared. Indeed, 'that is virtually what it is from the women's point of view,' insisted Hannah Sheehy-Skeffington, 'so long as the Nationalist leaders fail to recognise explicitly our claim to equal citizenship.'[30]

Reports of suffragist meetings sometimes read like accounts of *The Playboy* riots. On 16 April 1912, the Irish Women's Franchise League assembled at the Antient Concert Rooms to hear Sarah Cecilia Harrison speak on the 'present position of the suffrage movement in Ireland'.[31] Margaret Cousins's opening remark on the exclusion of the suffragists from the Home Rule Bill was 'the signal for an outburst in a part of the room where a number of women, boys, and girls, all of the working class, were seated together'.[32] The audience shouted for nearly half an hour. They chanted 'We want Home Rule', called out the names of John Redmond and Joseph Devlin, and 'ever and anon above the storm was heard the cry of "No votes for women" which seemed to have been thoroughly learned by heart'.[33] Neither Margaret Cousins, nor S. C. Harrison or the actress Helen Laird (Honor Lavelle) succeeded in pacifying the crowd. According to the *Irish Times*, they were drowned 'by a perfect babble, out of which once voice was heard advising the suffragists to attend to their domestic duties and "lave the votin' to the gintlemen"'.[34]

Suffragists provided the nationalist communities with spectacles that, much like Synge's plays, conflated the issues of nationalism and gender. Nationalist objections to Synge and to the suffrage movement revolved around the question of artistic and political misrepresentation of the nation. The playwright and the suffragists exposed the Ireland of virtuous women, gentlemanly patriots and patriotic artists as a 'doll's house' – a false construct, which they refused to serve. The artist's duty was to realise his artistic potential, not to promote nationalism. The Irish politicians' primary duty was to their society – which included women – not to the abstract concept of a nation. Submerged in the opposition to these ideas was the question of female sexuality. The sight of a woman in conversation with her lover and the mention of the word 'shift' (in *The Playboy*) were as offensive to some nationalists as the allegedly immodest acts of the militant suffragists.

The notion of obscenity (or Ibscenety) was central to the 1890s London controversy over Ibsen's plays. The opposition to Ibsen's anti-idealistic politics and poetics found expression in the belief that his plays were indecent treatises of venereal diseases and sexual deviance. *Ghosts*, which contains only a few veiled references to Oswald's congenital syphilis, was described by its critics as 'loathsome and fetid', 'gross almost putrid indecorum' and 'literary carrion'.[35] Ibsen's plays hardly ever incited the Irish imagination to similar outbursts. Yet, the reception of Synge's plays and the suffragist militancy reveals a similar tendency to see artistic and political radicalism as indecent or, more precisely, as sexually transgressive.

This tendency is worth bearing in mind as we examine, in the following sections, the reception of the plays by Ibsen and his Irish followers in the transitional period in Irish history, from 1916 to 1926. The First World War, the Easter Rising, the War of Independence and the Civil

War were severe shocks to Irish society, affecting, among other things, the development of Irish feminism and Irish nationalism. The complex relationship between the significant social changes that occurred and the reception of theatrical and literary works is revealed in the often inconsistent and contradictory responses to Ibsen and the Ibsenite playwrights of this period.

Ghosts, An Enemy of the People and *John Gabriel Borkman*: conflicting responses, 1917–19

In the summer of 1916, Lady Gregory wrote to her long-time friend Shaw, asking his permission to stage a selection of his plays at the Abbey Theatre. Possibly motivated by a desire to challenge the Abbey's now well-established image as a theatre of peasant comedies, Lady Gregory wanted to produce *John Bull's Other Island* (which had been written for and rejected by the Abbey in 1904), *The Devil's Disciple, The Doctor's Dilemma* ('not her favourite', she wrote, 'but which ... acts best of all') and *Androcles and the Lion*, provided they could 'borrow a lion'.[36] Shaw, however, was not enthusiastic. He felt that Ibsen's plays were better suited to the Abbey's needs. 'I believe [Ibsen] might give the theatre a new lease of life,' he insisted. 'And it would be a labour of piety too: he is the greatest of educators; and Ireland needs him badly.'[37]

Shaw's reply acknowledged the possible motives behind Lady Gregory's request. Over the past few years the Abbey had staged few original works of theatrical merit. The relative dearth of new talent in Dublin meant that the theatre had to recycle old material – plays by Yeats, Lady Gregory and Synge. The theatre desperately needed a 'new lease of life'.

The Abbey was frequently criticised for its conservatism and its patronage of peasant drama. It had to compete with several new companies that sprang up in 1913–16 and openly contended to fill voids in the Irish theatrical world. The Irish Theatre, the Independent Dramatic Company and the Repertory Company turned their backs on peasant drama and wanted instead to stage plays by foreign authors alongside Irish plays of modern life. In Martyn's words, they wanted to prioritise 'native works dealing with the lives and problems of people more complex at all events, if not more refined, than the characters represented by the Abbey dramatists'.[38] Notably, *The Devil's Disciple* was among the first produced by the Repertory Company in 1913. By staging Shaw's plays, Lady Gregory might have hoped to remind Dublin intellectuals of the Abbey's place among the city's theatres. She would also prove that the Abbey was not merely a folk theatre; it would appear as modern, cosmopolitan and yet intrinsically Irish – everything, in fact, that was associated with the figure of Shaw.

Shaw loved the pose of a self-sacrificing Ibsenite. In 1896, for instance, he told Henry Irving, who had offered him £50 for *The Man of Destiny*, that he would waive the fee on condition Irving also produce *Peer Gynt* or *The Pretenders*. (Irving did not accept the offer).[39] However, Shaw's suggestion that the Abbey take on Ibsen probably had more to it than his reverence for the Norwegian playwright or even a wish to taunt Lady Gregory, who had never been an fan of Ibsen. (She later compared him to the stone walls of County Galway: 'if you take a stone the rest fall, if you take out the rope at the beginning of an Ibsen play there is nothing for the hero to be hanged with at the end'.)[40] Shaw emphasised the theatre's educational role. Ibsen was a 'teacher whom the Irish especially need, and whom they have a right to know as part of their culture'.[41] He realised that, by 1916, Irish theatregoers had inadvertently absorbed a great deal of Ibsen's ideas and technique through the plays of his imitators. 'If Ibsen has set Robinson and Co. imitating him, all the more reason to give the original,' Shaw wrote. Moreover,

> [t]he north of Ireland should hear *Brand*, and the south *Peer Gynt*. And Merrion Square and Rathmines and Kingstown need *A Doll's House* and *The Wild Duck* to save their souls. Dreamers all round the coast need *The Lady from the Sea*; and *Hedda Gabler* needs shewing-up everywhere as much as *Blanco Posnet*.[42]

Shaw's attempt to Ibsenise Ireland failed. His unsolicited advice was rejected by Lady Gregory. A newly appointed theatrical manager, Augustus Keogh, transformed the Abbey into a Shaw theatre, much to the dismay of Holloway and several other regulars.

Between 1894 and 1916, Dubliners had seen several Ibsen plays. There had been performances of *An Enemy of the People, A Doll's House, Hedda Gabler*, Act 4 of *Brand, The Master Builder, The Lady from the Sea, Little Eyolf, Rosmersholm* and possibly *Ghosts*. Yet, productions by Dublin amateurs and touring companies did not convince Shaw that Ireland was even aware of Ibsen. His letters to Lady Gregory raise the question whether, almost thirty years after the controversy over Ibsen plays in England, Ibsen could still be regarded as a novelty in Ireland. Did Ibsen still have the power to shock, inspire and educate the rising generation of Irishmen for whom stage realism had become a convention and who had seen at the Abbey the plays by Ryan, Colum, Murray and Robinson, all inspired by Ibsen?

On 13 October 1917, a 'flying matinée' of *Ghosts* was given in the Theatre Royal by the London Company of Victor Lewis. The scandal that ensued demonstrates that Dublin, in spite of the regular doses of Ibsenism it had received, was not yet fully immune. The performance awakened the conservative forces in Dublin society. A reminder of how little things may change in over twenty years, the affair is a throwback to the controversy over *The Countess Cathleen* in 1899.

The play was first staged in Belfast, where the negative reactions were limited to the groans of boredom of the theatre critic of the *Northern Whig*.[43] The little troupe, consisting of Hilda Esty Marsh, Helen Temple, Ernest Milton, H. A. Young and Henry Scatchard, were not, if we can hazard a guess, serious devotees of intellectual drama – they probably simply wanted to capitalise on the relative backwardness of the two Irish cities. The play was advertised as 'Ibsen's forbidden play' being produced 'for the first time in Ireland'. Just like the two rogues in *Huckleberry Finn*, they proclaimed the play as being 'For Adults Only', thus ensuring that the hall was filled with curious teenagers and, as Holloway put it, 'strange looking men' who 'came thinking the [play] would be bawdy'.[44]

For their financial success in Dublin, the company had to thank Cardinal Logue, who had opposed the staging of *The Countess Cathleen* in 1899, and the Very Reverend E. J. Meehan. At the annual meeting of the Catholic Truth Society on the eve of the performance, Meehan singled out Ibsen as one of the 'insidious dangers' threatening Ireland: 'Hendrik [*sic*] Ibsen, the protagonist of the freedom of the individual, the iconoclast of every sacred institution and foundation who said there was a culture to supplant the culture that Christ brought on earth, was brought to Dublin to teach and to show by stupid immorality what morals were.'[45] 'If he were a young man', Meehan was reported as saying, 'he would stand at the door of the Theatre Royal and would take the names of every Catholic who went into the place to hear Ibsen – the would-be destroyer of Christian traditions.'[46] Meehan concluded his fiery speech by calling on all Irishmen to resist the foreign filth. Cardinal Logue endorsed his speech, averring that 'evil literature' was 'one of the most horrible scourges that afflicted people'.[47] To the sound of loud applause, the cardinal declared that 'he had never crossed the threshold of a theatre in his life, [b]ut he read the notices in the papers of these plays, and he had the feeling that if the devil came and gave such plays in Dublin he might rely upon a bumper house'.[48]

Meehan's speech and Logue's reply were reproduced in the Dublin press. 'Ibsenism Condemned' announced the *Irish Times*; 'Dangers to

Faith in Ireland / Ibsen Play Denounced / Cardinal and Women's Attire' declared the *Irish Independent* (the latter remark referred to the cardinal's reference to the scanty clothing of Dublin women). The next day saw crowds of people streaming towards the Theatre Royal. 'Jacques' of the *Irish Independent* arrived at noon.[49] It was a bright autumn day. A few young men and ladies were standing outside the theatre 'busily noting those that passed in'.[50] Inside a lone young woman was reading a book in the dress circle. But soon other women arrived, 'staid women and young women',[51] a woman carrying a poodle and a young woman accompanied by an old, feeble nanny.[52] By '12.30 when the curtain rose at the Theatre Royal there was not a vacant seat at the auditorium'.[53] Most of the audience, 'Jacques' observed, were women, 'largely representative of the professional leisured and military classes'.[54] 'The Dublin literati' who, according to Holloway, usually turned up when Ibsen was produced were either mostly absent or swallowed up in this festive crowd. As he was hurrying to get in, Holloway noticed the actor Paul Farrell looking for somewhere to leave his bicycle. Farrell was soon approached by a man who (along with the chairman of the Dublin Tenants' Association, William J. Larkin) decided to carry out Meehan's suggestion that the names of Catholics who came to see *Ghosts* be recorded. The man threatened to inform all branches of the Gaelic League, to which Farrell replied that 'that they might publish it in English or Irish as much as they liked'.[55]

Once the play began, Holloway soon became bored (as he was at most Ibsen productions). The rest of the audience became very quiet and 'leaned forward in their seats to catch'[56] every word. Not a 'murmur escaped them till the act drop fell'.[57] A curtain was thrown open at the back of the gallery, and a big shaft of sunlight illuminated the spectators. The play of light among the joyful, curious, youthful mob seemed in strange contrast with the grim subject of the play. For most of them, Holloway believed, the play 'proved as dull as ditch water'.[58] They giggled a little in Act 2, and there was occasional applause. But by the end of final Act, the audience 'became cool and bitter', and when the play ended remained seated. 'The only amazing thing of the afternoon,' Holloway concluded, 'was the disappointment of those who went to revel in [obscenity] to be bored almost to death.'[59]

There is a phrase in *Finnegans Wake* that alludes to the title of Ibsen's play while suggesting the idea of frustrated curiosity. It sums up the reaction of the audience on this occasion: 'Go away, we are deluded, come back, we are disghosted.'[60] While the play received a relatively good review in the *Irish Times*, the general opinion was negative.

A moderate review in the *Freeman's Journal* found that 'lack of nobility makes *Ghosts* a savage indictment of a social evil rather than a dramatic masterpiece'.[61] J. H. Cox found the play far less agreeable: '*Ghosts* was the gloomiest thing I ever witnessed – and all the time it preached for *joie de vivre*.'[62] 'Jacques', writing for the *Irish Independent* and *Evening Herald*, had a field-day describing his boredom and disappointment. Reviewing *Ghosts*, 'Jacques' mentally travelled to the time of the London Ibsen controversy. In its inventive coarseness his criticism surpasses that of the supposedly 'great' critic Clement Scott, whose famous line – 'Shut up your windows! The ghouls are about' – Jacques also quoted for good measure. He described Helen Alving as 'a strumpet in her heart and a lunatic in her actions' and Oswald as 'a painter [who] has inherited his father's rottenness and his mother's imbecility'.[63] The other characters appeared to him as 'a thoroughly bad, inhuman, sneak souled, muddied, small-brained crew', while the play was 'a masterpiece of mire moulded in theatrical mud!'[64]

The whole episode seems to follow the same pattern as the public and press reactions to Beerbohm Tree's production of *An Enemy of the People*, seen in Dublin for the first and only time in 1894. In both cases, rumours of Ibsen's obscenity drew crowds to the theatre. In both cases the audience left disappointed, while journalists were licking their lips at a chance to run an amusing article. Were this the only Ibsen production of the year, we might conclude that the twenty and more years of slow exposure to Ibsen had not had any effect. However, just a few months earlier, from 23 to 28 April 1917, the Irish Theatre staged *An Enemy of the People*, and the production was successful enough to make them stage it again just after the *Ghosts* fiasco on 4–9 February 1918 (although, it must be admitted, on that occasion, they played to an audience of just fifteen people).[65] William J. Feeney has detected the contrast in tone between the 1894 reviews and the 1916 reviews of *An Enemy of the People*. In 1894, the complaint was that the play was 'a common-place story of local politics ... the work of a man who has been unduly impressed with the importance of small things'.[66] Conversely, in 1917 it was said that '*An Enemy of the People* is one of the very few [plays] in which we feel that in a dispute about the parish pump or the town sewer the conflict of ideals may be as moving and tragic as if the fate of a kingdom were at stake'.[67]

Shortly before the first performance of *An Enemy of the People*, John MacDonagh asked Holloway about the 1894 production. Holloway replied that he had been disappointed with Beerbohm Tree's comic interpretation, for he considered the play to be a 'profound tragedy'.[68] The Irish Theatre's version proved much more to his taste. After seeing the February revival of the play, he wrote to tell MacDonagh that it was the best thing the theatre had done: 'the originally fine impersonations of the Doctor, the Burgomaster, and the printer have now ripened and mellowed into finished studies'.[69]

The only actor who detected the comedy in the play was Norman Reddin, who 'introduced much quiet humour into his interpretation of the character of Aslaksen'.[70] Peter, Dr Stockmann's brother, was played by Joseph MacDonagh who, according to the *Freeman's Journal*, made 'the burgomaster as impassive as Stockmann is impetuous'.[71] 'It was difficult to remember at times', wrote the same critic, 'that one was listening to a Norwegian official, and not to a disciple invoking Buddha'.[72] The town newspaper editor, Hovstad, was played by Kerry Reddin who 'seemed to agree with Dr Stockmann's indictment of his own hypocrisy, whereas the real Hovstad had no doubt of his own integrity'.[73] Francis Purcell, who played Billing, and Katherine MacCormack, who played Stockmann's daughter Petra, received less praise. And Nell Byrne in the role of Mrs Stockmann was 'altogether too stiff'[74] (something that Holloway thought as well).

What seems to have carried the play through was Paul Farrell's interpretation of Stockmann. He 'struck the right note of tempestuous vitality, and while he was on the stage the interest never flagged'.[75] Farrell emphasised the heroic aspect of the play. At its revival in February 1918, Farrell 'fought through the hostile meeting [in Act 4] in fearless style'.[76] Notably, the same *Young Ireland* review also compared Stockmann to 'a Sinn Feiner of six years ago, in a provincial Irish town'.[77]

There was thus a contrast between the Irish reception of *Ghosts* and *An Enemy of the People*, an English production and an Irish one, a première and a revival, a tragedy turned comedy, and a comical drama performed as a tragedy. *Ghosts* was a commercial undertaking put on for the benefit of curious youngsters. *An Enemy of the People* was produced by the company whose founders could proudly declare: 'We don't want the general public. We want the people who believe in non-commercial plays.'[78] *An Enemy of the People* was staged for Dublin's intellectual community. Its success indicates that the play reflected the concerns of that community in a way that Victor Lewis's *Ghosts* did not. It must also be noted that *An Enemy of the People* is always topical, whereas *Ghosts*, in a sense, never is. For all its concern with debunking social hypocrisy, the play's real concern is psychological and, as we have seen, that dimension of Ibsen's work was not generally understood or appreciated in Dublin. Raised on a diet of plays by the Cork Realists, Dubliners were particularly receptive to the social satire and the tragic heroics of Stockmann.

The date was barely a year after the Easter Rising in which two of the founders and directors of the Irish Theatre, Thomas MacDonagh and Joseph Mary Plunkett, had lost their lives. This was a play about an accidental revolutionary whose actions are the result of his uncompromising pursuit of truth. It is a parable of a man who discovers that things are not as they seem, that a democratic society harbours a latent evil that may spring up should one stray across the line defined by the compact majority. Was Farrell's tragic-heroic conception of Stockmann a tribute to his friends who had recently been executed as 'enemies of the people'? One wonders also whether one of the reasons for the success of the production was the shock experienced by most Dubliners at the unexpected savagery of the British reaction to the Easter Rising.

There is one anecdote which reveals the politically charged atmosphere in which this play was rehearsed. As Lady Gregory recounted it, Edward Martyn's

> Dublin house had been raided, because Paul Farrell having borrowed his upper room for a rehearsal of *The Enemy of the People*, the windows being open, the shouts and strong language in the scene of the meeting had reached the windows of Kildare Street Club and the authorities were informed he was holding a Sinn Fein meeting.[79]

On 4 December 1917, the Abbey staged *Blight* by 'Alpha and Omega' (pseudonyms for Oliver St. John Gogarty and the Dublin journalist Joseph O'Connor). The play, which 'reveal[ed] the horrors of slumdom in the naked light of truth',[80] was an ambitious departure from the Abbey's usual repertoire – the theatre rarely staged problem plays, let alone problem plays of Dublin life.[81] Even the more conservative critics approved. The review in the *Irish Times* seems at first sight to echo the famous summary of the 1891 London production of *Ghosts* as 'a loathsome sore left unbandaged'.[82] The 'insight into the results of tenement life ... is given in a brutally realistic way ... There is not a symptom of the disease which is left undiagnosed', wrote the author of the *Irish Times* review. 'The ugly sore is painfully disclosed by searching surgical rays.'[83] Yet this brutal realism was welcome. '[A]s a piece of propagandist work it cannot be lauded too highly,' concluded the *Irish Times* critic. 'It is hoped that it will attract the attention of citizens generally and fix their thoughts on an insistent and persistent problem.'[84]

'Jacques', however, complained that 'the playwrights have allowed their personal prejudices ... to outplace their judgement.'[85] He concluded: 'Just as I come to a close, a note reaches me from a gentleman whose views I hold in esteem. "Would you not put *Ghosts* and *Blight* in the same zoo category?" he asks. No, *Ghosts* is a slimy snake that crawls and poisons; *Blight* is a barking bull pup.'[86]

The *Saturday Herald* also drew a distinction between Ibsen's drama and *Blight*: '[O]ur alphabetical Ibsens ... are terribly earnest in their subject.' 'Will this Ibsen-like method of placarding the evil destroy the demon?' it asked:

> As well ask has *Ghosts* succeeded in anything better than filling theatrical coffers with gold, and filling our public mind with curiosity. But there comparison must end. *Blight* may not be a 'nice' play in the accepted meaning of the term, indeed parts of it might have been relegated to the discarded matter, but its meaning is clear, its lessons powerful, and its influence – well that remains to be seen.[87]

Blight features a family of four. The father is an alcoholic, the son is disabled and the daughter has been driven to prostitution. Yet this play, horrific as it is, gave less offence to conservative critics such as 'Jacques' than Ibsen's classic. This was a reversal of the usual pattern: ordinarily plays by Ibsen's Irish followers were received with more hostility than productions of Ibsen's plays. The reaction of 'Jacques' is also a testimony to *Ghosts'* perennial ability to shock, even when (as on this occasion) acted by an unexceptional ensemble. When he saw *Ghosts* in 1908, Joyce writhed in pain as he witnessed Oswald's final collapse into madness.[88]

On 10 June 1918, Dubliners finally saw Ibsen in the Abbey, but it was not staged by the Abbey Company. Frank Dyall and Mary Merrall were a married English couple who took over the Abbey for a five-week session. Dyall's theatrical career was not glamorously successful, but it stretched as far back as 1894. He had played Rank in *A Doll's House* (1911), Brack in *Hedda Gabler* (1911) and the title role in *John Gabriel Borkman* (1910), which he now staged in Dublin.[89] In contrast to Dyall and Merrall's other productions, *John Gabriel Borkman* was a disaster. It attracted only a handful of people (even though those who did come seemed to enjoy it) and was withdrawn after three days. 'Jacques' complained that 'not one of [the players] was word perfect except the prompter, who was robustly audible'.[90] 'The players strove very hard to give the Ibsen touch to this muddle of morbidity,' he wrote in another review, adding, 'Dyall used voice and gesture to interpret strength of will and mastery of action'.[91]

The Abbey actor Arthur Shields was also irritated by having to listen to the prompter. By contrast, Holloway, who had taken the trouble to read *John Gabriel Borkman* before seeing it, was quite impressed by the performance. He noted that 'Ibsen's different and talky play was lovingly interpreted by this company.'[92] The *Evening Telegraph* also praised the actors:

> While one may not endorse the enthusiast's declaration that the conception of the three leading figures is one of the great things in literature, there is no doubt that they make great demands on the players. Last night those demands were met with marked ability.[93]

The same critic also recorded the 'cordial reception' and the 'numerous curtain calls' from the audience.[94] However well the play might have been received on the first night, soon the following notice appeared in *Sport*: '*John Gabriel Borkman*, by one Ibsen, established a record run at the Abbey of an undesirable character.' 'It was rather rough on Franklin Dyall, after all the trouble rehearsing and performing,' added this critic, 'but by now he must know the sort of stuff to give 'em in Dublin.'[95]

One gets the impression that Shaw was right after all. Thirty years after the London controversy, Ibsen remained the famous highbrow playwright whom Dublin famously rejected time and time again. This was not an indication of the supposedly philistine inclinations of Dublin audiences, however. Dublin was sufficiently open-minded and intellectually alert to enjoy *Blight* or the plays by the Cork Realists. One gets the impression also that if the Irish Theatre crowd had been able to secure a less cramped hall and advertised more, their *An Enemy of the People* would have been as great a success at bringing in audiences as it was at drawing complimentary reviews. The problem was that Ibsen, for the most part, was presented by visiting English companies. More professional local productions were needed for Ibsen to succeed in Dublin.

One of the Abbey Theatre's significant achievements, as Robinson pointed out in 1919, was in creating 'an appreciative audience',[96] who were literarily inclined and who came to the theatre not merely to be amused, but to judge the aesthetic and political merits of the plays. Such an audience would have formed the basis for Ibsen's popularity in Dublin. Yet the Abbey policy became in the late years of the decade even more staunchly exclusive.

The staging of international drama at the Abbey became a subject of the widely publicised 1919 debate between Yeats and Robinson, who had just been re-employed by the theatre as a business manager. At a discussion on 'The Abbey Theatre, Past Present and Future' held at the theatre on 30 March 1919, Robinson 'pleaded for a more international drama'. He thought that the theatre should draw on the world's masterpieces rather than furthering bad writing by producing third-rate plays.[97] Yeats, however, pointed out that he himself had once planned to stage foreign masterpieces but had been persuaded by Synge that this would be detrimental to the development of Irish drama.[98]

The Yeats–Robinson discussion was a reverberation of the 1890s debates on the future of the Irish drama and the role of the National Theatre in shaping public taste. And again, as in the argument between Yeats and Eglinton, or as in Moran's criticism of the Irish Literary Theatre, Ibsen's name was evoked. 'The dramatists must get their inspiration and form from this country – from Murray or Synge rather than Ibsen,'[99] argued Yeats. Robinson countered: 'If Dublin gave young people no chance of seeing great plays by Shakespeare, Ibsen and others, it failed in its duty.'[100] As of old, Ibsen was used as a collective noun for foreign literature and good education; and his plays remained barely known to Dublin audiences.

With the exception of the Metropolitan Players, the new amateur theatrical groups that had sprung up in Dublin, such as the Independent Dramatic Company established by Count and Countess Markievicz in 1908, or its successor, the Dublin Repertory Company, which was founded in 1913 and numbered Flora MacDonnell among its founders, avoided Ibsen. Of all Ibsen's plays, the Irish Theatre staged only *An Enemy of the People*. The Drama League was founded in 1918, by, among others, Yeats and Robinson, specifically for the purpose of staging commercially unviable foreign plays. It also shrank from producing Ibsen, choosing instead more contemporary and lesser known authors such as Paul Claudel, Gabriele D'Annunzio, and Srgjan Tucic. It was not until the next period, which Hogan and Burnham call 'the years of O'Casey', that Ibsen finally made it to the Abbey Theatre.

The Abbey entered: *A Doll's House* and *The Plough and the Stars*, 1923–28

Joyce's semi-autobiographical *Stephen Hero* contains an amusing story of the protagonist's attempts to introduce his parents to Ibsen. While Mrs Daedalus was mildly interested in the plays, becoming particularly fond of *The Wild Duck*, his father was soon disappointed. He 'suspected that *A Doll's House* would be a triviality in the manner of *Little Lord Fauntleroy*' and thought that '*Ghosts* would probably be some uninteresting story about a haunted house'; he 'chose *The League of Youth* in which he hoped to find the reminiscences of like-minded roysterers and, after reading through two acts of provincial intrigue, abandoned the enterprise as tedious'.[101] The incident illustrates the degree to which Ibsen was unknown in the late 1890s.

A quarter of a century later, Sean O'Casey included almost exactly the same joke in *Juno and the Paycock* (1924). 'Whose is the book?' asks Joxer Daly, picking a book from the table in the Boyles' house 'Aw, one of Mary's; she's always reading lately – nothn' but thrash too,' answers Captain Jack Boyle. 'There's one I was lookin' at dh'other day: three stories, The Doll's House, Ghosts, an' The Wild Duck – buks only fit for chiselurs!'[102] Boyle's remark is primarily O'Casey's jocular acknowledgement of his literary roots. Ibsen's plays are not merely alluded to in the play, but (assuming that the book that Joxer picks up is the same one that Boyle had earlier chanced upon) are literally present on stage. This episode also suggests that, by the 1920s, Ibsen, although not universally read or understood, had become part of the fabric of Dublin life.

A Doll's House was first given at the Abbey between 22 and 24 March 1923, less than a month before *The Shadow of the Gunman* (12–14 April 1923) – the first of O'Casey's plays to be presented there. Starring Eileen Crowe as Nora, her husband F. J. McCormick (off-stage known as Peter Judge) as Torvald Helmer, Michael J. Dolan as Dr Rank and Arthur Shields as Krogstad, *A Doll's House* was revived several times over the course of the next six years. The part of Mrs Linde was usually filled by Christine Hayden, although on one occasion, in December 1923, Sara Allgood took her place. Helen, the maid, was played by May Craig, Maureen Delaney and, on one occasion, Ria Mooney; the children were played by May Craig's children, Edna and Raymond Fardy, and a certain P. Brennan, who was later replaced by Vera Fardy. The 1923 playbill names Dolan, who was then the manager of the Abbey theatre, as a producer. On subsequent playbills, Robinson is the producer and McCormick the stage manager. However, Holloway, writing his diary on the night of the performance, names Robinson as the producer. It is likely, therefore, that Robinson was the driving force behind the production, even if on some occasions Dolan was officially responsible.

The performance was a success. It was revived on 18 December 1923 and became part of the Abbey repertoire for the next few years. Some doubted that the young Eileen Crowe, known to the public as the flighty heroine of Colum's *Grasshopper* and Columbine in Harold Chapin's *The Marriage of Columbine*, would be able to carry off the more complex role of Nora.[103] But Holloway, who attended every performance of the play, thought she did 'wonderfully well'.[104] 'It was only in her monologue ... that her words escaped from her lips somewhat mechanically,' he observed. However, '[s]he almost reached greatness in her episodes with Helmer in act 3, and her change from doll wife to woman on hearing her husband's outburst on learning of her forgery was cleverly conveyed'.[105] Yeats was also full of praise for the production and its star:

> I thought the Abbey performance of *The Dolls House* [*sic*] astonishing – one of the best Ibsen performances I have ever seen. I told Miss Crow [*sic*] that she had the makings of a great actress. I had expected it to be bad & only went at the last moment. A Nora who is really young & plays young transforms the play & her husband was given a touch of caricature which gives life to it all.[106]

McCormick said that he 'revelled in playing Helmer'.[107]

According to Holloway, 'he was inclined to be somewhat jerky in delivery' at first, becoming quite passionate by Act 3. In the scene when Helmer first learns of Nora's forgery, McCormick shook the stage so much that a vase of daffodils flew off the piano. (Apparently, his wife was also full of acting zeal; after dancing her tarantella in Act 2, she 'dashed the tambourine into the stalls'.[108])

Holloway wrote that 'Ibsen's play was followed with ardent interest by the big horde present';[109] the *Freeman's Journal* added that 'the audience were most generous in their applause'. Several people, including the well-known Dublin wit Susan Mitchell and John MacDonagh (who had played John Fitzmaurice in *Pagans*), confessed to Holloway (at the December revival of *A Doll's House*) that they had never seen this play before.[110] One person told him how he had been asked whether the play would be suitable as Christmas entertainment for young children.[111] This confirms that the impact of earlier performances of Ibsen's plays in Dublin had been limited. Shaw was right when he urged Lady Gregory to introduce Ireland to Ibsen – and the Abbey was the only company that was up to the task.

An Abbey production of *A Doll's House* had been long overdue. After all, the theatre owed much of its reputation to its alleged 'Ibsenity' (the similarity of the plays of its leading dramatists to Ibsen). The rumour started with Nora Burke in 1903 when she shut the door on her husband, and it never quite dissipated. The heroine of Padraic Colum's *Broken Soil* (1903) was called an 'Irish Hedda Gabler'[112] and the heroine of Martyn's *Grangecolman* (1912) was described as 'one of those introspective Ibsen women who don't know exactly what they want'.[113] The most direct literary engagement with *A Doll's House* since Synge's play was Robinson's *The Cross Roads* (1909), in which a liberal-minded woman remains in a loveless marriage out of the sense of duty.[114] While Dublin critics did not see the connection, their objections to Robinson and other Cork Realists echoed early English judgements of Ibsen's plays: the characters were abnormal, the men unmanly and the women unwomanly. It was high time that the prototype of these Irish unwomanly women appeared on the stage of the national theatre.

One gets the impression that the 1923 production of *A Doll's House* should have been a significant turning point in the history of the Abbey Theatre. Yet, apart from Holloway's notes and the newspaper reviews, there are hardly any surviving records of the production. It is not mentioned in Lady Gregory's *Journals* for instance, or in O'Casey's *Autobiographies*. Robinson, to whom we owe the myth (not entirely unfounded) of Yeats's prolonged resistance to staging Ibsen, and who, in 1919, fought with Yeats on the subject of productions of foreign masterpieces at the Abbey, is also noticeably silent. In *I Sometimes Think*, *Curtain Up* and *The Abbey Theatre*, he speaks of his being 'Ibsen-foolish', mentioning the impact the playwright had on him and other Cork Realists. He tells again and again how, during his first spell as a manager of the Abbey, he managed to persuade Yeats to stage *Little Eyolf* and how he was halfway through rehearsing it when he had to give way to Murray's *Birthright*. Yet the story of his directing *A Doll's House* remains untold.

In the case of *A Doll's House*, objects have conspired with the people for the promptbook of the production has also disappeared (it was probably lost in the 1951 fire that destroyed the theatre). In its absence, perhaps it is useful to turn to what Robinson wrote about the play over twenty years later in *Towards An Appreciation of the Theatre* (1945). The following remarks on the staging of the play may reflect the 1923 production: 'I ignore Ibsen's direction that the room should be "not extensively furnished"', writes Robinson,

> the room should give a sense of stuffiness, the curtains should be heavy, there are too many cushions, the pictures are mediocre and sentimental ... There would be one or two gimcrack tables and the upright piano would be draped, the vases on it [we know that there was at least one vase which McCormick knocked over]; and on the mantelpiece would be bright, bad imitations and there might be a comic group of little figures – they would appeal to Torvald and Nora copies his taste in everything. The light is bright ... and the lampshades are gaily painted.[115]

It is quite possible that Crowe and McCormick played in such surroundings.

Their performance style was probably quite sombre. Unaware of the many humorous touches in *A Doll's House*, Robinson wrote: 'we can pay our highest tribute to the dramatist and forgive him for the fact that there is no humour'.[116] The *Freeman's Journal* review could not see the humour of the play either: 'The actors who can grip their audience with *The Whiteheaded Boy, The Eloquent Dempsey* ... or such like real and wholesome transcripts from nature must seem at first to be out of the picture when transplanted into the vapid region of Helmer and Krogstad.'[117] Not a single laugh escaped from the audience during the 1923 December performance of *A Doll's House*; only the occasional thump of a dropped umbrella and the munching of chocolates were heard.[118]

Robinson's interpretation of Nora is conservative. He insists that the heroine should not be mistaken for a prototype suffragette: 'Nora ... would never bother to fill up a voting-paper, or if she did so (at her husband's bidding) would most likely make a mess of the transaction and it would go into the wastepaper basket as a spoiled vote.'[119] For Robinson, the play is devoid of politics; it is a straightforward and brilliant character study of a person who should be pitied rather than admired. 'There is a genuine touch of thoughtless kitten in [Nora],' he writes:

> [h]er reasoning faculty is very narrow; her sense of wrong and right very limited. Torvald is deathly ill, his life must be saved; this is sound reasoning, but the means by which she saves him shows her to be entirely deficient of worldly wisdom, not to mention common morality.[120]

What Robinson does not see is that to discredit Nora's morality is as dangerous a misreading as turning her into a martyr for female emancipation.

In Act 3, when Torvald tries to prevent Nora from leaving by appealing to her sense of religion, her conscience and her moral sensibility, Nora replies:

> I really don't know – I am all at sea about these things. I only know that I think quite differently from you about them. I hear too, that laws are different from what I thought; but I can't believe that they can be right. It appears that a woman has no right to spare her dying father, or to save her husband's life! I don't believe that.[121]

The questions implicit in these words are examined throughout the play: how can the country's laws, meant to protect its citizens and uphold morality, be deemed more important than human life? The world which Nora finds so bewildering is represented by Torvald. He cannot accept her desire to save his life as a justification for the act of forgery. For him, certainly, social disgrace is worse than death.

With her belief in the overriding importance of human life and in the value of human relations, Nora is an instinctive humanist. Humanism is also what the play demands of the audience. It enlists their sympathy for a heroine who is a petty criminal, besides being vain, deceitful and prone to hysteria. Still, as Robinson himself stated, '[f]rom the first our sympathies are with Nora'.[122] We accept her and might even mistakenly idealise her in spite of her obvious flaws.

In her analysis of the most common criticisms of *A Doll's House*, Joan Templeton notes that critics often accuse Nora of being frivolous without taking into consideration that, on the one hand, 'being frivolous' is essential to the part of addle-brained doll that is Nora's role in her marriage,[123] and, on the other, that by saving Torvald's life Nora demonstrates that she is serious and determined. 'Nora's detractors,' writes Templeton, 'conveniently forget the bottom line of Nora's crime: Torvald would have died if Nora had not forged.'[124] What is notable about Robinson's interpretation of *A Doll's House* is that he does not actually commit the mistake that Templeton describes. Robinson does acknowledge that Torvald would have died if Nora had not intervened, but for him, as for Torvald, this is not sufficient.

'There are [in *A Doll's House*] mistaken notions of what morality means, idealised scenes of flagrant selfishness, material heartlessness and such like spread over the three acts with very little to redeem the picture,'[125] wrote the theatre critic of the *Freeman's Journal* after seeing Robinson's production. He praised Crowe for her success in the 'most difficult, exacting and responsible part' of Nora, 'the lady who possesses to such a rare degree the art of deceit, who is treated as a "Doll" and a great deal of whose part in the dialogue is rather dull and incomprehensible'.[126]

It is likely, therefore, that the Abbey's *A Doll's House* was a tame version of the play. This might be one of the reasons why there are so few eyewitness accounts of this production: it was not offensive enough to write about. Moreover, for the Irish theatre chronicler, such as W. G. Fay or Máire Nic Shiubhlaigh, the production was irrelevant – it was not a celebration of the notorious Abbey realism. In comparison to Lennox Robinson's *A Doll's House*, the Ibsenite Irish plays (including Robinson's own) appeared more provocative and their female characters more problematic. One such character is Nora Clitheroe from O'Casey's *The Plough and the Stars*.

While *The Plough and the Stars* is not modelled on a play by Ibsen, its Nora resembles her Norwegian namesake more than the heroines of other Irish plays inspired by *A Doll's House*.[127] Like Nora Helmer, Nora Clitheroe seems at first glance to be a frivolous and slightly childish woman. We first see Ibsen's Nora fresh from a shopping trip, laden with packages, nibbling on macaroons. In O'Casey's play, we first hear of Nora when her neighbour, Mrs Gogan, finds her new hat: 'I wondher what's this now? A hat!' she exclaims, taking out a black hat with red and gold trimmings, 'God, she's goin' to th' divil lately for style! That hat, now cost more than a penny. Such notions of upperosity she's gettin''.[128]

O'Casey originally intended his Nora to be middle-class.[129] Transplanted into the tenement, Nora still acts out the middle-class obsession with respectability and keeping up appearances. She strives to improve her standard of living, training her relatives in basic hygiene and putting locks on the door. She is as protective about her tenement room 'furnished in a way that suggests an attempt towards a finer expression of domestic life' (135) as Ibsen's Nora is about her own doll's house. Like Nora Helmer, Nora Clitheroe hides her serious side from her husband, preferring to appear to him as his 'little red lipped Nora' (155).

Most importantly, however, the two Noras, while seemingly satisfied with the social role that they are supposed to play, are ready to break all social rules and taboos in order to save the life of those dear to them. Ibsen's Nora borrows money behind her husband's back to pay for his life-saving trip to Italy. O'Casey's Nora burns the letter announcing her husband's appointment as commandant of the Irish Citizen Army in a futile attempt to keep him safe at home. When her deception is disclosed and her husband is summoned to lead a battalion in the 1916 Rising, Nora, risking herself and her unborn child, runs in search of him through the streets of Dublin. In both plays the husband's reaction to the wife's behaviour is fear of personal disgrace. 'You have destroyed my whole happiness. You have ruined my future!' shouts Helmer, who fears that '[p]eople will think [he] was at the bottom of it all and egged [Nora] on'.[130] Jack Clitheroe castigates his wife in a similar manner: 'What possessed you to make a show of yourself like that ...? They'll say now that I sent you out th' way I'd have an excuse to bring you home ... Are you goin' to turn all th' risks I'm takin' into a laugh?' (196).

Like Nora Helmer, Nora Clitheroe proves to be extremely articulate when speaking in self-defence: 'They told me I shamed my husband an' th' women of Ireland to be carryin' on as I was ... They said th' women must learn to be brave an' cease to be cowardly ... Me who risked more for love than they would risk for hate' (184). For Nora Clitheroe, as for Nora Helmer, something is deeply wrong with the world in which human life is less important than social disgrace and the love of an ideal of national freedom is more important than the love of a woman for her husband. O'Casey's Nora rebels against the traditional wifely role that society expects of her in a desperate attempt to save her 'babby house' (138) from the onslaught of idealism.

Grene warns against misreading *The Plough and the Stars* as 'promoting a sentimental humanity represented by women and the family over against a stigmatised but unexamined politics of men'.[131] Nora should not be read as O'Casey's spokesperson. According to Grene, Nora's 'possessiveness, the emotional excess of her performance in Act III and her final collapse into madness suggest a fragility in the ideal of home and personal values for which she stands, a weakness associated with what remains of the bourgeois colouring of her character'.[132] Nor should *A Doll's House* be seen as a panegyric to Nora Helmer's abandonment of her home. The emotionally unstable, self-centred heroine of Ibsen's play has made it easy for some early critics, such as Robinson, to reject the feminist ideas which she represents. 'For *A Doll's House* to be feminist,' writes Templeton, 'it would, apparently, have to be a kind of fourth wall morality play with saintly Everyfeminist, as heroine, and not this ignorant, excitable, confused – in short, human – Nora Helmer.'[133] *A Doll's House* and *The Plough and the Stars* are thus similar in that their radical ideas seem to be accidentally discovered by a character seemingly unfit to sustain their weight.

'I am at sea about these things,' says Nora Helmer as she explains to her husband that she has different views on morality, religion, and individual conscience than the rest of her society. As Templeton has demonstrated, in the final scene of *A Doll's House* Nora seems to quote 'a compendium of everything that early modern feminism denounced about a woman's state', from Mary Wollstonecraft to Camilla Collett and Harriet Martineau.[134] But Nora is unaware of the existence of feminist writings. As she leaves her home, she is only secure in the knowledge that her past life has been a sham and is no longer bearable. O'Casey's Nora is also oblivious to the political nature of her views. In her insistence that Jack's life and their family should be more important than the rebellion, Nora represents a view directly opposed to that of Padraic Pearse as echoed in the following exchange in Act 2:

CAPT. BRENNAN We won't have long to wait now.
LIEUT. LANGON Th' time is rotten ripe for revolution.

CLITHEROE	You have a mother, Langon.
LIEUT. LANGON	Ireland is greater than a mother.
CAPT. BRENNAN	You have a wife, Clitheroe.
CLITHEROE	Ireland is greater than a wife.

(178)

In Act 2, Pearse (seen as a dark silhouette from the pub) calls for a revolutionary war: 'There are many things more horrible than bloodshed, and slavery is one of them' (162). In an unconscious reply to this statement, Nora tells her neighbours of her experience of bloodshed:

> At th' barricade in North King Street I saw fear glowin' in all their eyes ... An' in th' middle o' th' sthreet was somethin' huddled up in a horrible tangled heap ... His face was jammed again th' stones, an' his arm was twisted against th' terrible thing that had happened to him ... An' I saw that they were afraid to look at it ... An' some o' them laughed at me, but th' laugh was a frightened one ... An' some o' them shouted at me, but th' shout had in it th' shiver o' fear ... I tell you they were afraid, afraid, afraid!'
>
> (185)

As Grene points out, the author of *The Plough and the Stars* did not subscribe to Nora's worldview or advocate her behaviour; but nor did Ibsen vindicate forgery or call on the women of Norway to leave their husbands. Both plays use the flawed female heroines to point to the wrongs within their societies without ascribing to them the role of social reformers.

The promptbook of the 1926 Abbey production of *The Plough and the Stars* was discovered by the Abbey archivist Mairead Delaney in 1997 and has since been transferred from the Abbey Archive to the National Library.[135] It contains a typescript of the play with several crossings out, corrections by O'Casey and many more jottings, corrections and signatures which, as Grene notes, suggest that it was used for the 1940s revivals of the play, as well as for the 1951 revival.[136] What I would like to focus on are some cuts to the original typescript, especially the way these affect O'Casey's original conception of Nora. The promptbook contains a variety of crossings and additions, reflecting the sensibilities of diverse actors and producers.[137] The particular deletions in question, however, are all executed in pink ink. Textual alterations and directorial instructions to actors are added in the margins in the same pen, and in Robinson's hand. It is therefore likely that he also made the cuts.[138]

It is unclear whether these changes were made before the first production in the hope of forestalling public antagonism, or whether they were made after the riots in an attempt to appease the public. Whatever the case, the careful pruning of O'Casey's play in the promptbook was motivated by a desire to free the play of the charges of indecency on the one hand, and anti-nationalism on the other. In Act 1, for instance, O'Casey had Jack Clitheroe call Bessie Burgess an 'old bitch'; in the promptbook Clitheroe refers to her as an 'old one'. A similar alteration can be found in Act 3, where Peter and the Young Covey argue about the looting of Dublin shops during the rebellion. In the original Peter shouts at Covey: 'You lean, long, lanky lath of a lowsey bastard .... Lowsey bastard, lowsey bastard!' (192) In the prompt book, Peter says the words 'lowsey bastard' only once; Robinson must have liked the alliteration of Peter's curses, yet wished to de-emphasise these words, which were particularly offensive to the audience and the actors.[139]

In the same scene, Peter (who was too afraid to join in the looting) refuses to open the door to Covey, Bessie and Mrs Gogan as they return from their expedition. In the promptbook Peter shouts: 'Don't be assin' me to open any door, don't be assin' me to open any door for you .... Makin' a shame an' a sin o' th' cause that good men are fighting for.' But the rest of Peter's speech is crossed out: 'Oh, God forgive th' people that, instead o' burnishin' th' work th' boys is doin' to-day with quiet honesty an' patience is revilin' their sacrifices with a riot of lootin' an' roguery!' (192).

It is not difficult to guess why this was cut. First, it was simply too funny. Even though it does not directly ridicule the leaders of the Rising, some might have taken offence at such a light-hearted treatment of the subject. Moreover, Peter's glorification of his own cowardice and his insistence that by staying at home he somehow 'burnished the work' of the fighters made fun of the sustaining myth of the newfound Irish Free State, namely the belief in shared sacrifice and the mythical conviction that all of Ireland had somehow taken part in the Easter Rising. Finally, the structure of Peter's remark makes a carnivalesque jumble of the looters, the fighters and the stay-at-homes. 'The boys who are doing the work', the people who are 'burnishing that work with quiet honesty' and the people who are 'reviling their sacrifices with a riot of looting' appear as equally ridiculous inhabitants of a mad world.

Nora Clitheroe was the one character to suffer most from the cuts made to the play. The promptbook Nora is less articulate and sympathetic, but more selfish and unreasonable than the Nora of the published text. In other words, she begins to resemble Robinson's conception of the heroine of *A Doll's House*.

The change is especially apparent in the central scene in Act 3. Captain Brennan, Jack Clitheroe and the wounded Lieutenant Langon find themselves on the steps of the tenement where the Clitheroes are living. Nora, who has spent the night searching for Jack and calling his name in the streets, sees them and 'rushes wildly out of the house and flings her arms around the neck of Clitheroe with a fierce and joyous relief'. In the original she shouts out wild praises to God while madly kissing the husband she thought she had lost:

> Jack, Jack, Jack; God be thanked ... Be thanked ... He has been kind and merciful to His poor handmaiden ... My Jack, my own Jack, that I thought was lost is found, that I thought was dead is alive again ... Oh God be praised for ever, evermore! ... My poor Jack ... Kiss me, kiss me Jack, kiss your own Nora!'
>
> (194)

Almost all of this is crossed out. The promptbook Nora appears much more reserved in her passion for Jack; she only says: 'Jack, Jack, ah God be thanked, be thanked.'

In the original text Clitheroe kisses Nora, but then reprimands her and asks her not to make a scene. In the promptbook the following reply is edited out: 'I won't, I won't; I promise, I promise, Jack; honest to God. I'll be silent an' brave to bear th' joy of feelin' you safe in my arms again ... It is hard to force away th' tears of happiness at th' end of an awful agony' (194). This makes clear Nora's pathetic misunderstanding of the situation. Jack has not yet returned home from the fight; her suffering is far from over. The crossing out of these lines might have undermined the audience's perception of Nora's agony. In O'Casey's text, Nora is hysterical, already driven half insane by her ordeal. Her exuberant, transgressive language matches her reckless behaviour. In the cut version of the play, Nora's clinging to her husband is inconsistent with her peculiarly laconic utterances.

While Nora passionately clings to Jack, the wounded Lieutenant Langon is groaning for an ambulance and Bessie Burgess, the Clitheroes' Protestant neighbour, shouts abuse at the three soldiers. Captain Brennan urges Jack to leave Nora so they can find help for Langon. Jack tries to gently let go of his wife, saying: 'Loosen me, darling, let me go.' In the cut version Nora responds: 'No, no, no, I'll not let you go.' The following lines have been crossed out: 'Come on, come up to our home, Jack, my sweetheart, my lover, my husband, an' we'll forget th' last few terrible days! ... I look tired now, but a few hours of happy rest in your arms will bring back th' bloom of freshness again, an' you will be glad, you will be glad, glad ... glad!' (195). The urgency of her appeal is lost in the cut version; what is highlighted instead is her insensitivity to Langon.

Nora's character is central to the play's attack on idealism in two ways; she is both a victim and an accuser. Further cuts include some of the lines in which she makes her most powerful condemnations. When Jack again entreats her to let him go, asking if she wants him to be untrue to his comrades, Nora replies: 'No, I won't let you go ... I want you to be thrue to me, Jack ... I am your dearest comrade; I'm your thruest comrade.' Crossed out in the promptbook is the rest of her speech: 'They only want th' comfort of havin' you in th' same danger as themselves' (196).

The rest of the scene is almost completely edited out. Gone is the short exchange in which the Clitheroes sound peculiarly like the Helmers. While it is unclear from the markings in the promptbook whether Jack, in the cut version, asks Nora when shaming her for 'bawlin ... at th' barricades': 'What are you more than any other woman?'[140] Nora does not get to reply to him: 'No more, maybe; but you are more to me than any other man, Jack' (196). Like the Nora of Ibsen's play, she is not able to understand that, for her husband, concepts of honour and manhood belong to the world outside their marriage. In his reply, Jack reveals an insecurity and fear of scandal that rival Torvald Helmer's. This too is edited out: 'They'll say now that I sent you out th' way I'd have an excuse to bring you home ... Are you going to turn all th' risks I'm takin into a laugh?' (196).

Moreover, all references to violence towards Nora are struck out. Her description of the night at the barricades is heavily edited. 'All last night I asked for you everywhere', says Nora in the promptbook, 'and I screamed and screamed your name.' What she does not say is 'some of them laughed ... I was pushed away, but I shoved back ... Some o' them even sthruck me' (196). That the heroes of 1916, or even their supporters, could have hit a woman was blasphemy in 1926. In the promptbook, Jack does not physically hurt Nora. In the original text, Jack is urged by Brennan to break his wife's hold on him. He asks Brennan to 'hold [his] gun ... for a minute', roughly loosens her grip and, despite her pleadings, pushes her to the ground. In the promptbook, Brennan does not say to Jack: 'break her hold on you man', nor does Jack ask him to hold the gun. Nora's pitiful wailing: 'Please, Jack ... You're hurting me, Jack ... Honestly ... Oh, you're hurting ... me! .... I won't, I won't, I won't! ... Oh, Jack, I gave you everything you asked o me ... Don't fling me from you now!' (197) is crossed out.

In his analysis of *A Doll's House*, Robinson refused to believe that Nora's plight was caused by anything other than her limited sense of right and wrong, dismissing the view of the play as a social commentary. The cut version of *The Plough and the Stars* similarly separates the heroine's behaviour from its social causes and implications. In both cases what is undermined in the transferral of the original text to production is the female protagonist's role in debunking idealism.

As seen earlier, Joyce and O'Casey made practically the same joke to emphasise by comic exaggeration the idea formulated by Shaw – that Ibsen's plays can be easily misunderstood by an idealistic reader who 'misses the meaning altogether ... and proceeds to substitute a meaning congenial to his own ideal of nobility'.[141] In the case of the production of *The Plough and the Stars,* O'Casey and contemporary interpreters of his play emerge as readers of Ibsen's *A Doll's House.* O'Casey's humanism, his distaste for idealism and the similarity of his outlook to Ibsen's (and indeed Shaw's) are noticeable in his conception of Nora Clitheroe. Robinson's approach to *A Doll's House* as a perfectly structured character study of a person with imperfect understanding of right and wrong rather than an attack on the inherent inhumanity of common morality was transferred also to the play-text of *The Plough and the Stars*.

Neither O'Casey's alterations to the playscript nor the changes made by the directors prevented riots on the fourth day of the performance of *The Plough and the Stars*. One of the most eloquent and least violent opponents of the play was Hannah Sheehy-Skeffington, who had been widowed during the Rising. In an attempted speech at the performance, in a letter to the press and in public debate with the author she contended that 'the play was a travesty of Easter Week ... it concentrated on pettiness and squalor, unrelieved by a gleam of heroism'.[142]

Her husband, Francis, who was a nationalist and a committed pacifist, was picked up by a British soldier while trying to organise an anti-looting committee and executed without trial. Hannah did not know that O'Casey had paid tribute to Francis in *The Story of the Irish Citizen Army* (1919), declaring him 'the living antithesis of the Easter Insurrection' and its 'terrifying madness'.[143] In her grief, she had resorted to idealism. Recounting the details of her husband's death to an American audience in 1917, Hannah insisted that he 'would have gone to his death with a smile ... knowing that by his murder he had struck a heavier blow for his ideals than by any act of his life'.[144] Calling for American support for Ireland's fight for independence, she described her husband as a victim, not of militarism, but of specifically British militarism (and not as an almost accidental victim of the Rising). As she was leaving the performance of

The Plough and the Stars under police protection, she declared: 'I am one of the widows of Easter Week. It is no wonder, that you do not remember the men of Easter Week, because none of you fought on either side.'[145] That her husband did not fight on either side, and that his beliefs were reflected in O'Casey's pacifist and socialist play, did not seem relevant.

The similarity between of O'Casey's play and *A Doll's House* allows us to see the breakdown of communication between O'Casey and Hannah Sheehy-Skeffington which occurred at the performance of *The Plough and the Stars* in the context of the history of Irish feminism. As we have seen in the case of *In the Shadow of the Glen*, in pre-1916 Ireland there was a degree of affinity between Irish suffragists and the controversial playwright of the Abbey Theatre. Anti-idealism, which Shaw regarded as Ibsen's quintessence, the refusal to subordinate one's duty to oneself to the duties prescribed by society, permeated Synge's drama and Irish suffragist thought.

For Irish suffragists and their English supporters, 'Home Rule without women would be a false sort of Home Rule'.[146] For Synge, the supposed 'unripeness' of the Irish nation was a false excuse for its idealistic misrepresentation on stage. However, after 1916, things changed. As Rosemary Cullen Owens explains, 'the post-1916 wave of nationalism, which swept the country, submerged women's groups'.[147] Cullen Owens quotes a 1918 report of the Irish Women's Franchise League which explained that the 'passing of the Conscription Act and the militarist reign of terror then inaugurated rendered the carrying on of suffrage activities impossible'.[148] Suffragists now operated in a radically different world. The human losses incurred during the First World War, the 1916 Rising and the two Irish wars that followed made it nearly impossible to maintain the kind of anti-idealism that had informed the Irish struggle for women's rights. The story of Nora Helmer is impossible in the conditions of war: a character similar to Nora would find herself not a feminist, but, in her refusal to see life as less important than current ideology, an unconscious pacifist – like O'Casey's Nora. Irish feminism had thus become divorced from Irish Ibsenism.

In a letter to the press, addressing Hannah Sheehy-Skeffington's criticism of his play, O'Casey urged her and the Republican Party to recognise that 'people that go to football matches are as much a part of Ireland as those who go to Bodenstown'[149] (where the Irish revolutionary Theobald Wolf Tone is buried). Otherwise Ireland would become 'a terrible place fit only for heroes to live in'.[150] This 'terrible place' was real for Hannah; its reality possibly a greater reason for the diminishment of feminist activities in Ireland than the granting of the female

vote in 1918. As she wrote in 1920, 'In Ireland at present we are in a state of war, and all the conditions prevailing in other countries during the later European War now apply at home. Just as then the woman's movement became patriots and heroes' wives or widows, rather than human beings, so now in Ireland the national struggle overshadows all else.'[151] According to Cullen Owens, such 'sublimation of women's issues to controversial national questions ensured that the position of Irish women remained subservient, a situation compounded by the deepening Catholic ethos of the state'.[152]

The late 1920s and 1930s saw the consolidation of the doll's house; female emancipation and artistic freedom were secondary to nationalist ideals. In 1920s, a performance of *A Doll's House* was a near-annual event at the Abbey Theatre. That it was received well by the press and the audience does not mean that Ibsen's ideas were universally understood or accepted. 'Ibsen's play,' went a 1923 review in the *Irish Times*, 'does not mean all to audiences of to-day that it must have meant to those of a generation ago, when it seemed to stand for then current ideas about the emancipation of women.'[153] Yet, if Ibsen seemed outdated, it was not because of the widespread success of the feminist movement. According to the 1923 *Irish Independent* review of the play, *A Doll's House* showed 'the disastrous results to the happiness and contentment of family life caused by the moral depravity, duplicity, and secret intriguing of a clever wife, and in this there is a moral which might be well learned by some modern civilisations'.[154]

The Abbey's second Ibsenite experiment was *John Gabriel Borkman*. Starring McCormick and Crowe as the Borkmans, Dolan as Foldal, May Craig as Ella, Arthur Shields as Erhart, Meriel Moore as Fanny Wilton and Kitty Curling as Frida, it was produced on 3–7 April 1928 to mark the centenary of Ibsen's birthday. This performance being the only official celebration of the occasion, the wife of the Governor General, members of the Executive Council and many foreign consuls were present on the opening night. While there was some disagreement whether McCormick was 'comfortable in the ill-fitting frock coat of the bourgeois Napoleon',[155] overall the play was a success. 'As one sat in the crowded theatre last night,' wrote the correspondent of the *Irish Times*,

> it was hard to reconcile oneself to the admitted fact that Ibsen in these countries is not popular in the ordinary accepted meaning of the term. ... Stalls were filled, and the pit and balcony were packed. From both sections there came at the end a unanimous and pronounced expression of approval. Ibsen was popular.[156]

The upsurge of interest in Ibsen occasioned by the anniversary of his birth is evident in the rumour that Sara Allgood proposed to give a performance of *Ghosts* in 1928.[157] While anecdotes about Ibsen were circulated in the newspapers, several people observed that the Irish experience of his plays had been rather one-sided. 'We see all too little of the later Ibsen in whom the imaginative poet reinforces the realist to produce a type of drama which has no parallel in the history of the theatre,'[158] wrote J. W. Good in a review of *John Gabriel Borkman*. Robinson expressed the same idea in relation to Ibsen's influence on Irish drama: 'We Irish have learned, let it be admitted, more from the early Ibsen that the late – more from *The Enemy of the People* and *The League of Youth* than from *Little Eyolf*.'[159] An article by T. G. Keller (earlier known as Keohler, the one-time honorary treasurer of the Theatre of Ireland) marked a change of direction in the Irish reception of Ibsen. 'Ibsen,' insisted Keller, 'was born a poet. He made himself a dramatist. And this is why he is not merely a playwright, but a great imaginative seer, who used the dramatic form for his visions.'[160]

In a brief survey of Ibsen's plays (ending with *The Master Builder*), Keller emphasised Ibsen's poetic imagination, his eschewing of didacticism and the unrealistic aspects of his plays. Of *The Wild Duck* he said that it 'has touches of matchless lyricism but exists chiefly in a unique word of inversion where anything might happen, and where everything, even the death of poor little Hedvig, belongs to the category of things which are not what they seem'. Of Ibsen's women he said that they are conceived as 'the motive power behind destiny'. He also highlighted the importance of paradox in Ibsen's drama, from which 'we can draw no moral, political, social or any other so-called teaching ... Ibsen, like all seers, climbed instinctively to the towering summit of paradox where simplicity reigns'. With his interest in the paradoxical and the absurd, and scorn for didacticism or sham morality, and his delight in the 'opening of the finite sense to infinity, a realization of the incredible mystery of creation', Keller is a modernist reader of Ibsen. The Abbey Theatre 1923 and 1928 Ibsen productions were Victorian in their outdated naturalist settings, and, more importantly, their conservative interpretation of the plays. It was the Gate Theatre that on its opening in 1928 interpreted an Ibsen play in a way that resonated with more modernist sensibilities.

6
A Farewell to the Revival and the Beginnings of Irish Modernism

Peer Gynt in Irish writing

In 'The Circus Animals' Desertion' (1939), Yeats bids farewell to the Irish Revival. The 'masterful images'[1] of his poetry and drama – Oisin, Countess Cathleen and Cuchúlain – are mocked in the poem's title. They have deserted the poet whose mind begot them; now, one imagines, they are wandering the streets of modern Dublin as clumsy and helpless as exotic lions and elephants that have been trained to perform outmoded tricks. The poet confesses that his flight into the realm of fancy has ended. He has emerged from the state in which 'the dream itself had all my thought and love',[2] a state in which the only reality was that of the fantastic forms of his imagination to return to the wasteland that he now recognises as his homeland, the place where the masterful images of his mind had come to life out of

> A mound of refuse or the sweepings of a street,
> Old kettles, old bottles, and a broken can,
> Old iron, old bones, old rags, that raving slut
> Who keeps the till. Now that my ladder's gone
> I must lie down where all the ladders start
> In the foul rag and bone shop of the heart.[3]

Here, and indeed throughout *Last Poems*, Yeats unveils an uncanny aspect of the Irish Literary Revival. He suggests that in his attempt to reshape Irish life through the revival of the fantastic images of mythology he somehow lost control and must now take responsibility for his inner impoverishment and the spiritual devastation of the community.

By 1938, it had become clear that poetry could affect politics in ways not always envisaged by the poets. 'Did that play of mine send out / Certain men the English shot?' Yeats asked in 'The Man and the Echo'. Even more troubling than the thought that his poetry literally inspired others to acts of violence was the fear that the Revival might have affected Ireland in ways yet unknown. Thus in 'The Statues', Yeats wondered:

> When Pearse summoned Cuchulain to his side,
> What stalked through the Post Office? What intellect,
> What calculation, number, measurement, replied?[4]

The fear that reality may be unpredictably impacted by poetry is also one of the major themes of *Peer Gynt*, a play that explores the pitfalls of romanticism and, more specifically, national revivalism.

The final stanza of 'The Circus Animals' Desertion' resembles the auction scene in *Peer Gynt* (4. 5) where Peer Gynt, now an old man, returns to the Hegstad farm, the site of the adventures of his youth, to find a 'ruined mill-house beside the stream. The ground is torn up, the whole place waste.'[5] Outside an old farmhouse, an auction is in progress: a crowd of drunks are 'squabbling for rags and clouts' (220), the detritus of the woman who 'is laid in a wormy bed' (219). This scene, like Yeats's poem, piles up images of death, drink, litter and money. Dispersed among the rubbish are relics of Peer's childhood and his adult dreams. There is a metal casting ladle in which 'Peer Gynt cast his silver buttons' (220), a bearskin which he apparently used to overcome trolls, a reindeer skull belonging to 'the wonderful reindeer that bore ... Peer Gynt over edge and skree' (222), and an 'invisible cloak / Peer Gynt and Ingrid flew off through the air with' (222). To his shock, Peer discovers that during his long absence from Norway he has become a feature of local folklore, a half-forgotten legend. All that the drunks at the auction vaguely remember is that Peer was 'an abominable liar' (224) who came to a bad end overseas.

This scene is also a surprise for the audience. It distorts the already complex relationship between fairy-tale and reality established in the previous four Acts. Taking the name of a legendary troll hunter in Asbjørnsen and Moe's *Folk Tales of Norway*, Ibsen created a character whose second-hand heroics critique the revivalist ideology that furthered such folklore collections. In the first Act, Peer Gynt appears as a self-deceiving liar, a nineteenth-century man whose fascination with folktales leads him to identify himself with their heroes. He boasts of riding a reindeer through the air, of cramming a devil into a nutshell and of fighting trolls. Villagers are amused that he claims the acts of folk heroes as his own, until he infuriates them by re-enacting an old fairy-tale and abducting a bride, Ingrid, from her wedding feast. The abduction, like Christy's wounding of his father in *The Playboy of the Western World*, exposes the gap between a gallous story and a dirty deed. Instead of flying through the sky with Ingrid, wrapped in an invisible cloak, Peer seduces her in the mountains and then abandons her. The objects that the drunks brandish about the stage in the auction scene cannot exist; they are mementoes of events that never took place, except in Peer's imagination.

'The Circus Animals' Desertion', like the auction scene, articulates a sense of loss through its conflation of the subjective and the objective realities. In Yeats's early poetry, the treasured 'image that blossoms a rose in the deeps of my heart' is distinct from 'things uncomely and broken, all things worn out and old'.[6] By contrast, the late poem ends with the discovery that poetry's masterful images are inseparable from the dirty rags of human life. The drab shop with its 'raving slut who keeps the till' is not only the image of modern Ireland, which has outlived its need for legends. It is also the interior of the poet's mind. The land of drunks, auctioneers and dead dreams to which Peer returns in Act 5 is both nineteenth-century Norway and Peer's personal purgatory.

Peer Gynt prefigures those texts of the Irish Revival that, like 'The Circus Animals' Desertion', are concerned with the dynamics of myth-making. Peer, the parodic embodiment of literary revivalism, affects his world in ways that he has not deemed possible and is consumed by the reality that he creates. 'We were to forge in Ireland a new sword on our old traditional anvil for that great battle that must in the end re-establish the old, confident, joyous world,' wrote Yeats in 'Poetry and Tradition' (1908). Yet the societies that Yeats founded for this purpose 'became quickly or slowly everything [he] despised'.[7] Moreover, the changes wrought by the Irish Literary Revival were vastly different from the creation of 'the Ireland in the heart',[8] proposed by AE at the outset of the movement. In *Ulysses*, Joyce critiques the misdirected revivalist efforts. In 'Circe', Dublin is depicted in a way markedly similar to the dreamscape of Act 5 of *Peer Gynt*. In the drab city, the images of the Irish Revival acquire dimly malevolent life.

Noting the substantial number of incidents and techniques that 'Circe' has in common with *Peer Gynt*, Tysdahl concludes that 'Joyce had Ibsen's play in mind when he wrote and rewrote it'.[9] Bloom's fantasy of Bloomosalem, 'a golden city', 'the Nova Hibernia of the future',[10] is a direct allusion to Peer's empire of Gyntiana and its capital Peeropolis, which he plans to found in Act 4. 'Circe' recalls the madhouse episode, occurring at the end of Act 4 of *Peer Gynt*, as well as Act 5, scene 6 where bird cries, thread-balls, fallen leaves and the voice of his dead mother all accuse Peer of having squandered the emotional and creative possibilities of his life. This scene seems to be the backdrop to the sequence in 'Circe' in which yew trees, a nymph, a calf and the echo accuse Bloom of a horrendous but vaguely defined crime (which at times seems to have been masturbating while on a school trip).[11] Yet what links 'Circe' explicitly with *Peer Gynt* is its approach to literary revivalism.

Both Ibsen's play and Joyce's 'Circe' distort the boundaries between the inner world of the protagonists and the physical world they inhabit. Thus Stephen's conversation with the ghost of his mother is interrupted by the prostitutes' casual remarks which seem to relate to the ghost's words. For instance, Zoe's remark on the temperature of the room – 'I'm melting' – is soon followed by Stephen's mother's angry words on the 'fire of hell'.[12] Similarly, during Bloom's subjection by the fantastic Bello, his metamorphosis into a pig and a woman, his giving birth to 'eight male yellow and white children [who] appear on a red-carpeted staircase adorned with expensive plants',[13] the reader never quite loses sight of Bloom's actual whereabouts – Mrs Cohen's brothel. As in Act 5 of *Peer Gynt*, we are never certain whether the magical occurrences of 'Circe' should be interpreted as actual hallucinations experienced by Bloom and Stephen, or whether the mental landscape painted by this episode is an exaggeration of the protagonist's psyche.

This oscillation between the objective and the subjective in both works builds up to a critique of the romantic idealism of national revivalists. Instead of merely presenting the realm of the trolls in Act 2 of *Peer Gynt* as a beautifully animated piece of Norwegian folklore, Ibsen suggested that the trolls are also part of Peer's subconscious (Peer knocks his head against the rock in the scene immediately preceding the appearance of the trolls). Ibsen thus subverted the nationalist romantic approach to folklore as the purest expression of the national consciousness. His magical world is anything but a revival and celebration of what Wagner called 'that native, nameless poem of the folk'.[14] Rather, it is the dark interior of the individual's mind.

As William Archer pointed out in 1909,[15] the troll scenes contain a 'jibe at Norwegian national vanity':

> The cow gives cakes and the bullock mead
> Ask not if its taste be sour or sweet
> The main matter is, and you mustn't forget it,
> It's all of it home-brewed ...
>
> (72)

Folklore is revived not to foster national consciousness but to ridicule certain forms of nationalism. Those who turned to Ibsen's text in the hope of finding their ancestral past found only distorted images of themselves. It might be added that in an early draft of *Peer Gynt*, the trolls danced and sang Johan Nordahl Brun's 'For Norge, Kjæmpers Fødeland' (1771) adopted in the nineteenth century as the unofficial anthem of Norway.[16]

A passage in 'Circe' that betrays a similarly subversive approach to folklore is the appearance of the Celtic sea-god Mananaan MacLir:

> (*In the cone of the searchlight behind the coalscuttle, ollave, holyeyed, the bearded figure of Mananaan MacLir broods, chin on knees. He rises slowly. A cold seawind blows from his druid mouth. About his head writhe eels and elvers. He is encrusted with weeds and shells. His right hand holds a bicycle pump. His left hand grasps a huge crayfish by its two talons.*)
> MANANAAN MACLIR (*With a voice of waves*) Aum! Hek! Wal! Ak! Lub! Mor! Ma! White yoghin of the gods. Occult pimander of Hermes Trismegistos. (*With a voice of whistling seawind*) Punarjanam patsypunjaub! I won't have my leg pulled. It has been said by one: beware the left, the cult of Shakti. (*With a cry of stormbirds*) Shakti Shiva, darkhidden Father! (*He smites with his bicycle pump the crayfish in his left hand. On its cooperative dial glow the twelve signs of the zodiac. He wails with the vehemence of the ocean.*) Aum! Baum! Pyjaum! I am the light of the homestead! I am the dreamery creamery butter.[17]

Joyce's Mananaan MacLir combines the traditional attributes of the sea-god with those of AE. The god's evocation of Hermes Trismegistos is an allusion to the Hermetic society of which AE, as well as Yeats, was a member. AE had to rely on a bicycle during his journeys in search of Ireland's old gods (as described in George Moore's *Hail and Farewell*) and in his work for the Irish Agricultural Organization Society; this bicycle is materialised in the pump that the god grasps in his left hand. The final lines allude to the setting up of the cooperative creameries by the society and to its official organ, *The Irish Homestead*, which was edited by AE.[18]

This passage, similar to the troll scenes in *Peer Gynt*, and indeed to 'The Circus Animals' Desertion', emphasises the inauthenticity of revivalism. It suggests that the bicycle pump-wielding sea-god haunting the minds of confused Dubliners is the only result of the revivalist crusade. The attempts to bring the legendary past to life and to instil in the lives of the bourgeoisie the imagined purity of peasant lore have ended in the creation of a new mythology and a false one. The warped creations of the revivalist attempts to create a new world are Yeats's run-away circus creatures, and Joyce's vision of Kathleen Ní Houlihan as '*Old Gummy Granny in sugarloaf hat appears seated on a toadstool, the death-flower of the potato blight on her breast*'.[19] Their literary ancestor is Ibsen's impoverished troll-king, who tells Peer in Act 5 that he hopes to get a place in the theatre because the papers are clamouring for national talents (250).

In *Peer Gynt*, Ibsen's own earlier fascination with folklore (in 1892 he was granted a stipend by the Akedemiske Kollegium which allowed him to spend over a month collecting folklore in northern districts of Norway) and with the revivalist aesthetics, which had produced such works as *Olaf Liljekrans* (1856) and *The Vikings of Helgeland* (1857), are subjected to ironic scrutiny. *Peer Gynt* articulates the discovery that, as Castle argues, informs such revisionist works of the Irish Revival *The Playboy* and *Ulysses* (to which we may add Yeats's later poetry), namely 'the realization that the problem of authenticity is less one of finding the appropriate technique for unearthing cultural essences ... than it is one of coming to terms with the fact that authenticity is, in a sense an impossible goal'.[20]

Yet, it was not only his emigration or his growing dissatisfaction with the politics of his native country that provided Ibsen with a double-look at romantic nationalism. Like the earlier *Brand*, *Peer Gynt* was not written for the stage. Unrestricted by the limitations of stagecraft, Ibsen felt free, writes Meyer, 'to move uninhibitedly in time and space', and, more importantly, to 'ignore the ... the frontiers between reality and fantasy between ... the conscious and the unconscious'.[21] Meyer's point makes it easier to see why we should find echoes of *Peer Gynt* in those texts of the Revival that revisit the theatrical traditions of the movement. 'Circe' is Joyce's unstageable play, which, as Len Platt argues, is a 'kind of hijacking of revivalist theatre'.[22] 'Circe' takes the central tropes, rituals and images of the Revival out of the confines of the Abbey Theatre and projects them into the city slum. The rules of the revivalist game are broken; the distance between the drama and the audience is abolished. Ancient myths are no longer revived by actors for the benefit of the public. Instead the distorted myths are constantly revived and mutated by the inhabitants of Nighttown.

Correspondingly, Yeats's 'The Circus' Animals Desertion' questions the problem that preoccupied Yeats throughout his involvement with the Abbey theatre: the unsuitability of the representational style to his drama:

> My circus animals were all on show,
> Those stilted boys, that burnished chariot,
> Lion and woman and the Lord knows what.[23]

The ornate artificiality of the 'players and painted stage' mocks the 'things which they were emblems of'.[24]

Throughout his career as an artistic director of the Abbey, Yeats attempted to find a non-representational style. Dismissive of the naturalistic scenic paintings of William Fay,[25] Yeats hoped to employ coloured light and abstract patterns of colour, pioneered by Gordon Craig. As early as 1905, Yeats wrote that the scenery for Synge's *Well of the Saints*, then in preparation by the theatre, should consist of 'mountains in one or two flat colours and without detail, ash trees and red salleys with something of recurring pattern in their woven boughs' in an attempt to 'express what no eye has ever seen'.[26] Between 1910 and 1912, Yeats's short-lived partnership with Craig brought about innovative revivals of *The Countess Cathleen* and *The Hour-Glass*. In these productions, atmospheric effects were achieved through the use of coloured lights. Craig's moveable screens, invented in 1910, allowed for greater freedom in the use of light and space. For a while Yeats believed that with the help Craig he would find a 'means of staging everything that is not naturalistic' and foresaw the development of a 'new method even for our naturalistic plays'.[27] Yet, even while he anticipated expressionist theatre, Craig was limited by the as yet rudimentary technology, especially in his use of stage lighting.[28] His partnership with Yeats ended soon after 1912. Yeats's interest in revolutionising the Abbey Theatre gradually gave way to the opportunities offered by the theatre of the drawing room.

'Dublin was never more theatre conscious than it was when pulling out of its civil disorders,'[29] recalled C. P. Curran. However, to most of his contemporaries 'it seemed that for the Abbey, [the] European stage with all its new wealth and colour and experiment did not exist'.[30] Nor did the other theatrical societies, including the Drama League, established by Yeats and Lennox Robinson specifically to produce plays by foreign dramatists, bring Dublin any closer to the theatrical trends of mainland Europe. For Curran, the Drama League was merely 'coquetting with the avant-garde ... carr[ying] into the theatre the atmosphere of brilliant drawing room charades'.[31]

The literature of the Irish Revival had developed in an increasingly self-critical direction. Yet Irish theatre lacked the means to stage self-reflexivity and involve the audiences in the process of re-examining revivalist myths. Free State Dublin badly needed expressionist theatre.

Peer Gynt at the Peacock, 1928–32

Peer Gynt was first staged in Ireland at the Peacock Theatre on 14–27 October 1928. With this play Micheál MacLiammóir and Hilton Edwards opened the first season of the Gate Theatre. The production was a runaway success. Curran later referred to it as a 'watershed in Irish theatre': 'On the tiny Peacock stage Hilton and Micheál revealed a whole new world flooded with colour but edged in silhouette, crafty and imaginative inventions always significant, always bearing directly on the action of the play.'[32]

The production incorporated several elements peculiar to expressionist theatre. Hilton Edwards fashioned a rudimentary cyclorama and equipped the minuscule Peacock Theatre with expensive footlights, projectors and spotlights. A dense and carefully scripted lighting plot allowed him to make the interplay between coloured light and shadow integral to the play. Reflecting the early 1920s designs of Jürgen Fehling and Leopold Jessner, Edwards relied on a set of two steps to indicate mountain peaks, valleys and house interiors.[33] The expressionist approach was particularly well developed in the 1932 revival. As he explained, the first production had attempted a style that 'was at once pictorial and suggestive'; the style of the 1932 production was 'consistently austere rather than pictorial' in that it relied on 'shapes and of masses of colour in costume and setting as well as by lighting which symbolizes rather than portrays'.[34]

In *All for Hecuba*, MacLiammóir provides an ironic, behind-the-scenes account of the change in approach from 'pictorial and suggestive' to purely expressionistic. He set out to portray 'the enormity of Norwegian mountains and Moroccan deserts on a stage whose measurements were sixteen feet eight' and produced a series of coloured designs 'showing certain qualities of pattern and colour and dramatic value'.[35] Edwards, however, with 'a rigidity of theory alarmingly purist in one so young', came up with a different solution to the problem of stage space and 'insisted on the use of steps for mountains'.[36] The two sets of steps formed a pyramid when placed back to back and thus, as Edwards explained, 'visually ... gave a perfect suggestion of a peak and structurally ... allowed figures mounting them to be thrown into the postures of ascending and descending great heights'.[37] MacLiammóir loved the idea and designed the steps. As an actor he admired their theatrical potential; as a painter he was impressed by their stark beauty. But, he confessed, 'a third and not very promising factor in me decided to have other mountains, superior things, built of three-ply wood and designed, shaped and painted by me to resemble what I could imagine of Norway'.[38] The result, he believed was a 'mixture, and a bad one, of the constructionist principle and postcards of lovely Lucerne'.[39] MacLiammóir explained that the early set failed because 'two principles were at work, and they would no more mix than oil and water, – the principle of using suggestive, significant shapes, and that of pictorial realism'.[40]

As a seemingly romantic work that critiques romanticism, *Peer Gynt* invites the kind of ambivalent response evidenced in MacLiammóir's first stage designs. As F. J. Marker and Lise-Lone Marker demonstrate, the earliest productions of the play captured its romantic aspect in terms of stagecraft and character conception. Conversely, post-Second World War approaches to *Peer Gynt* were non-representational; their aim was to emphasise its anti-romantic exploration of egoism.

Thus an 'impressively three-dimensional Norwegian log house' was constructed by Theodor Andersen for the 1886 production at Dagmar Theatre, Copenhagen. After his flight into the woods, Peer was found to have built a cabin 'decorated with reindeer's antlers above the door'.[41] A pair of wooden blocks mounted on a track hidden behind the hut enabled Solveig to ski towards it. This production, typical of the nineteenth-century approaches to the play, returned *Peer Gynt* to the fairytale world from which it originated. As Marker and Marker put it:

> even the trolls ... whom Peer encounters in the abode of the Mountain King – appeared to be as 'real' in their world as ... Aase [and] Solveig, were in theirs. Rather than inhabiting a symbolic and disturbing dream world, these ... figures ... were comfortably familiar elves of the *eventyr* tradition of adventure and romance.[42]

The more disturbing and complex facets of Peer's personality were neglected by nineteenth-century directors: 'Ibsen's Peer the fraud and self-deceiver who goes roundabout remained ... primarily the dreamer of romantic dreams that crystallised into a dream vision of the redemptive Solveig.'[43]

In 1933 and 1944 the Danish critic Frederik Schyberg highlighted the discrepancy between the picturesque productions of *Peer Gynt* and the play's critique of romanticism. He argued particularly against the use of Greig's incidental music, which had accompanied nearly every production since the world première in 1876: 'Greig makes *Peer Gynt* romantic – but *Peer Gynt* is an anti-romantic work.'[44] Aase's death scene and the ending of the play are particularly vulnerable to such distortion. Peer lulls his mother to her last sleep with a fantastical account of their ride to St Peter's gate. In doing so he acts selfishly, persisting in his playmaking even as his mother calls for the parson and asks for her prayer book. Yet Greig's music lends a sense of nobility and grief to the scene. Tyrone Guthrie similarly argued that Greig's music places undue emphasis on Solveig's song about redemptive hope, faith and love through which, supposedly, Peer would be given some kind of life after death. The final words of the play, the Button Moulder's warning that he will look for Peer at the last crossroads, are thus easily ignored: 'If Greig's intention is to succeed, Ibsen's must fail.'[45]

Hans Jacob Nilsen, who produced the play in 1948, believed that '*Peer Gynt* is no journey through Norway; it is a journey through a human mind'.[46] This idea dominated many post-war approaches; they dispensed with Greig's music and the pictorial realism of the earlier productions. In Ingmar Bergman's 1957 production all stage props and sets are gradually removed as the 'doubt-ridden Peer' journeys towards 'final disillusionment and nothingness', so that the final image of the play is 'two human beings on the immense stage, and in the background the mute, bent figure of the Button Moulder, his casting ladle in his hand and his box of tools upon his back'.[47]

The Gate Theatre production reflected the romanticism of the earliest interpreters of the play while anticipating the non-representational style of the post-war productions. Greig's *Incidental Music* for *Peer Gynt* was used in 1928 and 1932. In 1928, there being no room for an orchestra, it was performed on a piano, much to the disgust of Curran, who complained that it 'brought down the mountain-tops into the suburbs'.[48] Aase's death and Peer's reunion with Solveig were thus invested with the kind of optimistic romanticism that characterised the earlier productions. The *Evening Mail* critic observed that while the text leaves little doubt as to whether Peer escapes the casting ladle in the end of the play, the final scene 'is full of such a lofty and fragrant perfume of assurance that one can only assume that Ibsen meant that his hero was saved by the life-long sacrifice and fidelity of the woman'.[49] Evidently, Edwards's staging of the ending conformed to this reading of the play.

Of Aase's death, the same critic observed that 'the depth of that scene is impenetrable'. Edwards, he observed, 'suggested without overstating the right mood that made it a memorable performance'.[50] May Carey, who played Aase, showed an 'instinctive appreciation here, on her

Figure 1 Aase's death. May Carey as Aase and Hilton Edwards in *Peer Gynt*, Dublin Gate Theatre, 1928 or 1932. Photograph by Harry Braine.

part, of the unimaginative woman meeting death with joy, borne on a childish fancy'.[51] Curran also singled out this scene as 'one of the most moving ... of the modern stage' and praised Carey's 'picture of this fantastic, pathetic and truculent old mother, charioted at last to Paradise'.[52]

Edwards's approach to Aase's death seems to have been similar to that of the Copenhagen actor who particularly angered Schyberg in 1944. 'Mogens Wieth acted Aase's death scene according to the music, not the intent of the words,' he declared. 'It was excusable, it was beautiful, and it will become popular – but it was wrong.'[53]

Edwards's restrained, grief-stricken version of Peer at his mother's death-bed survives in a recording of the 1958 Radio Éireann production, commemorating the thirtieth anniversary of the play. Greig's music is heard from the start. It blends with Edwards's quiet, calm recitation of the sleigh-ride to Paradise. His voice is that of an adult seeking to reassure an invalid, not that of a spoilt child unable to face her death. He seems to be determined to hide his grief and mask the horror of death from his mother, guiding her carefully and safely on her imaginary journey.

Perhaps, after all, Edwards's reading is not that far from Ibsen's intentions. If Peer's last white lie to his mother is presented in a positive light, the retrospective judgement of Peer's actions is particularly forceful in Act 5, where, in scene 6, as Peer runs across the heath, fleeing withered leaves and tumbleweed that whisper to him of his wasted life, he hears the voice of Aase:

> Fie, what a post boy!
> Hu, you've upset me
> Here in the slush, boy!
> Sadly it's smirched me. –
> You've driven me the wrong way.
> Peer, where's the castle?
> The Fiend has misled you
> With the switch from the cupboard.
> (233)

Even though he cut most of the scene, Edwards, still retained Aase's accusations.

'Edwards,' wrote Holloway (who had the opportunity to talk with him before the première), 'had a lot of work cutting down *Peer Gynt* from [an] eight hour show into [a] reasonable length.'[54] Edwards's promptbook reveals his fascination with the imaginative quality of Ibsen's poetry; Ibsen's philosophy he found less interesting. Edwards retained most of the first three Acts, which deal with Peer's youth and his adventures with the trolls. He also kept some of Act 4, which differs from the rest of the play in style, setting, tone and its portrayal of the protagonist. In Edwards's version, Act 4 becomes primarily a satire of Peer's youthful romanticism. Peer is a middle-aged millionaire bragging of slave- and idol-trading. In what Brian Johnston calls a parody of Byronic romanticism, Peer endeavours to supply money and ammunition to the Turks rather than support the Greeks' fight for freedom.[55] He then plays the role of a prophet to a Bedouin tribe and enters a humiliating love affair with Anitra. This desert beauty strips him of his jewels and abandons him in the dunes. As Peer is cursing women as a 'worthless crew' (170), a vision of the faithful, patient Solveig appears. This is also the point where Edwards brings an end to Peer's adventures abroad. In Edwards's version Peer did not embark on a nonsensical journey as a would-be historiographer and did not see the singing statue of Mnemon or the Sphinx. Even more significantly, Edwards dispensed with the whole episode of Peer's entrapment among the suicidal and fanatic inmates of the Cairo madhouse, who crown him Emperor in a mockery of his early ambitions.

The madhouse episode is particularly significant to an interpretation of the play that sees it as an exploration of the human psyche. It is a reminder of Peer's fight with the trolls in the end of Act 2; and like that earlier episode, it occupies the uncertain middle ground between objective and subjective reality. It also contains satirical passages that might have been offensive to Dublin audiences: the madman Huhu's campaign for the revival of the language of the orang-utans, and Peer's recommendation to 'emigrate to serve your country' (185).

Edwards's Act 5 begins *in medias res*, with the protagonist safely in Norway. There is no shipwreck; the Strange Passenger does not appear to prophesy his death and ask for his corpse; nor does Peer drown the ship's cook to save his own life. There are also some changes to the later scenes. Peer's frenzied search for witnesses to testify that he has remained himself all his life is considerably shortened. Peer encounters only two of the three figures that he meets in the text – the troll king, the devil and Solveig. Edwards's Peer meets the Old Man of the Dovre, the troll king, whom Paul Farrell made 'infamously witty' and 'a joy to hear and gaze upon'.[56] Consequently, Peer finds out that in his egoism he had lived like a troll all his life. However, there is no meeting with 'The Lean One' (the Devil). The Dublin of 1928 was perhaps not quite the place in which Peer could exclaim: 'A priest I must catch, if it be with the tongs' (254), let alone mistake the Devil for a parson. Peer's following remark would have been similarly inappropriate:

> I'd have taken my oath you were simply a parson;
> And I find I've the honour –. Well, best is best; –

When the hall door stands wide, – shun the kitchen away;
When the king's to be met w ith, – avoid the lackey.
(257)

With the devil's excision from Edwards's version, Peer's anguish in the face of complete oblivion appears to be less tragic. Edwards's Peer does not have to ask for a sanctuary in hell. Edwards also cut what Johnston calls the 'most moving speech of the entire play'[57] in which Peer first realises the imminence of his death:

Is there no one, no one in all the whirl,
In the void no one, and no one in heaven
...
So unspeakably poor, then, a soul can go
Back to nothingness, into the grey of the mist.
(265)

Edwards's Peer does not ask forgiveness of the earth and the sun for squandering their gifts of light and beauty, nor does he make his last dignified farewell to life:

... dearly one pays for one's birth with one's life. –
I will clamber up high, to the dizziest peak;
I will look once more, on the rising sun,
Gaze till I'm tired o'er the promised land;
Then try to get snowdrifts piled over me.
(265)

MacLiammóir considered *Peer Gynt* a tragedy and described the end as the adventurer's return 'to the patient imperishable fire that is so close to himself and that may not save him at the end of all from the waiting dark'.[58] Yet Peer needs to speak his monologue for the play to be taken seriously. If Peer does not stir in the audience their own fear of mortality, the play is no tragedy at all. The Button Moulder then becomes a bogeyman, an empty threat in a fairy-tale on its way to an inevitable happy ending when 'old Peer Gynt lies at the feet of Solveig in the Easter dawn'.[59]

Edwards's textual alterations, his reliance on Greig's music, as well as his interpretation of the scenes of Aase's death and Peer's reunion with Solveig, suggest a brand of romanticism similar to that of the earliest productions. However, through his use of stage space and lighting,

Edwards managed to impress on the audience a dimension of the play that had hitherto escaped many directors.

Edwards believed that the 'essential quality of *Peer Gynt* is imaginative'.[60] The audience needed to be able to participate in the protagonist's mind game of poetic self-deception. The mainstay of his approach was the two sets of steps silhouetted against the cyclorama. The backdrop was painted in a neutral blue-grey and flooded 'with light from 500-watt lanterns, thus achieving an illusion of shadowless and infinite sky'.[61] The steps were placed back-to-back pyramid-fashion for the mountain scenes, allowing 'figures mounting them to be thrown into postures of ascending and descending great heights'.[62] 'These figures,' Edwards wrote, 'either silhouetted or picked out imperceptibly by spots which were carefully graduated in colour, associated the light on the stage with the lighting of the sky beyond.'[63] For the hut scenes, the space between the steps was 'fitted with a wall with a door and a little gable shaped roof'.[64] Once the steps were divided and pushed towards the wings, the stage became a valley where the wedding scenes could be played. The steps were removed for the desert scenes, and the cyclorama was 'lit below with sandy ambers and above with deep tropical blue'. The troll scenes 'were also played upon the steps, which became a towering and rhythmically moving mass of trolls'.[65]

Curran was particularly impressed with the suggestive power of this arrangement – it conveyed the 'freshness of the mountain farms, the dark encounters of the night' and 'the grotesque horror of the trolls' hall within the hill'.[66] In 1932 MacLiammóir's original sets, including 'decorative scheme of mountains and silhouetted trees', were abandoned and replaced by abstract patterns echoing the central step structure. The effect 'on the imagination', wrote Dorothy Macardle in 1932, was 'wizard-like: jagged, ascending lines create alpine summits about us; cold blues and greys hold us in Norway, weird greens and grotesque masks evoke the trolls of the mountains, brilliant reds and yellow sands'.[67]

In enabling the audience to imagine the fantastic landscapes depicted in the play, the Gate production operated in the middle ground between the different modes of reality – between pure reality and pure fiction or, to put it differently, between the imaginary world of the protagonist and the world of the spectators. This was an entirely novel approach. Something similar would be attempted twenty years later by Nilsen, who aimed to prove that Ibsen's play was a journey through the human mind. Nilsen had the stage designer, Arne Walentin, create stylised rock formations which were set on a revolving stage and seen from different angles and against various back projections. According to Marker and Marker, '[b]y utilizing the values of space, light, color, and form in varying combinations, Walentin's technique succeeded in evoking an atmosphere of dream and fantasy that would be unattainable with conventional painted scenery'.[68] Yet Walentin's designs, which included a stylised hut and an impressive mountain formation, show more traces of the tradition of pictorial realism than Edwards's simple, austere steps.

The two sets of steps appeared as a kind of mental gymnasium or a playroom for Peer, the eternal child. Moreover, the use of the same steps to suggest various locations intimated that Peer's adventures are, as Johnston says,[69] merely repetitions of the same tale. Peer's abduction of Ingrid from her wedding celebrations, his courtship of the Green Clad One in the kingdom of the trolls and his love affair with Anitra appear as variations on the same theme. The love question could be approached in several ways, just as the steps could be turned in various directions while still remaining the same steps. This idea was reinforced by most actors' taking several roles in the play. Gearóid Ó Lochlainn, for instance, played Aslak the smith in Act 1, Trumpeterstrale in Act 4 and the Button Moulder in Act 5. The reason was quite simply the very small cast, yet the effect of such doubling and trebling was to draw the audience's attention to the artificiality of Peer's fairy-tale world.

'I have come to the conclusion,' wrote Edwards in 1958, 'that it is desirable to discover how un-realistically, how true to the theatre, a play can be treated, and yet carry conviction and serve the author's intentions.'[70] In the case of *Peer Gynt*, the unrealistic style helped to restore what was lost during the process of cutting the play for the stage. While Edwards's abridgement indicates that he believed Peer to be a romantic hero and a poet rather than the 'perplexed and suffering anti-hero'[71] of the modern age, the stage design suggests otherwise. He delivered the play from the kind of pictorial realism that obscures the importance that it places on shifting conceptions of reality – the play's exploration of the boundaries of reality and perception.

In this production Edwards and MacLiammóir confronted their own romantic attitudes to the folkloric world of the play. As they abandoned the picturesque images of peasant Norway in favour of the interplay of light and shadow, they discovered and made apparent to their audiences that *Peer Gynt*'s romanticism is illusory. Peer Gynt does not inhabit a fairy-tale world; he imagines it into being, with disastrous consequences for himself. The audiences of the Gate production, in particular as it developed by 1932, were invited to share in his creative process; the abstract pattern of light and colour made them imagine the nonexistent, fantastic landscapes.

The expressionistic style of the Gate Theatre production of Peer Gynt conceptualised the play's self-reflexive attitude to the representation of folklore. With this production, Edwards and MacLiammóir demonstrated on stage the core idea that of the revisionist literature of the Revival namely that 'the *in*authentic is the authentic'.[72] Instead of presenting the Dublin audience with a picturesque fairy-tale, Edwards and MacLiammóir invited them to take part in reviving *Peer Gynt.* The result was that some could see their own thoughts and concerns reflected in the Gate *Peer Gynt.* This was particularly apparent in the case of the 1932 production and was practically the first time since the 1894 production of *An Enemy of the People* that spectators responded to a play by Ibsen as if it were an Irish play and not an imported or outdated curiosity.

The decade of the Button Moulder and the Norwegian Playboy

Holloway observed that the 'crowded and distinguished audience followed the strange and weird play with wrapt attention, and though [it] ... wasn't over till 10.30 yet none of the spectators left before the [final] curtain'. He was full of praise for Edwards, who 'was the play and carried it through all difficulties to success'. He liked Paul Farrell's 'droll ... Old Man of the Dovre with his long nose and shaggy beard', Bridie Folan's portrayal of Solveig, 'the meek mannered maiden whom Peer wooed so strangely', and Coralie Carmichael as Anitra, 'the slave-girl' and the Green Clad One. Gearóid Ó Lochlainn as Aslak the Smith gave an impression 'of brute strength', 'while [as] the Button Moulder silhouetted against a glowing background he suggested the uncanny as remarkable as when ... his face ... [was] seen, De Valera flashed into the mind on beholding him.' The tall, gaunt Gearóid Ó Lochlainn was indeed somewhat similar in appearance to the man nicknamed the Long Fellow. 'The resemblance', wrote Holloway, 'was remarkably like Dev.'[73]

The opening of the Gate Theatre coincided with the beginning of the 'De Valera's decade' (1928–38),[74] and it was a miracle that it survived in the shadow of his government. De Valera by his own admission went to the Abbey Theatre for the first time when he was in his fifties and suggested once that he 'couldn't see any reason for playing the work of foreign composers in Ireland, as we already had our own beautiful Irish music'.[75] To some Irish intellectuals he might indeed have appeared as a Button Moulder of Irish culture. Sean O'Casey's description of the unseen presence of the young mathematician in pre-civil war Dublin is particularly evocative of the kind of bureaucratic deadliness represented by the Button Moulder:

> Though Sean knew not even of De Valera's existence, there he was walking beneath the gentle clouds caressing Dublin's streets: a young man full of the seven deadly virtues, punctual, zealous, studious, pious, and patriotic, cautiously pushing a way through crowds of queerternions, stopping occasionally to put them through their paces, numbering them off, making minus double exes of them, forming them into plus fours, and sending them forth in a hurray of feshelons so that one day they might make Ireland a nation of restraints and scollars.[76]

In his enthusiastic review of the Gate *Peer Gynt*, Curran pointed out that in the play, Ibsen 'fuses human allegory with a localised, political satire'. '*Peer Gynt*,' he explained, 'was written in 1867, when Ibsen was in full reaction from the national movement, which, separatist in politics, was on its literary side stocking the Norwegian Parnassus with idealised peasants.'[77] This remark might well have been a tongue-in-cheek criticism of the Fianna Fáil policy of cultural and economic self-sufficiency which went hand in hand with practical idealism. In the late 1920s, idealistic and romantic images of the Irish Revival were coalescing into state policy and the image of industrious, pure and Irish peasant-dominated political speeches and schoolbooks. 'Ibsen had no interest in political upheavals which do not liberate the soul,' continued Curran. '*Peer Gynt* is Norway, which Ibsen would free from the domination of trolls.'[78] Curran did not explain that, in *Peer Gynt*, Ibsen had satirised the narrow-minded nationalists of his day in the crude joke of the trolls' eating the 'home-brewed' bovine excrement in order to avoid importing goods from the human world. (This episode was retained in Edwards's version.) Like his fellow graduate James Joyce, who in 1901 accused the Irish Literary Theatre of 'surrender[ing] to the trolls',[79] Curran let his readers decipher the metaphor for themselves.

Curran presented the play as a parable of the development of the Norwegian nation:

> Peer ... lives on grandmother's stories, on 'lies and trash and moonshine' ... and imagines vain things in torn breeches. Ibsen will teach him that to build houses he must hew wood and quarry stones, and

> likewise in the edification of his soul. In this larger operation he opposes to the troll's device: 'Troll to thyself be enough', the wider 'Man be thyself.' As an egoist, a hill-troll man, Peer-Gynt sets his life's design at defiance; he sinks to the fodder of the button-moulder ... if not redeemed by the faith, hope, and love of Solveig, mother of Norway's future.[80]

Curran's point that a nation can be destroyed by vain idealism as well as by narrow-minded notions of self-sufficiency had immediate relevance to his readers. These were the dangers concurrent with de Valera's rise to power. In 1933, he made a remark in his defence whose very phrasing confirmed the accusations levelled against him: 'You sometimes hear Ireland charged with a narrow and intolerant nationalism, but Ireland today has no dearer hope than that, true to her own holiest traditions, she may humbly serve the truth and help the truth to save the world.'[81]

The Gate Theatre revival of *Peer Gynt* ran for three weeks from 25 September to 15 October 1932, seven months after de Valera was appointed president of the Executive Council (9 March 1932). Once again, *Peer Gynt* provided journalists with an opportunity for political commentary. The correspondent of the *Donegal People's Press* did not see the play, but knew something of its history, and what is more, found one Dublin review of the play particularly provocative:

> *Peer Gynt* ... is a satire on idealistic and national extravagances. The extremists of Norway did not like it. It savoured of 'sedition' and anti-nationalism. But Norway has since learned to laugh at its ... follies. Be that as it may, President de Valera's organ [the *Irish Press*] devoted a large page to a review of the play. The review reads uncommonly like a satire on the antics of the present Government.[82]

The 'review' in question was Dorothy Macardle's and dealt with the satirical content of the play and its reception in Dublin. The passage that drew the attention of the *Donegal People's Press* referred to the madhouse episode, which was not part of the performance. It ended:

> It is in a lunatic asylum and there Peer Gynt is Emperor ... Peer Gynt has been a vain and idle idealist while he pursued crazy day dreams, he wrought cruel injury on simple and faithful people and reality passed him by.[83]

The *Donegal People's Press* added:

> In these few lines, the *Irish Press* contributor has summed up not *Peer Gynt* but the leader of the Fianna Fail Party. 'While he pursued crazy day dreams, he wrought cruel injury on simple and faithful people and **reality passed him by**.' That is precisely what is happening to-day. And what is happening to-day is merely a repetition of what happened ten years ago.[84]

To reinforce this point, the *Donegal People's Press* pointed to *An Enemy of the People* and provided a particularly curious misreading of the play:

> The dramatist chooses as an example of destructive egoism the medical officer of a Norwegian town who discovers that the water of the local baths is contaminated and instead of setting about to devise remedies, he determines to advertise the fact far and near to the probable ruin commercially of the community which he is supposed to serve.[85]

Macardle's article, 'The Playboy in Drama', showed more intelligence and subtlety in its relation to Ibsen's work and Irish politics. Like Curran, who in his 1928 review called *Peer Gynt* a 'Northern Playboy',[86] Macardle found an affinity between Ibsen's play and Synge's. The similarity had earlier been remarked on by Cornelius Weygandt in 1913. He wondered what 'a certain element of Irishmen' would have done had Synge made *The Playboy* 'as biting as Ibsen made *Peer Gynt*'.[87] Working from the opposite end of the critical spectrum, Macardle explained to the (largely republican) readers of the *Irish Press* that the fantastic foreign play shown at the Gate was as mordant and satirical as the infamous *Playboy*.

'The Norwegians of [Ibsen's] time did discover in *Peer Gynt* a satire upon themselves,' she wrote. 'In Peer they saw a caricature of their whole national movement, of their attempt to free Norway politically from Sweden and culturally from Danish influence.'[88] Macardle emphasised the satirical content of the troll scenes (which might have escaped the audience) and, moreover, alluded to those passages in the play which did not make it to the stage:

> They found their effort to secure the use of Norwegian produce satirized in the Troll King's nonsense; their effort to purify and restore the old language mocked in the figure of Huhu, who would revive

> the screech of he aboriginal orang-outang; their desire for a self-sufficing nation parodied in the lunatic scene; they believed that one of the greatest of Norwegians as using his gifts to ridicule and retard his country's progress and they ere very angry indeed.[89]

To emphasise the connection between the original reception of *Peer Gynt* and *The Playboy*, Macardle summed up Ibsen's attitude to the Norwegian criticisms of the play in a way that would have reminded some readers of Synge's plea that his play was only an 'extravaganza':[90] 'At the time the writer resented the resentment of his countrymen. He complained that they had read into the poem more satire than he had intended: he thought they ought to have been content to read it as a piece of pure poetic fantasy.'[91] And, writes Macardle, casting off her mask of a coolly detached literary critic: 'It was a great deal to ask.'[92]

Macardle was a republican, a friend of de Valera's and a member of the Fianna Fáil Executive. She was also a gifted historian and talented author. Her extensive knowledge of world drama is evidenced in a series of lectures she gave in 1928, shortly after the opening of the Gate Theatre. Macardle spoke of Ibsen, Tolstoy, Chekhov, Turgenev and Andreev, as well as Pirandello, Claudel and Maeterlinck, Susan Glaspell, O'Neill and some Jewish dramatists.[93] Her education and culture, however, did not prevent Macardle from protesting against *The Plough and the Stars*, along with her friend Hannah Sheehy-Skeffington. Hogan notes that Macardle's attack on O'Casey's play is a 'fact ... not without its ironies', as in her own play *Ann Kavanagh*, she had made 'the point that an allegiance to general humanity was more important than patriotism'.[94] In her article on *Peer Gynt*, Macardle attempted to solve the conflict between her political convictions on the one hand, and her literary humanism on the other. The article is thus an inquiry into the nature of the clash between the rights of the artists and those of their publics:

> Inevitably, at such a time, those who are labouring, unselfishly and sincerely against immense difficulties, for their nation, feel that their talented countrymen should help them – should at least, encourage and sympathize. But the men of talent, sometimes, look on at the struggle with a cool detachment, acutely aware of the excesses and weaknesses which it generates, strangely blind to its grander aspect, its necessity and its truth. They become interested in certain crudities of human nature which reveal themselves at such crises, and about these they write. The work so produced is resented in their

> own country, where it hurts and discourages the national effort but is admired abroad.[95]

It remained up to the readers to decide whether this paragraph was an allusion to O'Casey's work (who by now had said farewell to Inisfallen) or whether it referred merely to those named: Ibsen and Synge.

The article concluded on a reconciliatory note. In the spirit of 'let bygones be bygones', Macardle asserted that the survival of a satirical work depends on 'a universal truth of its theme' which becomes apparent once the satire loses its bite: 'It is as dramatic extravaganza, rich in humour, gaiety, fancy, wisdom and laughter, with an under-current of universal truth, that Synge's *Playboy* is famous in Scandinavia as in his own country, while *Peer Gynt* delights audiences in Ireland today.'[96]

The critical responses to *Peer Gynt* indicate that one of the aims of the Gate Theatre has been fulfilled. In 1929, Hilton Edwards explained that Dublin needed a theatre devoted to international drama; this was 'essential in the city if only to enable the public to appreciate native drama'.[97] Moreover, Macardle's point that dramatic works are susceptible to different interpretations as they travel across several countries and generations was timely. On 15 September 1927, *The Playboy* was produced at the Nationaltheatret in Oslo and received mixed reviews. The similarity of Synge's play to *Peer Gynt* was noted by several commentators, although some claimed that Ibsen's criticism of the national character was deeper and more serious than Synge's.[98] Meanwhile *The Playboy* was revived by the Abbey on 12 March 1928, and again on 7 May 1929 and 21 January 1930. On the last occasion The *Irish Times* presented the success of the play with the audience as a sign of social change: 'Everything that was at first taken to be objectionable has been blunted by familiarity; a newer and possibly less sensitive generation stays to laugh where their predecessors threw turnips.'[99]

The nature of the relation between *Peer Gynt* and *The Playboy* has intrigued several of Synge's contemporaries as well as modern-day critics.[100] The authors draw on common tropes and motifs from the European literary tradition. While endless similarities can be found at different ranges of textual depth, they do not in themselves prove a relation of influence or parody. Peer and Christy are both at times Falstaff, Hamlet, Oedipus and Don Quixote. Both plays toy with the themes of death and resurrection, folk tales and superstitions, madness and imagination. Their explorations of the individual's relationship to society are also similar. As his sketch for Act 2 of *Peer Gynt* reveals, MacLiammóir's was aware of this affinity. The sketch could work as an illustration for

Figure 2 Peer Gynt and the crowd, Dublin Gate Theatre 1928, Design by Micheál MacLiammóir. Reproduced from Bulmer Hobson, *The Gate Theatre Dublin.* Dublin: The Gate Theatre, 1934. Courtesy of MacLiammóir Estate and the Gate Theatre.

Synge's play. A solitary figure emerges on the right of the drawing. His arms are thrust upwards and outwards in an attitude that could signify joyous inspiration, but which also resembles the pose of the condemned in Francisco Goya's famous *The Third of May 1808*. The rifles aimed at the man in Goya's painting are replicated in the outstretched arms of the mob, who (depending on how one interprets the picture) may also be lined up to greet their saviour and messiah.

The most important similarity between *Peer Gynt* and *The Playboy*, however, lies in their authors' satirical exploration of romantic nationalism through the figure of the mock-hero. The protagonists of *Peer Gynt* and *The Playboy* are artificially revived folk heroes, who fail to live up to the romantic ideal. The similarities between Christy and Peer – their boisterousness, their roguishness, their tendency to believe in their own lies, their poetic language – are all marks of the familiar folk stereotype. Christy and Peer are descendants of the glorious liars of European folk tradition.[101] Their charm (which is as likely to seduce the reader as it does the fictional characters) lies in their ability to mediate between the drabness of modern life and the lost world of fairy-tales.

However, both characters are also profoundly insecure and dependent on others' admiration for the propagation of their image. Peer's greatest lines are spoken to his adoring mother, from whom he then flees; Christy develops a belief in his legendary prowess when speaking to a gaggle of admiring girls of whom he is slightly afraid. Indeed, instead of indulging their readers and audiences in poetic fantasies, Ibsen and Synge treat their comic heroes seriously, exposing the illusory nature of their heroism. Eglinton was right when he wrote in 1899 that should mythological heroes 'appear once more in literature ... [they] must be expected to take up on their broad shoulders something of the weariness and fret of our age'.[102] The charming, light-hearted Peer commits a series of crimes and suffers the existentialist horror of a modern, godless universe where death means an end of consciousness. The bumbling, amiable Christy almost commits a murder, and in doing so incites the hitherto comic Mayo villagers to acts of savage violence. *Peer Gynt* and *The Playboy* are written out of the failure of romance and in retaliation against a particular branch of applied Romanticism – literary revivalism. And yet both plays also have been read as crowning achievements of the national literary movement in their authors' respective countries.

By 1932 *The Playboy* had become a regular feature of the Abbey repertoire; yet these popular revivals occluded the most controversial and interesting features of the play. On the occasion of its performance on 13 March 1928, the *Irish Times* commented that it attracted 'quite a large number of admirers'[103] in spite of the bad weather. The brief review also noted 'the warmth of the applause at the end of each curtain'.[104] The audience 'forgot the slush and discomfort of the city streets in the picture of elemental life on the wild shores of Erris'. The Abbey actors were 'completely satisfying in the poetry of the play as in the semi-barbarity of its setting'.[105] The play that had once turned the theatre into a battleground now provided an escape from Dublin's bad weather into a fantastic Erris.

In an article on the 1961 film version of *The Playboy*, Frazier argues that Synge's play lost its sexual dimension, its humour and all traces of intelligence, as it was turned into a vision of de Valera's 'Ireland We Dreamed Of, with comely maidens step-dancing at the cross roads'. Scenic shots replaced excised passages in the film in which 'everyone ... puts on a face of hyper-naïve, wondering innocence, like so many simpletons'.[106] With some caution, it may be possible to suggest that the process which had resulted in the 1960s in such a lobotomising of Synge's play had already started in 1928. After the initial hostility had been overcome (and the more troubling passages had been deleted), *The Playboy* became a picturesque journey through the peasant Ireland of imagination. It was subjected to the same limiting approach as *Peer Gynt* on its first appearance on the Scandinavian stage, ten years after its publication.

Was the new public of the Free State more tolerant of plays critical of the ideal of nationhood than previous generations had been? Were the audiences now more aware of the international dimension of theatre? Were they less insular in their criticism of local drama? During the decade of de Valera, the questions posed by the Irish Revival were re-examined. Several hundred people, for instance, attended a symposium hosted on 7 November 1932 by the Gate Theatre which addressed the question: 'Should the Theatre be International?'[107] At this event, Frank Hugh O'Donnell was heard to denounce the Protestant Synge for attempting to represent Irish life, in spite of his being a Protestant. The playwright David Sears defended Synge, yet he also suggested that certain common themes of world theatre were unavailable to Irish playwrights: 'There was ... no use in an Irish dramatist writing a play dealing with the problem of divorce because divorce does not exist in Ireland.'[108] Old misconceptions persisted. Edwards and MacLiammóir laboured to impress on the audience that 'sexual and religious problems in Ireland were grave enough to warrant discussion' or that the 'whole danger to drama in Ireland lay in their consciousness of the national drama which had been ... developed by the Abbey Company'.[109]

In declaring their interests in the theatre to be 'neither international nor national but purely theatrical',[110] the directors of the Gate Theatre offered a new way of engaging with international drama. The Gate Theatre *Peer Gynt* was the first production of an Ibsen play in Ireland to reflect the concerns of the public and also to show them new facets of Ibsen's art. In other words, it was the first Irish production of an Ibsen play that mattered. The imagery and concerns of *Peer Gynt* resonate in several revisionist works of the Irish Revival, from Synge's famous play to Joyce's novels and Yeats's late poetry. Through their expressionistic approach to the play, MacLiammóir and Edwards allowed this resonance to be felt by the audiences. The production was part-payment of the Irish Revivalists' long overdue debt to Ibsen. It was also the long-deferred fulfilment of Yeats's 1899 promise to stage Ibsen's poetic plays. Yeats's dream of 'total theatre', inspired by Gordon Craig's innovative stage designs, was also actualised in the style of the Gate production.

Unlike Yeats or the founders of the Theatre of Ireland, MacLiammóir and Edwards did not set out to teach, reform, inspire or represent the nation. Their relationship to theatre was not ideological but practical – they wanted to stage plays by foreign authors and plays of experimental nature using local actors. When asked why they had chosen to put on *Peer*

Gynt, MacLiammóir replied: 'We wanted to do it. We always had. *Peer Gynt* was one of the first ideas Hilton and I found we had in common.'[111]

For a trained Shakespearean artist like Edwards, Ibsen's verse drama was undoubtedly of special interest. Besides, he had played a small part in a production of *Peer Gynt* when still a boy and longed for a chance to correct the flaws of that production. As for MacLiammóir, he was emotionally invested in the play. Ibsen's charming liar who fashions his personality out of myths and fairy-tales appealed to the London-born actor who was so enthralled by the Irish legends in his youth that he decided to become Irish, adopting a Gaelic name and becoming proficient in the Irish language.[112]

MacLiammóir arrived on the Irish scene soon after the lights of the Revival were extinguished. By the time the Gate opened, Ireland had gained independence. Pursuit of cultural independence based on the love of folk legends and racialist longings seemed no longer politically necessary. The Abbey Theatre was then state-run. It had lost its zest and zeal. As the theatre critic A. E. Malone wrote in 1928, the 'great days of the Abbey Theatre [were] in the past', 'the pioneers have grown weary of pioneering'.[113] This strange English impostor who gave a new lease of life to the Dublin stage and established the first Irish-speaking theatre in Galway (it opened in 1928 with the production of his own *Diarmuid and Graine*), MacLiammóir embodies the very spirit of the Revival, while at the same time parodying its artificiality. He was living proof of the longevity and the beauty of the ideal of Irishness created by the Revivalists and, at the same time, proof that the Irishness that they celebrated was merely a beautiful construct, rather than something inherited and 'racy of the soil'. In a way, MacLiammóir was the Playboy, or indeed the Peer Gynt, of the Irish theatre.

Epilogue: Dreams of Resurrection – Ibsen and George Moore

'Ibsen's New Drama' (1900), a review of *When We Dead Awaken*, was Joyce's first significant publication, ensuring his reputation as a genius among his fellow students. His pamphlet 'The Day of the Rabblement', published a year later in 1901, derided the literary efforts of the leading figures of the Irish Revival. In it Joyce conceded that George Moore's early novels had some originality, but asserted that 'his new impulse has no kind of relation to the future of art'. By contrast, the artist of the future would follow in the footsteps of Ibsen and 'carry on the tradition of the old master who is dying of Christiania'.[1] Yet Joyce's representation of Moore as Ibsen's antithesis was unfair. In 'In the Clay' and 'The Way Back', two stories from *The Untilled Field* (1903), as well as their 1931 retelling, 'Fugitives', Moore parodies and examines the plot of *When We Dead Awaken*, the play that received Joyce's unreserved enthusiasm in 1900. What is more, Moore turns Ibsen's last play into the judgment day of the Irish Revival, exploring several core issues of *When We Dead Awaken* in relation to the movement.

Ibsen, rarely named in Moore's fiction, is briefly mentioned in 'Fugitives'. Harding tells the Irish sculptor Rodney of his meeting with his former model, Lucy Delaney. The girl has run away from Ireland to start a stage career. Harding tries to help and takes her to one of London's theatres, but the manager is busy; soon the conversation turns to Ibsen and the possibility of 'getting the public to see a good play' and Harding realises the futility of his enterprise.[2] 'Fugitives' is set around 1900, judging from the mention of the Boer War in the latter story. It was in that year that Ibsen's *When We Dead Awaken* was first published in English. The mention of Ibsen in 'Fugitives', therefore, might indicate Moore's acknowledgement of the similarity of the subject matter of his story and Ibsen's last play: both deal with the relationship of a sculptor and his model. In both texts, the protagonist's name is assonant with Rodin – Rubek in Ibsen, Rodney in Moore.[3]

What Rubek experiences with Irene, and Rodney with Lucy, is a perfect communion of minds, whereby the model lives for the emerging masterpiece, guessing every need of the artist. At the end, the woman is rejected. In Ibsen's play, Irene perceives that Rubek thinks of her as a mere episode in his artistic career and vanishes from his life. And Rodney, in Moore's story, refuses to take Lucy with him as he prepares to leave Ireland because, as he realises in the earlier version, 'he would have to look after her till the end of this life. This was not his vocation.'[4] The beautiful clay image is also altered. In Ibsen's play Rubek finds his vision of the sculpture of the Resurrection Day challenged by the disappearance of the model. Instead of figuring it as 'a young unsullied woman ... awakening to light and glory without having to put away from her anything ugly or impure', Rubek creates a group figure: 'men and women with dimly suggested animal faces' swarm from 'the bursting earth'; and in the foreground appears a mournful figure of the artist himself who is unable to extricate himself from the ground.[5] In Moore's story, the statue is turned into a lump of clay. Two little boys, the brothers of the model, have heard a priest denounce her to her parents. Without quite understanding the nature of their sister's transgression or the priest's anger, they steal into the studio and break the statue. Rodney feels 'like he could never do sculpture again' (292), echoing Rubek, who has become a mere craftsman after completing his only masterpiece.

According to Errol Durbach, Ibsen's play 'investigates ... that specifically Romantic attitude to art as creative solution to life's dilemma, a substitute religion in which a god-like creator locates the redemptive hopes of a now effete Christian dispensation'.[6] This play might well have struck a chord with Moore, who confessed himself, in *Hail and Farewell*, to be the messiah of Ireland called to deliver the land from the empty dogma of Catholicism and awaken it into personality – 'personal love and personal religion, personal art, personality for all, except God'.[7] Yet this new religion must have its sacrifices, and Ibsen's play, which in Durbach's words measures the 'promise of personal and cultural redemption ... against the humanity that must be sacrificed to the ideal',[8] anticipates Moore, who writes in *Hail and Farewell* how he was asking himself 'again and again' whether he was 'capable of sacrificing brother, sister, mother, fortune, friend, for a work of art'.[9] Like *When We Dead Awaken*, 'Fugitives' explores the consequences of the artist's rejection of humanity through the inversion of the Pygmalion and Galatea myth. The tragic dialogue of Irene and Rubek reverberates in Moore's comic prose.

When after years of estrangement the two meet again, Rubek tries to explain to Irene that he did love her, but 'the superstition took hold of me that if I touched you, if I desired you with my senses, my soul would be profaned so that I should be unable to accomplish what I was striving for'. But she scorns him for putting 'the work of art first – then the human being' (372). Irene is obsessed with the idea that she is dead and that Rubek's statue is her child, the only legacy of her empty life. 'I hated you', she tells the artist, 'because you could stand there so unmoved'.

> RUBEK Unmoved? Do you think so?
>
> IRENE – at any rate so intolerably self-controlled. And because you were an artist and an artist only – not a man ... But the statue in the wet, living clay, that I loved – as it rose up a vital, human creature, out of those raw shapeless masses – for that was our creation, our child mine and yours.
>
> (411–12)

This is how the artist's predicament in relation to the sexual attraction of the model is described in Moore's story:

> The word tomorrow chilled his ardour, so far away did it seem from Lucy, like centuries, and he wished that he could sleep all day, for how the time would pass without her he did not know … he did not care to see other sculpture, and dared even to breathe to himself: 'All I see is dry and insipid compared to what I am doing from Lucy!' … he went to bed hoping he would sleep the time away. But his desire to be at work again on his statue of the Virgin and Child was so great that he slept hardly at all. Lucy was a little late … but he forgot his loss when she had taken the pose, and many days passed in the same excitement, the same exaltation, till one morning she arrived wheeling a perambulator.
>
> (289–90)

The play on the words 'excitement' and 'desire' and the frequent mention of the word 'bed' culminates in the unexpected image of a woman with a pram – a literal transfiguration of Ibsen's idea of the woman thinking of the work as a child and thus proclaiming the importance of her contribution and the wrong done to her by the artist's neglect of her body. (The child in Moore's story is discovered to be Lucy's baby brother whom she has thoughtfully brought with her to pose as the infant Christ.)

Much of the power of *When We Dead Awaken* lies in the comic debasing of the reunion of Rubek and Irene through the developing relationship between Maja, Rubek's clever, vivacious and much patronised trophy wife, and Ulfheim the bear-hunter. The latter couple, far more interested in the joys of the body than works of art, have been described by Shaw as the man and woman of the 'stone age'.[10] According to Shaw, Ibsen's play asks the following questions: 'What is there to choose between those two pairs? Is the cultured gifted man less hardened, less selfish towards the woman, than the Paleolithic man? Is the woman less sacrificed, less enslaved, less dead spiritually in the one case than in the other?'[11]

In fact Ulfheim and Maja offer each other more by demanding less than do Rubek and Irene. Rubek promises Irene all the glory of the world and she swears to 'go with [him] to the world's end and to the end of life' and to 'serve him in all things' (369). Ulfheim merely suggests to Maja to 'try and draw the rags' of their tattered lives together and 'make some sort of a human life out of them' (442) and asks her to go with him only 'as far and as long as [he] wants her' (445).

The contrast between celibate romanticism and realistic acknowledgement of sexuality is also found in the bipartite structure of 'Fugitives'. Harding's account of his bemused seduction of Lucy undermines the pathos of Rodney's story. When Harding comes across the girl wandering in London, he feeds her, tries to get her a place in the theatre and finds her somewhere to live. The seduction process (involving an attempt to get Lucy to pose for him) takes some time, during which two detectives are spotted at Harding's club. He panics – the girl is only seventeen and a court case would destroy his reputation. He journeys to Ireland, where Lucy's parents welcome him as a Galahad come to the rescue of their daughter. He returns to London to tell Lucy that she must return to Ireland where her marriage to a Chicago businessman has been arranged, and the two spend the night together (or at least this is what Harding implies).

Harding's story makes Rodney realise an aspect of his past model that he has missed earlier: 'Lucy wanted life', Rodney says, 'and perhaps she will get her adventure sooner or later' (310). This desire for life, 'for the beautiful, miraculous earth life', is what both Maja and Irene of *When*

We Dead Awaken have in common with Lucy. Both accuse Rubek of denying them the opportunity to experience life fully. Maja decides to leave Rubek to go in search of adventure and 'let life take place of all the rest' and describes their marriage as like living in a 'clammy cage' without 'sunlight or fresh air, but only gilding and great petrified ghosts of people all round the walls' (442); Irene describes her mental disorder or nervous breakdown as something 'that always happen[s] when a young warm-blooded woman dies' (367).

Both Ibsen's play and Moore's story (in its various versions) ask whether such awakening to life is possible or whether, as Irene puts it, 'when we dead awaken ... [w]e see that we have never lived' (431–2). However, while Ibsen is concerned with the ideal of the revival in general human terms, Moore's story examines this subject in the specifically Irish context. There are several references in the story to the Irish Revival, in its different forms as the movement for the restoration of the Irish language, political independence and cultural awakening. Rodney's friend Harding refers sceptically to his proposed 'wandering from cabin to cabin storing country idiom' (299) and Edward Martyn is mocked by both men for imagining the future Gaelic Ireland as a 'spring wood: burgeoning trees, nests in the branches, sculptors carving all day and perhaps all night in their studios ... and painting of sea shores and forests' (298). Negative references to the movement for whose sake Moore returned to Ireland and wrote *The Untilled Field* are more numerous in the earlier version of the story. In 'In the Clay', as Rodney contemplates his imminent departure from Ireland, we are told that '[t]hey were talking about reviving the Gothic, but Rodney did not believe in their resurrections or in their renaissance or in their anything, "The Gael has had his day. The Gael is passing"'.[12] By using the word 'resurrection' of the Irish Revival, Moore links his story of the destruction of the statue of the Virgin to the artist's inability, in Ibsen's play, to sculpt the allegorical representation of the Resurrection Day as a pure, unsullied woman.

This idealist dream of Resurrection is impossible; the people's small-mindedness and avarice stand in its way. The statue in Ibsen's play becomes, in Durbach's words, 'a cancelled vision of Resurrection, [revealing] the Land without Paradise and man's fallen state – mired in guilt and mortality'.[13] And Moore's *The Untilled Field* became, not a collection of celebratory stories of Irish folk life suited for translation into Irish, but a depiction of the land of failed possibilities in which sexuality, conjugal happiness and art are stunted by the inbred obeisance to dogma. Thus Rodney learns that his statue was not wrecked, as he first assumed, by a religious fanatic sent by the enraged priest, but by 'two stupid little boys who have been taught their Catechism and will one day aspire to the priesthood' (297). In *Hail and Farewell* Moore speaks of his initial excitement about the Irish Revival as Ireland's long-awaited awakening 'out of the great sleep of Catholicism'.[14] In his comic autobiography as well as the earlier *The Untilled Field*, he demonstrates how wrong he was to hope for this awakening. Catholicism, in its pernicious form, unique to Ireland, is so deeply entrenched that no resurrection is possible. In the words of Pat Connex, a character from 'The Wedding Feast' (the fifth story of *The Untilled Field*): 'We are a dead and alive lot' (100).

However, Moore's story of the destruction of a masterpiece is not merely a simplistic allegory of art's demise in the Catholic climate of Ireland. 'In the Clay' contains a passage which, in its resemblance to a line from *When We Dead Awaken*, indicates the complexity of Moore's response to the problem of the artist's relation to his country. Rodney remembers telling Harding that

> he had given up the School of Art, that he was leaving Ireland, and Harding had thought that this was an extreme step, but Rodney had said that he did not want to die, that no one wanted to die less than he did, but he thought he would sooner die than go on teaching ... he was going ... to where there was art, to where there was the joy of life, out of a damp religious atmosphere in which nothing flourished but the religious vocation.[15]

The passage recalls Rubek's confession to Maja that he began to value life more than the hollow 'talk about the artist's vocation and the artist's mission':

> is not life in sunshine and in beauty a hundred times better worth while than to hang about to the end of your days in a raw, damp hole, and to wear yourself out in a perpetual struggle with lumps of clay and blocks of stone.
>
> (396)

The damp hole of the artist's studio becomes in Moore's story the 'damp religious atmosphere' of Ireland. The implicit comparison to Ibsen's play suggests, however, that Rodney's choice of Italy in preference to Ireland might be as hollow as Rubek's desire for the simple joys of life. Rubek eventually realises that he is not 'at all adapted for seeking happiness in indolent enjoyment'. 'Life does not shape itself that way for me and those like me,' he tells his wife: "I must go on working – producing one work after another – right up to my dying day' (398).

In 'The Way Back', Rodney's flight from Ireland is counterbalanced by Harding's proposed return there. His friends suggest that Harding's biographer 'will be puzzled to explain this ... episode': 'You knew from the beginning that Paris was the source of all art ... And having lived immersed in art till you're forty, you return to the Catholic Celt' (397). Rodney is unable to understand why Harding would wish to return to the country which is soon to be 'dead beyond hope of resurrection'.[16] Harding's search for a way back to Ireland is comparable to Rubek's decision in Ibsen's play to be reunited with Irene, his former model, who in her insanity believes that she has died because Rubek has rejected her. Both men return to their roots. Rubek takes Irene as his wife, in spite of her insanity and dubious past: 'Be who or what you please, for aught I care! For me you are the woman I see in my dreams of you' (453). And Harding is drawn to the newly discovered pathetic, dear, wistful and intimate beauty of the country and its people.[17] In Ibsen's play, the couple know that they face death as they ascend a mountain in a storm. Such melodramatic devices are alien to Moore's vision, yet there is a hint of morbidity in Harding's saying in 'The Way Back' that 'No man wanders far from his grave sod'.[18] His return to Ireland, like Rubek's union-in-death with Irene, is acceptance of his mortality.

Ibsen's meditation on the contrast between the promise of immortality offered by art and its life-denying power allowed Moore to review his position within the Irish Literary Revival. 'Fugitives' demonstrates that the romantic ambitions of the Gaelic League and the Celtic twilight are doomed to failure, not only because of the deep-seated religious conservatism of the country. Idealistic revivalism – the creation of an Ireland of imagination – is inherently flawed. Harding, who says in 'The Way Back' that he treasures what 'Paddy Durkin and Father Pat will say to [him] on the roadside'[19] far more than the discussions of the Italian renaissance, exemplifies a different approach to the Irish Revival. A true masterpiece of the movement would subject the country to realistic scrutiny. Accepting the country's prejudices and the dogmatic morbidity of its culture, such a masterpiece will not let any ideas of purity stand in the way of an honest depiction of its men and women. Rubek, in Ibsen's play, becomes an acclaimed genius for a group statue of 'men and women as [he] knew them in real life' (416) – not for his original idea of the awakening of a pure, unsullied woman. And Moore's realistic collection, as he claimed, was a landmark departure in Irish literature, not least for modifying the Celtic Twilight approach to the depiction of Ireland and anticipating Synge and Joyce. Yet, what Moore has in common with Ibsen is the knowledge that anti-idealist modernist art, in spite of its promise of freedom, may be as enslaving and deadening as the idealism that it has rejected.

At the end of *When We Dead Awaken* Rubek and Irene are killed in an avalanche as they climb a mountain in the hope of a glorious life through death. Meanwhile Maja and Ulfheim take the dangerous route down the mountain. Maja sings triumphantly, rejoicing in her new freedom. But, as Durbach explains, 'there is fine irony in her confidence. No one on the *dodsens vei* [the deadly path] is free. To move into the abyss of process, sexuality and change is to embrace death as surely as to transcend life in mythical constructs of the Romantic imagination.'[20]

In the earlier version of the story Harding may well believe that as an artist he is different from Rodney, that empathy with his countrymen and unabashed interest in their lives provide a way back to Ireland. Yet 'Fugitives' implies that just as Rodney and Harding's contrasting relationships with Lucy end with a similar inability to fulfil her desire for life, so may the two men's artistic engagements with Ireland prove to be opposite versions of failure. Consequently, in the final version, Harding is not planning to return to Ireland. Nor does he give a lengthy explanation of this decision; he is only going with Edward Martyn for a few, boring weeks to collect peasant idiom. In the final version, the way back is closed, the model has fled and the participants of the Irish revival wake in London to the realisation that Ireland has never let them live.

Conclusion

Ibsen's works were rarely discussed in Ireland until the mid-1890s. The playwright who had wrought a revolution in the European theatrical world and who had shaken the foundations of social institutions was known in Ireland mainly as a London fashion craze and the author of the only unspectacular play staged by Beerbohm Tree on his Irish tour in 1894. Some five years later, the story was different. By then, Ibsen had become a significant influence on Irish writing and a catchword in theatre criticism. From 1899, playwrights and the public in Ireland were simultaneously subjected to two opposing facets of Ibsen's drama. He was proclaimed as a great romanticist and the progenitor of dramatic realism, revered as a model patriot and feared as a cosmopolitan artist. Ibsen's ambivalent role in the Irish Revival reflects the unique nature of the movement that was at once a belated reverberation of national romanticism – a phenomenon that had occupied European imagination since the late eighteenth century – and the beginning of Irish modernism.

With all its search for authenticity, its hope for a regeneration of the lost folk culture and its belief in mythology as the purest expression of the national psyche, the Irish Revival was an extremely self-conscious movement. Its leaders were aware that what they were hoping to achieve in Ireland had already been attempted elsewhere – in Germany and in Norway, for example. Moreover, in the years since then, new artistic forms had superseded revivalism. It was apparent that these new forms had to be accommodated within, or spurned by, the Revival in order for the movement to succeed in Ireland. Yeats responded to the challenge in his 1899 speeches and articles, which implied that Ibsen's worldwide fame was due to his early saga dramas, such as *The Vikings at Helgeland*. By means of this half-truth Yeats might have hoped to counteract the effects of the revolution brought about by Ibsen's realist drama; romanticism could once again have its turn if the public became convinced that it had always been the most authentic way to approach reality. Synge's response was quite the opposite. *In the Shadow of the Glen* demonstrates that Ibsen is omnipresent. While drawing on Irish folklore and his own experiences of peasant life, the author engages with the ideas of the great world. The once pastoral thatched cottages appear as so many doll's houses. In his discovery that in the modern age the only path to romanticism is through parody, moreover, Synge is a true disciple of the author of *Peer Gynt*.

Ibsen had an impact on two interrelated developments in Irish writing: the humanist tradition and modernism. His importance for Irish literary humanism begins with the publication of *The Quintessence of Ibsenism*. Shaw identified Ibsen's rejection of idealism as the most innovative and controversial aspect of his drama. For Shaw ideals are 'something to blind us, something to numb us, something to murder self in us, something whereby, instead of resisting death, we can disarm it by committing suicide'.[1] This was not a commonly held view in early twentieth-century Ireland. The widespread frustration with the humiliations of colonial rule translated into idealism of sacrificial intensity. The most extreme manifestation of this sacrificial idealism was the Easter Rising of 1916. As a consequence, Ibsen's anti-idealist humanism presented difficulties to some of his self-proclaimed Irish followers. This is evident in the Theatre of Ireland's staging of *Brand*, the dedication of Lennox Robinson's *Patriots*, the ending of Thomas MacDonagh's *Pagans* and Pearse's unusual reference to *Ghosts* in a 1915 article. Conversely, in George Moore's *Hail and Farewell* and O'Casey's *The Plough and the Stars*, as well as Synge's *Playboy*, allusions to his plays are enriched by the authors' ideological affinity with Ibsen. They do not believe that sacrifice has any redemptive power. In different ways, they protest against an ideology that neglects to account for its causalities.

Ibsen's rejection of idealism was not merely a question of ethics, as Shaw suggested, but a modernist rebellion against the predominant aesthetics of the nineteenth century. Ibsen's plays dispense with belief in the unity of truth, goodness and beauty. They do not attempt 'to uplift us' or 'point the way to the ideal',[2] even though some readers, such as the Irish writer Kathleen O'Brennan, thought they did. *Brand*, for instance, does not, as Shaw suggests, simply illustrate the inhumanity of the idealist that would sooner see his little son die of consumption and beloved wife as a result die from grief than abandon what he perceives to be his calling. While it scrutinises the consequences of the protagonist's actions in detail, the play does not pass an absolute judgment on Brand; nor does it clearly delineate the boundaries between the world of hallucinations and holy visions and that of reality. In Act 5, Brand wrestles with a phantom that assumes the form of his dead wife, but which the madwoman Gerd interprets to be the Spirit of Compromise. The phantom tempts Brand, telling him that his wife and son are alive. All he needs to do to reclaim happiness is awaken from his nightmare and repent of his former ways. Brand refuses and the phantom vanishes with a piercing scream. How are we to interpret this episode? Does it confirm or subvert the idea of Brand's inhumanity? What does it suggest about the authorial position on the subject? How, for that matter, should it be staged? Should the phantom appear as a madman's hallucination in a play about real life or as an otherworldly apparition in a fantastic morality play? Through its refusal to explain itself, *Brand* examines the very premises of the aesthetic tradition that informs its epic tone and verse form. The metapoetic and metatheatrical concerns of *Brand* emerge also in later plays. In Ibsen's drama, goodness, beauty and even truth are unreliable and dangerous clichés in a world in which language itself is unreliable.

While it is often assumed that in Ireland Ibsen's influence was strongest in the case of the Cork Realists, on closer examination it can be seen that the Cork Realists failed to learn from Ibsen his minute exploration of the interrelation between thought and fact and between the everyday and the mythical. By contrast, Ibsen had a profound influence on Yeats, who is commonly believed to have hated the Ibsenite theatre. Synge, who publicly declared his distaste for Ibsen, is in fact a particularly sensitive reader of his plays. And Joyce, whose youthful Ibsenism is usually considered to have inspired the realistic elements of *Dubliners* and *Ulysses*, also has an affinity with Ibsen when writing in the fantastic or surreal mode. In other words, the story of Ibsen's reception in Ireland extends beyond the development of dramatic realism. Ibsen's synthesis of the realistic and the fantastic modes, which is notable in *Peer Gynt* and such later plays as *Little Eyolf* and *Rosmersholm* – his discovery of the problematic presence of myth in the everyday reality – is echoed in some the most influential Irish works of the early twentieth century – *The Playboy of the Western World*, *Ulysses* and certain late poems of Yeats. Like Ibsen's plays, these works bring together and subvert the two opposing trends of early twentieth-century Irish writing – national romanticism and social realism. Even though news of Ibsen's fame reached Ireland not long before the playwright's death, and in spite of the fact that his plays were produced infrequently and usually by second-rate companies, his writings were a significant force in the development of Irish modernism.

In this book, I have used Ibsen and Ireland to examine the patterns of interrelation between literary influence and dramatic reception. The starting assumption was that a writer's engagement with a literary work, just like any other aspect of composition, does not take place in isolation. Therefore, I have made equal use of documents of two types. To one type belong eyewitness accounts of productions, newspaper reviews and various contemporary articles on Ibsen. Plays, works of fiction and poems that have affinity with Ibsen belong to the other type. Both types of documents have not only been cited as evidence of Ibsen's popularity or unpopularity in Ireland; they have also been examined for their knowledge and understanding of Ibsen's drama. One of the regular complaints in Ibsen criticism is how easily and frequently his plays are misread. The parody of romanticism in *Peer Gynt*, for instance, may be mistaken for the real thing; and *A Doll's House* may appear as merely a feminist pamphlet in dramatic form, or even – as was often the case in Dublin – reinterpreted as a tragedy of a righteous man and his unprincipled wife. In this way, I have used Ibsen's plays to explore the tensions between Irish writers and their audiences, and between the developments in the literary tradition and the stage tradition in Ireland. Thus the Theatre of Ireland's transformation of *Brand* into a panegyric to sacrificial idealism contrasts with Moore's humanist exploration of the same theme in *Hail and Farwell*. And the public outcry over *The Plough and the Stars* compares strangely with the placid reception of the 1923 production of *A Doll's House*. Edwards and MacLiammóir's production of *Peer Gynt* is so impressive because, among other things, it bridged the gap between the theatrical and the literary reception of Ibsen in Ireland. Through their expressionistic style, they captured a modernist dimension of the play, thus exposing for the public those elements of Ibsen's art that had hitherto been reflected only in certain self-reflective works of the Irish Revival.

This account of Ibsen's reception in Ireland highlights the international dimension of the Irish Literary Revival, a movement often misconstrued as a narrowly nationalist phenomenon. It also serves as a first step in suggesting that engagement with international playwrights constitutes an important aspect of the subsequent development of Irish dramatic tradition. Brian Friel's recent adaptation of *Hedda Gabler* acknowledges this. The off-stage Mademoiselle Diana is transferred in this version into a 'Mademoiselle Circe', thus bringing Ibsen's text into proximity with Joyce's *Ulysses*.[3] The translations and adaptations of his plays by Frank McGuinness and Thomas Kilroy, moreover, suggest that the problems that accompanied Ibsen's reception in Ireland are not quite laid to rest. Both McGuinness and Kilroy strive to break the link between Ibsen and Victorian England – a connection that turned so many nationalists against the playwright. McGuinness's translations are executed in Irish English, while Kilroy rewrites *Ghosts* to fit the social conditions of the 1980s Ireland. Dissatisfied with the British and American translations, both playwrights develop national responses to the classic dramatist. Ibsen still allows Irish writers to negotiate a way between the conflicting demands of modernity and tradition, nationalism and cosmopolitanism.

Appendix: List of Performances of Ibsen's Plays in Dublin, 1894–28

1894: 28 September. *An Enemy of the People* (1882) Beerbohm Tree. Gaiety Theatre.
1897: 14 December. *A Doll's House* (1879). The Dublin Players' Club. Molesworth Hall.
1903: 16 April. *A Doll's House*. The Dublin Players. Antient Concert Rooms.
18 June. *La Maison de Poupée*. Theatre Royal. Madame Rejane.
25–27 June. *A Doll's House*. Queen's Theatre. The Dublin Players.
1904: 20–21 April. *Hedda Gabler* (1890). Antient Concert Rooms. The Dublin Players.
1906: 7 December. Act 4 of *Brand* (1865). Theatre of Ireland. Molesworth Hall.
1907: 24 October. *Hedda Gabler*. Mrs Patrick Campbell. Gaiety Theatre.
1908: 11–16 May. Leigh Lovel and a Special London Company: *A Doll's House*, *Hedda Gabler*, *The Master Builder* (1892).
1911: 7 and 11 March. *A Doll's House*. Ben Iden Payne. The Gaiety Theatre.
1912: 17–18 May and 10 December. *Little Eyolf* (1894). The Metropolitan Players. Little Theatre, Sackville Street.
9–11 December. *The Lady from the Sea* (1888). The Metropolitan Players. Little Theatre, Sackville Street.
1913: 8–9 December. *Rosmersholm*. The Metropolitan Players (1886). Little Theatre, Sackville Street.
?1914 or 1915: *Ghosts* (1881). The Metropolitan Players. Unknown location.
1916: 11–12 February. *The Master Builder*. The Metropolitan Players. Little Theatre, Sackville Street.
1917: 23–28 April. *An Enemy of the People*, The Irish Theatre. Hardwicke Street.
13 October. *Ghosts*. Victor Lewis. Theatre Royal.
1918: 4–9 February. *An Enemy of the People*, The Irish Theatre. Hardwicke Street.
10 June. *John Gabriel Borkman* (1896). Frank Dyall and Mary Merrall. Abbey Theatre.
1923: 22–24 March. *A Doll's House*. The Abbey Theatre Company. Abbey Theatre. This production was revived on the following dates: 18–22 December 1923; 30 September–3 October 1925; 3 December 1926; 12–16 March 1929.
1928: 3–7 April. *John Gabriel Borkman* (1896). The Abbey Theatre Company. Abbey Theatre.
14–27 October. *Peer Gynt* (1867). Gate Theatre Company. Peacock Theatre.

Notes

Introduction

1. James Joyce, *A Portrait of the Artist as a Young Man*. Eds. Hans Walter Gabler and Walter Hettche (New York and London: Garland, 1993), p. 203.
2. Lady Gregory, *Our Irish Theatre: A Chapter of Autobiography*. Ed. Roger McHugh (Gerrards Cross: Colin Smythe, 1972), p. 17.
3. Toril Moi, *Henrik Ibsen and the Birth of Modernism: Art, Theater, Philosophy* (New York: Oxford University Press, 2006), p. 2.
4. George Bernard Shaw, *The Quintessence of Ibsenism* (London: Walter Scott, 1891), p. 5.
5. Ibid.
6. See Harold Bloom, *The Anxiety of Influence: a Theory of Poetry* (New York: Oxford University Press, 1973).
7. See Naomi Lebowitz, *Ibsen and the Great World* (Baton Rouge, LA: Louisiana State University Press, 1989).
8. See Toril Moi, *Henrik Ibsen and the Birth of Modernism: Art, Theatre, Philosophy* (Oxford: Oxford University Press, 2006).
9. Miglena Iliytcheva Ivanova, 'Staging Europe, Staging Ireland: Ibsen, Strindberg, and Chekhov in Irish Cultural Politics 1899–1922' (PhD thesis, University of Illinois at Urbana-Champaign, 2004).
10. Robert Hogan, James Kilroy, Liam Miller, Richard Burnham and Daniel P. Poteet. *The Modern Irish Drama, a Documentary History*, 6 vols. (Dublin: Dolmen Press, 1970–9).
11. William J. Feeney, *Drama in Hardwicke Street: A History of the Irish Theatre Company* (London: Associated University Press, 1984).
12. Ibid., p. 163.
13. Jan Setterquist, *Ibsen and the Beginnings of Anglo-Irish Drama*, 2 vols. (Cambridge, MA: Harvard University Press, 1951–60).
14. Bjørn J. Tysdahl, *Joyce and Ibsen* (Oslo: Norwegian Universities Press, 1968).
15. See, for example, Theoharis C. Theoharis, '*Hedda Gabler* and "The Dead"', *ELH* 50:4 (1983), 791–809; Robert Spoo, 'Uncanny Returns in "The Dead": Ibsenian Intertexts and the Estranged Infant', in Susan Friedman, ed. *Joyce: The Return of the Repressed*, (Ithaca, NY: Cornell University Press, 1993), pp. 89–113; Steven Doloff, 'Ibsen's *A Doll's House* and "The Dead"', *James Joyce Quarterly* 31:2 (1994): 111–13; Diana O'Hehir, *Ibsen and Joyce: a Study of Three Themes* (Baltimore, MD: Johns Hopkins University, 1970); and, more recently, William A. Johnsen, *Violence and Modernism: Ibsen, Joyce, and Woolf* (Gainesville, FL: University Press of Florida, 2003).
16. Kathleen A. Heininge, 'Ibsen and Yeats: The Establishment of a National Drama' (MA dissertation, California State University, Fresno, CA, 1993); Katharine Worth, 'Ibsen and the Irish Theatre', *Theatre Research International*, 15:1 (Spring 1990): 18–28; Johannes Kleinstück, 'Yeats and Ibsen', in Wolfgang Zach and Heinz Kosok eds. *Literary Interrelations: Ireland, England and the*

World, 3 vols. (Tübingen: Narr, 1987), vol. 2, pp. 65–74. For the influence of Ibsen on Shaw, see Keith May, *Shaw and Ibsen* (New York: St. Martin's Press, 1985).

17. Robert Welch, *The Abbey Theatre, 1889–1999: Form and Pressure* (Oxford: Oxford University Press, 2003); Ben Levitas, *The Theatre of a Nation: Irish Drama and Cultural Nationalism* (Oxford: Oxford University Press, 2002); Albert J. DeGiacomo, *T. C. Murray, Dramatist: Voice of Rural Ireland* (Syracuse, NY: Syracuse University Press, 2003).
18. The note reads: 'Land of Heart's Desire – Little Eyolf: 4th wall of theatre', cited in Tysdahl, *Joyce and Ibsen*, p. 131.
19. Robert Hogan and Michael J. O'Neill, *Joseph Holloway's Abbey Theatre* (Carbondale, IL: Southern Illinois University Press, 1967), p. 129.

Chapter 1

1. 'Notices of Books: E. Gosse's translation of *Hedda Gabler*', *Dublin Review*, 15:5 (April 1891), 485–6.
2. Katherine Newey, 'Ibsen in the English Theatre', in *A Companion to Modern British and Irish Drama*, ed. Mary Luckhurst (Malden, MA, Oxford and Carlton: Blackwell, 2006), pp. 35–47, p. 37.
3. G. B. Shaw's preface to William Archer's *Theatrical World for 1894.* Cited in James Woodfield, *English Theatre in Transition* (London: Croom Helm, 1984), p. 5.
4. The third Dublin theatre, the Theatre Royal, was burnt down in 1880 and reopened in 1897.
5. See Philip B. Ryan, *The Lost Theatres of Dublin* (Westbury, Wiltshire: Badger Press, 1998).
6. 'Ibsen's Plays', *Weekly Irish Times*, 31 October, 1891, 4.
7. 'A Wife Beheaded and Burned for Poisoning her Husband', *Irish Times*, 16 April 1892, 7.
8. See, for example, 'Stories of Noted People', *Weekly Irish Times,* 1 October 1892, 1.
9. Constantine P. Curran, *Under the Receding Wave* (London: Gill & Macmillan, 1970), p. 78.
10. 'Topics of the Month / *The Master Builder*', *Lyceum* 6: 66 (March 1893), 139–40.
11. Gretchen P. Ackerman, *Ibsen and the English Stage* (New York and London: Garland, 1987), p. 135. Moore's article was originally published in *The Hawk* on 24 June 1890.
12. George Moore, 'A Note on *Ghosts*', in George Moore, *Impressions and Opinions* (London: David Nutt, 1891), pp. 215–26. Reprinted in Michael Egan, ed. *Henrik Ibsen: the Critical Heritage* (London and New York: Routledge, 1972), p. 182.
13. Editorial comment, *Daily Telegraph*, 14 March 1891, 5. Reprinted in Egan, p. 189.
14. 'Reviews / Moore's Impressions and Opinions', *Dublin Evening Mail,* 18 March 1891, 4.
15. William Archer, '*Ghosts* and Gibberings', *Pall Mall Gazette,* 8 April 1891, 3. Reprinted in Egan, p. 209.

16. 'Dramatic Musical and Art Gossip', *Dublin Evening Mail,* 25 February 1893, 3.
17. 'Dramatic Musical and Art Gossip', *Dublin Evening Mail,* 4 March 1893, 2.
18. 'Dramatic Musical and Art Gossip', *Dublin Evening Mail,* 18 March 1893, 2.
19. W. G. Fay and Catherine Carswell, *The Fays of the Abbey Theatre: An Autobiographical Record* (London: Rich & Cowan, 1935), p. 108.
20. Vivian Mercier, 'Literature in English', in *A New History of Ireland,* vol.VI: *Ireland Under the Union, II 1870–1921*, ed. W. E. Vaughan (Oxford: Clarendon Press, 1996), pp. 357–84, p. 360.
21. 'Shanganagh', 'English Literature in Ireland', *United Irishman,* 7 January 1906, 3.
22. Joseph Holloway, *Impressions of a Dublin Playgoer,* National Library of Ireland, MS 1831, p. 830. All quotations from Holloway's manuscripts included in this work are reproduced with the permission of The Board of The National Library of Ireland.
23. Henrik Ibsen, *The Collected Works*, 11 vols., ed. William Archer (New York: Charles Scribner's Sons, 1908–10), vol. VIII, p. 153.
24. See Michael Meyer, *Ibsen: A Biography* (Garden City, NY: Doubleday, 1971), p. 498.
25. Levitas, *The Theatre of a Nation*, pp. 10–11.
26. Holloway's reaction to Parnell's downfall is unknown. He was, however, a Home Ruler.
27. A notice by 'Momus', *The Gentlewoman,* 24 June 1893, 835, rpt. in Egan, pp. 301–2.
28. Frank Swinnerton. *Background with Chorus* (London: Hutchinson, 1956), p. 98. Cited in Ackerman, p. 308.
29. Momus, 835.
30. Desmond MacCarthy, 'From the Stalls', in Max Beerbohm, *Herbert Beerbohm Tree: Some Memories of Him and His Art* (London: E. P. Dutton, 1920), pp. 216–27, p. 223. Cited in Ackerman, p. 307.
31. Ibid.
32 G. B. Shaw, *Our Theatres in the Nineties* (London: Constable, 1948), II, p. 33. Cited in Ackerman, p. 306.
33. *The Theatre,* 1 July 1893, 44, rpt. in Egan, p. 303.
34. *Times*, 15 June 1893, 10, rpt. in Egan, p. 298.
35. 'Of People's Enemies and Friends', *Dublin Evening Mail,* 29 September 1894, 5.
36. Fay and Carswell, *The Fays of the Abbey Theatre,* p. 108.
37. *Irish Daily Independent,* 29 September 1894, 5.
38. *'An Enemy of the People', The Irish Times*, 29 September 1894, p. 5.
39. *'An Enemy of the People', Daily Express*, 29 September 1894, 5.
40. *Freeman's Journal*, 29 September 1894, p. 5.
41. Both of these terms referred to those who were ashamed of their Irish Catholic origins and imitated British customs. The term 'West Brit', which is more generic, has survived in modern usage, whereas 'seonin', which referred more specifically to a young, male, pro-British snob, has not. The mawkish figure of the seonin was the butt of many jocular articles and sketches published in the *United Irishman* and *The Leader*.
42. *Irish Daily Independent,* 29 September 1894, 5.
43. Ibid.

44. 'Of People's Enemies and Friends', *Dublin Evening Mail,* 29 September 1894, 5.
45. Ibid. Gladstone's uneasy relationship with *An Enemy of the People* began in 1890, when his presence at Beerbohm Tree's public reading of the play drew a large audience. Gladstone fell asleep during the performance (Ackerman, p. 301, in reference to Elizabeth Robins, *Both Sides of the Curtain* [London: Heinemann, 1940], p. 265).
46. *Irish Times*, 26 September 1984, 4.
47. Ibid.
48. 'Unionist Meeting in Cork/Speech by Lord Templetown', *Irish Times*, 26 September 1894, 6.
49. 'Of People's Enemies and Friends', *Dublin Evening Mail,* 29 September 1894, 5.
50. Ibid.
51. 'Liberal Unionists at Birmingham', *The Times*, 27 April 1889, 8. The quotation is from Ibsen's 1885 address to the workers of Trondheim. This passage is quoted, in a different translation, in Havelock Ellis, *The New Spirit* (London: George Bell, 1890); I have not been able to find an earlier occurrence of this passage in English.
52. George Moore, *Hail and Farewell*, ed. Richard Allen Cave (Gerrards Cross: Colin Smythe, 1976), p. 76.
53. Ibid., p. 77.
54. Ibid., p. 76.
55. Ibid., p. 78. *Heather Field* was drafted before 1894 and later revised by Moore for its publication and production by the Irish Literary Theatre in 1889.
56. 'Ibsen in Dublin (by an Ibsenite)', *Daily Express*, 16 December 1897, 7.
57. 'The Players' Club / *A Doll's House*', *Irish Times,* 15 December 1897, 10.
58. According to John Kenny, editor of the *Collected Letters of W. B. Yeats*, Martyn's involvement with the Players' Club goes as far back as 1897. Jerry Nolan does not corroborate this view in Jerry Nolan, *Six Essays on Edward Martyn (1859–1923), Irish Cultural Revivalist, Irish Studies*, vol. 11 (Lewiston, NY, Queenstown and Lampeter: Edwin Mellen Press, 2004).
59. 'Ibsen in Dublin (by an Ibsenite)', *Daily Express*, 16 December 1897, 7.
60. Holloway, *Impressions*, MS 1795, p. 431.
61. Ibid.
62. 'The Players' Club / *A Doll's House*', *Irish Times,* 15 December 1897, 10.
63. 'Ibsen in Dublin (by an Ibsenite)', 7.
64. Ibid.
65. Elizabeth Robins, *Ibsen and the Actress* (London: Hogarth Press, 1928), p. 13. Cited in Ackerman, p. 45.
66. Holloway, *Impressions*, MS 1795, p. 431.
67. 'Nora Helmer off for the Antipodes', *Pall Mall Gazette* 5 July 1889, 1–2, rpt. in Egan, p. 125.
68. Evert Sprinchorn, 'Ibsen and the Actors', in Errol Durbach, ed. *Ibsen and the Theatre* (New York and London: New York University Press, 1980), pp. 118–30.
69. Holloway, *Impressions,* MS 1795, p. 431.
70. Ibid.
71. Ibid.
72. 'The Drama of the Year', *Irish Times*, 1 January 1897, 5.

73. John Kelly, gen. ed., *The Collected Letters of W. B. Yeats*, vol. 2 (Oxford University Press: IntelLex Electronic Edition, 1897), p. 124.
74. Adrian Frazier, 'The Irish Renaissance, 1890–1940: Drama in English', in *Cambridge History of Irish Literature*, 2 vols, eds. Margaret Kelleher and Philip O'Leary (Cambridge: Cambridge University Press, 2006), vol. 2, p. 183.
75. Arthur Clery, *Dublin Essays* (Dublin and London: Maunsel & Co., 1919), p. 119.
76. Letter signed by Lady Gregory, Yeats and Martyn and circulated in 1897. Reprinted in Robert Hogan and James Kilroy, *The Modern Irish Drama*, vol. I: *The Irish Literary Theatre* (Dublin: Dolmen Press, 1975), p. 25.
77. James Joyce, *Stephen Hero*. Eds. Theodore Spencer, John Slocum and Herbert Cahoon (New York: New Directions, 1944, rpt. 1963), p. 40.
78. Richard Ellmann, *James Joyce* (Oxford: Oxford University Press, 1983), pp. 53–4.
79. Bjørn Tysdahl, *Joyce and Ibsen, A Study in Literary Influence* (Oslo: Norwegian Universities Press/New York: Humanities Press, 1968), p. 40.
80. Padraic Colum, 'Ibsen in Irish Writing', *Irish Writing* 7 (1949), 66–70.
81. Skeffington's reading of Ibsen is satirised in *Stephen Hero* in the figure of McCann who says to Stephen that '*Ghosts* teaches abstinence' causing him to exclaim: 'You have connected Ibsen and Eno's Salt Fruit forever in my mind', *Stephen Hero*, p. 52.
82. Stanislaus Joyce, *My Brother's Keeper: James Joyce's Early Years* (New York: Viking Press, 1958), p. 128.

Chapter 2

1. John Eglinton, W. B. Yeats, AE and W. Larminie. *Literary Ideals in Ireland* (London: Fisher Unwin, 1899), p. 11.
2. Ibid., p. 12
3. Ibid., p. 17.
4. Ibid., p. 19.
5. Ibid., p. 25.
6. Ibid., pp. 25–6.
7. William Barrett 'Irish Drama?' *New Ireland Review*, 3 (March 1895), 38–41, 40.
8. Ibid., 113.
9. Henrik Ibsen, 'Professor Welhaven on Paludan-Müller's Mythological Poems', published in English under this title with an introduction by Rolf Fjelde, *The Drama Review:* 13:2 (Winter, 1968), 44–6.
10. William Archer, 'The Real Ibsen', *International Monthly* 3 (February 1901), 182–201, 184. Cited in Peter Whitebrook, *William Archer: a Biography* (London: Methuen 1993), p. 236.
11. *Literary Ideals in Ireland*, p. 82.
12. Ibid., p. 11.
13. Ibid., p. 83.
14. Ibid.
15. 'Dramatic Ideals and the Irish Literary Theatre', *Freeman's Journal*, 6 May 1899, 5.
16. Ibid.

17. Ibid.
18. Yeats, 'Plans and Methods', *Beltaine* 1 (May 1899), 6. All references to this journal are to *Beltaine: The Organ of the Irish Literary Theatre*, May 1899–April 1900, reprinted in one volume with an introductory note by B. C. Bloomfield (London: Frank Cass, 1970).
19. 'Irish Literary Theatre / *Countess Cathleen* and *The Heather Field* / Interesting Productions Next Week', *Evening Herald*, 6 May 1899, 6. This article referred to Yeats's lecture in London.
20. D. P. Moran, 'The Gaelic and Other Movement', *An Claidheamh Soluis*, 8 July 1899, 261.
21. Ibid., 261–2.
22. For an analysis of the reasons for the public reaction to the play and Yeats's own intentions in writing it, see Adrian Frazier, *Behind the Scenes: Yeats, Horniman, and the Struggle for the Abbey Theater* (Berkeley, CA: University of California Press, 1990), pp. 1–24.
23. James H. Cousins and Margaret E. Cousins, *We Two Together* (Madras: Ganesh & Co., 1950), p. 57.
24. See Ivanova, pp. 91–107 and Levitas, pp. 46–8.
25. Holloway, *Impressions,* MS. 1797, p. 228.
26. 'Irish Literary Theatre', *Irish Times*, 10 May 1899, 5.
27. Ibid.
28. See Marie-Therese Courtney, *Edward Martyn and the Irish Theatre* (New York: Vantage Press, 1956), pp. 86–7.
29. 'Stage Lighting', *Pall Mall Gazette,* 13 January 1911, 8. Reprinted in Robert Hogan, R. Burnham and Daniel P. Poteet, *The Modern Irish Drama, a Documentary History*. Vol. IV: *The Rise of the Realists 1910–1915* (Dublin: The Dolmen Press, 1979), p. 103.
30. Ibid.
31. Tore Rem, 'Nationalism or Internationalism: The Early Irish Reception of Ibsen', *Ibsen Studies* 7:2 (2007), 188–202, 190.
32. 'The Day of the Rabblement', in James Joyce, *Occasional, Critical and Political Writing,* ed. Kevin Barry (Oxford: Oxford University Press, 2000), pp. 50–2, p. 50.
33. Ibid., p. 52.
34. Ibid.
35. *Modern Irish Drama,* vol. I, p. 112.
36. Frank J. Fay, 'The Irish Literary Theatre', *United Irishman,* 2 November 1901, 2. Reprinted in *Modern Irish Drama,* vol. I, pp. 112–13.
37. Joyce, *Occasional, Critical and Political Writing,* p. 52.
38. Fay, 'The Irish Literary Theatre'.
39. Holloway, *Impressions,* MS 1801, p. 561.
40. Ibid.
41. *United Irishman,* 17 October 1903, 1.
42. 'Chanel' [Arthur Clery], 'Plays with Meaning', *Leader,* 17 October 1903, 124.
43. 'Chanel' [Arthur Clery], 'The Philosophy of an Irish Theatre', *Leader,* 31 October 1903, 155.
44. Holloway, *Impressions,* MS 1801, p. 561.
45. The mention of the police in Holloway's account does not mean that they were actually summoned to quell the unruly audience (as was the case at the

1907 performance of *The Playboy*). Performances in large theatres such as the Queen's were usually supervised by policemen.

46. Holloway, *Impressions,* MS 1801, p. 561.
47. Yeats's attendance at the play is confirmed by John Kelly in *The Collected Letters of W. B. Yeats*, vol. III (Oxford University Press, InteLex Electronic Edition, 1994), p. 307. The entry for 26 January 1903 in Synge's diary contains a reference to 'when we awaken from the dead', which is a literal translation of the play's title in French. Trinity College Dublin, MS 4420.
48. The production (15 April–14 May, 1903), starring the ageing Elizabeth Terry as the Viking Hjordis, was not a success. Yeats's verse translation of Ornulf's lament for his sons was omitted at the last moment, and the poem was subsequently lost. See *The Collected Letters of W. B. Yeats*, vol. III, pp. 323–7.
49. Padraic Colum, 'Ibsen in Irish Writing', *Irish Writing*, 7 (1949), 66–70, 66.
50. Robert Lynd, 'Ibsenising Ireland', *To-Day*, 24 June 1903, 276, in W. A. Henderson's Scrapbooks, National Library of Ireland, MS 1729, p. 329.
51. M. C. Joy, 'The Shadows of the Land', *United Irishman* 25 June 1903, 3.
52. Ibid.
53. Máire Nic Shiubhlaigh [Mary Walker], *The Splendid Years* (Dublin: J. Duffy, 1955), p. 40.
54. Ibid., p. 44.
55. Yeats to John Quinn, 15 February 1905, *The Collected Letters of W. B. Yeats*, vol. II, Accession letter no. 113.
56. [Arthur Griffith], 'All Ireland', *United Irishman*, 25 April 1903, 1.
57. 'Ibsen at the Theatre Royal', *Dublin Evening Mail,* 19 June 1903, 2.
58. 'Amateur Theatricals at the Queen's Theatre', *Irish Times* 26 June 1903, 5.
59. 'Rejane at the Theatre Royal', *Irish Times* 19 June 1903, 6.
60. See Levitas, pp. 85–7; and Christopher Murray, *Twentieth Century Irish Drama – The Mirror up to Nation* (Manchester and New York: Manchester University Press, 1997), pp. 75–7.
61. W. J. McCormack, *Fool of the Family: a Life of J. M. Synge* (London: Weidenfeld & Nicolson, 2000), pp. 160–1. Synge's diary for 1903 suggests that besides *When We Dead Awaken* he had seen Ibsen's *Ghosts* in André Antoine's *Théâtre Libre* on 21 March 1898 (TCD MS 4419).
62. J. M. Synge, *Collected Works,* vol. 2. *Prose*, ed. Alan Price (London: Oxford University Press, 1966), p. 66.
63. Ibid., p. 96.
64. D. P. Moran, 'A National Theatre', *Leader,* 26 October 1901, 138.
65. Kappa Mega [Hugh Kennedy], 'Immoral Literature at Popular Prices', *Leader*, 29 August 1903, 11.
66. Ibid.
67. Stephen MacKenna to Synge, January 1904, *The Collected Letters of John Millington Synge*, ed. Ann Saddlemyer, vol. I: 1871–1907 (New York: Oxford University Press, 1983), p. 75.
68. Synge to MacKenna, 28 January 1904, *Collected Letters*, p. 74.
69. Ibid.
70. Nicholas Grene, *The Politics of Irish Drama: Plays in Context from Boucicault to Friel* (Cambridge: Cambridge University Press, 1999), p. 109.
71. Gregory Castle, *Modernism and the Celtic Revival* (Cambridge: Cambridge University Press, 2001), p. 37. Original emphasis.

72. See *Modern Irish Drama*, vol. IV, p. 17.
73. Yeats, 'Windlestraws', *Samhain* 1 (October 1901), 7. All references to *Samhain* are to *Samhain October 1901–November 1908, Numbers One to Seven*, reprinted in one volume with an introductory note by B. C. Bloomfield (London: Frank Cass, 1970).
74. U. O R. 'I mBaile 's i gCein', *An Claidheamh Soluis*. 24 October 1903, 5. Also noted by Philip O'Leary, *Prose Literature of the Irish Literary Revival, 1881–1921, Ideology and Innovation* (University Park, PN: Pennsylvania State University Press, 1994), p. 83.
75. Lennox Robinson, *Ireland's Abbey Theatre* (Port Washington, NY: Kennikat Press, 1951), p. 4.
76. Lennox Robinson, *I Sometimes Think* (Dublin: Talbot Press, 1956), p. 26.
77. Yeats, 'The Stone and the Elixir', in *Uncollected Prose by W. B. Yeats,* vol. 1, ed. John P. Frayne (London: Macmillan, 1970) pp. 344–6, p. 346. My emphasis.
78. Yeats to Colum, 2 January 1903, *The Collected Letters of W. B. Yeats,* vol. III, p. 293.
79. Jerry Nolan, *Six Essays on Edward Martyn (1859–1923), Irish Cultural Revivalist,* p. 131.
80. All the following quotations relating to this story are to W. B. Yeats, *The Trembling of the Veil,* in *Autobiographies* (London: Macmillan, 1955, rpt. 1970), pp. 107–381, p. 279.
81. *The Collected Letters of W. B. Yeats*, vol. II, p. 350.
82. Tracy C. Davis, 'Ibsen's Victorian Audience', *Essays in the Theatre* 4 (1985), 21–38.
83. William Archer's *Ibsen's Prose Dramas,* which included the early plays, appeared in 1890; the eleven-volume *Collected Works of Henrik Ibsen,* edited by Archer appeared in 1906–8. See Egan, *Henrik Ibsen: The Critical Heritage.*
84. Yeats, 'The Reform of the Theatre', *Samhain* 4 (October 1903), 9.
85. Yeats, 'The Play, the Player, and the Scene', *Samhain* 5 (December 1904), 26.
86. Yeats, 'Windlestraws', *Samhain* 1 (October 1901), 7.
87. Yeats, 'The Play the Player and the Scene', 27.
88. Paul Ruttledge [George Moore], 'Stage Management in the Irish National Theatre', *Dana* 5 (September 1904), 151.
89. Moore is quoting from memory, or else referring to a text other than Archer's translation of *Ghosts.*
90. [George Moore], 'Stage Management in the Irish National Theatre', 151
91. Yeats, 'Plans and Methods', *Beltaine* 1 (May 1899), 6.
92. Ibid.
93. Yeats, 'The Play the Player and the Scene', 27.
94. Ibid.
95. J. M. Synge, *Collected Works*: *Plays*, vol. 4, ed. Ann Saddlemyer (Gerrards Cross: Colin Smythe, 1982), book II, p. 53.
96. Yeats, 'The Play the Player and the Scene', 26.
97. Yeats, 'Notes and Opinions', *Samhain* 6 (November 1905), 11.
98. Ella Young, *The Flowering Dusk: Things Remembered Accurately and Inaccurately* (New York, Toronto: Longmans, Green and Co., 1945), p. 95.
99. 'The Abbey Row' (Dublin: Maunsel, 1907), p. 10. Cited in Castle, p. 165.

100. An unreferenced clipping in Henderson's Scrapbooks, MS. 1720, p. 102.
101. Ibid.
102. Holloway, *Impressions*, MS 1805, p. 693.
103. Ibid.
104. J. H. Cox, 'Ibsen in Dublin / Mrs Patrick Campbell as Hedda / Verdict not Unanimous', *Irish Independent*, 25 October 1907, 5.
105. *Sinn Féin*, 27 October 1906.
106. 'The Poet is Pleased' / Interview with Mr. Yeats', in Henderson's Scrapbooks, MS 1730, p. 87; the source of the article is not clearly specified in the scrapbook.
107. 'Interview with Mrs Campbell', *Freeman's Journal*, 26 October 1907, 4.
108. Ibid.
109. Holloway, *Impressions*, MS 1805, pp. 692 and 697.
110. 'Mrs Patrick Campbell at the Gaiety / *Hedda Gabbler*', *Freeman's Journal*, 25 October 1907, 9.
111. J. H. Cox, 'The Irish Helen / Mr. W. B. Yeats's *Deirdre* / Mrs Campbell in Title Role', *Irish Independent*, 10 November 1908, 9.
112. 'Public Amusements / Abbey Theatre: Mrs Patrick Campbell as Deirdre', *Irish Times*, 10 November 1908, 7.
113. Yeats to John Quinn, 29 October 1907, *The Collected Letters of W. B. Yeats, Unpublished Letters*, accession no. 684.
114. 'Ikaros', '*The Unicorn from the Stars*', *Leader*, 30 November 1907, 236.
115. 'Dialogues of the Day / Recorded by F. Sheehy-Skeffington (Third Series) / Two Books and a Play', an undated clipping from *The Peasant* in Henderson's Scrapbooks, MS. 1730, p. 184.
116. Yeats, *The Player Queen*, in *The Collected Plays of W. B. Yeats* (London: Macmillan 1966), pp. 385–430, p. 408.
117. Gabriel Fallon, *Sean O'Casey the Man I Knew* (London: Routledge & Kegan Paul, 1965), p. 86.
118. *The Player Queen*, p. 404.
119. *The Writing of the Player Queen: Manuscripts of W. B. Yeats*, ed. Curtis Baker Bradford (DeKalb, IL: Northern Illinois University Press, 1977), p. 80, draft 8, version B.
120. Ibid., draft 8, version B.
121. Ibid., p. 115, draft 11.
122. Ibid., p. 83, version B, draft 8.
123. *The Player Queen*, p. 404.
124. Ibid., p. 409.
125. Ibsen, *Hedda Gabler*, trans. Edmund Gosse and William Archer, *The Collected Works*, vol. X, pp. 1–186, p. 146.
126. *The Player Queen*, p. 412.
127. *The Writing of the Player Queen*, p. 73, draft 7.
128. Ibsen, *Hedda Gabler*, p. 174
129. *The Player Queen*, p. 414.
130. Ibid., p. 424.
131. Ibid., p. 429.
132. Ibid., p. 425.
133. *The Writing of the Player Queen*, p. 88, draft 8.
134. Ibid.

135. Ibid., p. 89, draft 8.
136. *Hedda Gabler,* p. 174.
137. Ibid., p. 176.
138. Ibid.
139. Ibid., p. 185.
140. Ibid.
141. *The Writing of The Player Queen*, p. 80, version B, draft 8.
142. *The Player Queen*, p. 430.
143. Anthony Roche, 'Synge, Brecht, and the Hiberno-German Connection', *Hungarian Journal of English and American Studies,* 10: 1–2 (2004), 9–32, 15.
144. Joan FitzPatrick Dean, 'Bringing Abbey into Contact: The Ibsenite Theatre of Ireland', *Hungarian Journal of English and American Studies,* 10: 1–2 (2004), 33–40, 33.
145. The term 'alternative dramatic revival' is used by Karen Vandevelde in her study of the several lesser-known Irish theatre companies of 1897–1913. Karen Vandevelde, *the Alternative Dramatic Revival in Ireland 1897–1913* (Dublin: Maunsel, 2005).

Chapter 3

1. Edward Halim Mikhail, *The Abbey Theatre Interviews and Recollections* (Basingstroke: Macmillan, 1988), p. 52.
2. Edward Martyn, 'A Plea for the Revival of the Irish Literary Theatre', *Irish Review* (April 1914), 79–84, 81–2
3. Ibid.
4. R. M., 'The Players Club: Production of *Hedda Gabler*', unreferenced clipping in Henderson's Scrapbooks, MS 1730, p. 68.
5. Ibid.
6. 'The Players' Club: *Hedda Gabler*', *Irish Times* 21 April 1904, 7.
7. Spealadoir [James Cousins], '*Hedda Gabler*', *United Irishman,* 30 April 1904, 6.
8. Spealadoir [James Cousins], 'The Plays at Molesworth Hall', *United Irishman,* 12 December 1903, 6.
9. Oliver Gogarty, 'A Word on Criticism and *Broken Soil*', *United Irishman,* 19 December 1903, 6, reprinted in Robert Hogan and James Kilroy, *The Modern Irish Drama: a Documentary History,* vol. II: *Laying the Foundations* (Dublin: Dolmen Press, 1976), p. 91.
10. Ibid.
11. Ibid.
12. [Arthur Griffith], 'All Ireland', *United Irishman,* 17 October 1903. Reprinted in *Modern Irish Drama,* vol. II, p. 79.
13. 'Imaal' [John O'Toole], 'Henrik Ibsen', *Leader,* 2 June 1906, 231–2, 231.
14. 'Casual Notes', *Dublin Evening Mail,* 24 May 1906, 2.
15. 'Imaal', 'Henrik Ibsen', 232.
16. Ibid.
17. Ibid.
18. Ibid.
19. Synge to Stephen McKenna, 28 January 1904, *Collected Letters,* p. 74.

20. 'Samhain', *Sinn Fein*, 27 October 1906, 2.
21. Nicholas Grene, *The Politics of Irish Drama*, p. 86; with reference to James F. Kilroy, *The 'Playboy' Riots* (Dublin: Dolmen Press, 1971), p. 13.
22. 'The Passing of Ibsen', *An Claidheamh Soluis*, 2 June 1906, 8.
23. Peter Christen Asbjørnsen and Jørgen Moe, *Norske Folkeeventyr*, vols. I–II (Christiania: Johan Dahls Boghandel, 1842–3).
24. Ibsen, *Peer Gynt*, trans. William and Charles Archer, *The Collected Works*, vol. IV, pp.1–271, p. 184.
25. 'The Passing of Ibsen', *An Claidheamh Soluis*, 2 June 1906, 8. The mistaken notion that Ibsen wrote in the 'revived' dialect of Norwegian, the Norwegian Landsmaal (or nynorsk, in modern usage) persisted for a long time. The issue was clarified in 'The Language Question in Norway', *An Claidheamh Soluis*, 6 June 1911, 8. Philip O'Leary also notes an anonymous contribution to *An Claidheamh Soluis* 'An Da Teanga san Orbhuaidh', 3 January 1914, which also discusses 'the matter of Ibsen's language'. See O'Leary, p. 83.
26. Padraic Colum, 'Ibsen and National Drama', *Sinn Féin*, 2 June 1906, 3.
27. Ibid.
28. Ibid.
29. Ibid.
30. Ibid.
31. Ibid.
32. Holloway, *Impressions*, MS 1804, p. 278.
33. Vandevelde, p. 99.
34. 'Dramatic Ideals and the Irish Literary Theatre', *Freeman's Journal*, 6 May 1899, 5.
35. 'Irish Literary Theatre / *Countess Cathleen* and *The Heather Field* / Interesting Productions Next Week' *The Evening Herald*, 6 May 1899, 6.
36. Ibsen, *Brand*, trans. William Archer, *The Collected Works*, vol. III, pp. 1–262, p. 24. Hereafter cited in parentheses.
37. *Lady Gregory's Journals*, ed. Daniel Murphy (Colin Smythe: Gerrards Cross, 1978), vol. 1, p. 364; entry for 20 June 1922.
38. Yeats, *Cathleen ní Houlihan*, in *Samhain*, 2 October 1902, 31.
39. Shaw, *The Quintessence of Ibsenism*, p. 125.
40. 'Sinn Dicat', 'The Drama in Dublin', *Sinn Féin*, 15 December 1906, 3.
41. Grene, *The Politics of Irish Drama*, p. 53.
42. Holloway, *Impressions*, MS. 1804, p. 659.
43. Synge, *Collected Works*: *Plays*, vol. 3, ed. Ann Saddlemyer (Gerrards Cross: Colin Smythe, 1982), book I, p. 11.
44. Ellmann, *James Joyce*, p. 63.
45. Vandevelde, p. 105.
46. Ibid.
47. Frazier, *George Moore 1852–1933*, p. 322.
48. Moore, *Hail and Farewell*, p. 213.
49. Lennox Robinson, *Curtain Up*: *an Autobiography* (London: Michael Joseph, 1942), p. 22. The Lancashire dramatists is a term applied primarily to W. Stanley Houghton (1881–1913), Harold Brighouse (1882–1958) and Allan Monkhouse (1858–1936); the emergence of the Cork Realists and that of the Lancashire Realists are related phenomena. The Lancashire Realists' plays were first produced by the Manchester Theatre founded by Annie Horniman in 1908.

50. Robinson, *I Sometimes Think*, p. 26; also referred to in Robinson, *Ireland's Abbey Theatre*, p. 91.
51. Michael O'Dempsey, 'Two Plays from Ulster', *Leader*, 2 May 1908, 173.
52. Ibid.
53. Ibid.
54. Ibid.
55. 'The Gaiety Theatre', *Irish Times,* 12 May 1908, 6.
56. Holloway, *Impressions*, MS 1806, p. 491.
57. Kathleen M. O'Brennan, 'The Drama as a Nationalising Force', *Sinn Féin,* 10 November 1906, 3.
58. Ibid.
59. Padraic Colum, 'Ibsen in Irish Writing', *Irish Writing* 7 (1949), 66–70, 69–70.
60. O'Brennan, 'The Drama as a Nationalising Force'.
61. Padraic Colum, 'Muskerryism – A Reply to X', *Sinn Féin,* 23 July 1910, 3.
62. M. M. O'H, 'Mr. Padraic Colum at the Abbey Theatre / A Superb Play', *Evening Telegraph*, 6 May 1910, 3.
63. *Irish Nation,* 14 May 1910, in Henderson's Scrapbooks, MS 1733, p. 90.
64. Ella Young, '*Thomas Muskerry* in Court', *Sinn Fein*, 9 July 1910, 3.
65. 'X', 'Muskerryism', *Sinn Féin,* 16 July 1910, 3.
66. Ibid.
67. Ibid.
68. *Modern Irish Drama,* vol. IV, p. 32.
69. Ibid.
70. Padraic Colum, 'Muskerryism – A Reply to "X"'.
71. Ibid.
72. An unreferenced clipping in Henderson's Scrapbooks, MS 1733, p. 93. X's reply appeared in *Sinn Féin,* 30 July 1910, 3.
73. Riobard Ua Floin, 'Muskerryism – A Note on National Criticism', *An tEireanach,* an undated clipping in the Henderson Scrapbooks, MS 1733, p. 111.
74. Ibsen, *Ghosts,* trans. William Archer, *The Collected Works,* vol. VII, pp. 157–295, p. 225.
75. Padraic Pearse, 'Ghosts' (1915), in *Political Writings and Speeches* (Dublin: Phoenix, 1916), pp. 219–50, p. 221.
76. Shaw, *Collected Prefaces* (London: Paul Hamyln, 1965), p. 831.
77. Ibsen to Bjørnson, 12 July 1879. Henrik Ibsen, *Letters and Speeches*, ed. Evert Sprinchorn (New York: Hill & Wang, 1964), p. 179.
78. Niels Ravnkilde, *Dagbøger, Breve, digte og Noder,* Manuscript Department, The Royal Library, Copenhagen. My thanks to Aina Nøding for pointing out this passage to me.
79. Miss Byrne to Yeats, 15 April 1912. NLI MS 18, 722. Reprinted in *Modern Irish Drama,* vol. IV, p. 185.
80. Ibid.
81. Ibid.
82. Lennox Robinson, *Selected Plays*, ed. Christopher Murray (Washington, DC: Catholic University of America Press, 1982), p. 62.
83. Ibsen, *John Gabriel Borkman,* trans. William Archer, *The Collected Works,* vol. XI, pp. 153–324, p. 318.
84. A phrase that appears in Lennox Robinson's dedication of the play.
85. Robinson, *Selected Plays,* p. 13.

86. Ibid., p. 60.
87. *Lost Plays of the Irish Renaissance,* vol. 2: *Edward Martyn's Irish Theatre,* ed. W. J. Feeney (Newark, Delaware: Proscenium Press, 1979), p. 35.
88. Ibid.
89. Feeney, *Drama in Hardwicke Street,* p. 85.
90. Levitas, p. 216.
91. Feeney, *Lost Plays of the Irish Renaissance,* vol. 2, p. 53.
92. *Studies,* 10 June 1921. Cited in Feeney, *Drama in Hardwicke Street,* p. 87.
93. D. E. S. Maxwell, a note on Martyn's *Heather Field* in *The Field Day Anthology of Irish Writing,* vol. 2, p. 568.
94. Ibsen, *A Doll's House,* trans. William Archer, *The Collected Works,* vol. IV, pp. 1–156, p. 155.
95. Feeney, *Drama in Hardwicke Street,* p. 87.
96. Padraic Pearse, 'Ghosts', p. 221.
97. Shaw, Preface to *The Philanderer,* 1930, in *Collected Prefaces,* p. 835.
98. See Nelson O'Ceallaigh Ritschel, 'Shaw, Connolly, and the Irish Citizen Army', *SHAW: The Annual of Bernard Shaw Studies* 27 (2007), 118–34. Ritschel examines Shaw's belief in the strong socialist element of the Rising, and analyses the degree of Shaw's involvement in the event.
99. Meyer, *Ibsen: A Biography* (Garden City, NY: Doubleday, 1971), p. 636.
100. Moi, p. 4.
101. Ibid.

Chapter 4

1. Moore, *Hail and Farewell,* p. 593.
2. Jennette Lee, *The Ibsen Secret: A Key to the Prose Dramas of Henrik Ibsen* (New York: G. P. Putnam's Sons, 1907), p. 56.
3. Ibid.
4. Moore, 'Introduction' to Edward Martyn, *The Heather Field and Maeve* (London: Duckworth, 1899), p. xxii.
5. Ibid., p. xxv.
6. Martyn, *The Heather Field and Maeve,* p. 8.
7. Lee, p. 99.
8. Ibsen to Bjørnson, 9 December 1867, *Letters and* Speeches, p. 67.
9. Interview with J. J. Skordalsvold, *The North,* 9 April 1890, reprinted in Henrik Ibsen, *Hundreårsutgave: Henrik Ibsens samlede verker,* 21 vols., ed. Francis Bull, Halvdan Koht and Didrik Arup Seip (Oslo: Gyldendal, 1928–57), vol. 19, p. 182.
10. Conversation with Jules Claretie (Summer 1897), *Hundreårsutgave: Henrik Ibsens samlede verker,* vol. 19, pp. 210–11. Compare Kirsten Shepherd-Barr, *Ibsen and Early Modernist Theatre 1890–1900* (Westport, CT: Greenwood Press, 1997), p. 63. Shepherd-Barr notes Ibsen's approbation of Lugnë-Poe's symbolist approach to his dramas.
11. Maurice Bigeon, 'Profils scandinaves: Henrik Ibsen', *Le Figaro,* 4 January 1893, p. 3, reprinted in *Liberty* (New York), 4 February 1893, 3.
12. Ibid. The translation of the French text is cited in Evert Sprinchorn, 'The Transition from Naturalism to Symbolism in the Theater from 1880 to 1900', *Art Journal,* 45:2 (Summer 1985), pp. 113–19.

13. Lee, p. 54.
14. Meyer, *Ibsen*, pp. 272–3; Meyer also cites Francis Bull's Taylorian Lecture at Oxford (1954) to support his point.
15. See Frode Helland, *Melankoliens spill: en studie i Henrik Ibsens siste dramaer* (Oslo: Universitetsforlag, 2000), p. 33.
16. *The Standard Edition of the Complete Psychological Works of Sigmund Freud*, ed. James Starchey, vol. XIII (London: Hogarth Press, 1974), p. 85. 'The Uncanny', in *On Creativity and the Unconscious: Papers on the Psychology of Art, Literature, Love, and Religion*. Ed. Benjamin Nelson (New York: Harper & Row, 1958), pp. 122–61, p. 147.
17. Michael Bell, 'The Metaphysics of Modernism', in *The Cambridge Companion to Modernism*, ed. Michael Levenson (Cambridge: Cambridge University Press, 1999), pp. 9–32, p. 17.
18. Holloway, *Impressions*, MS 1806, p. 494.
19. Ibid.
20. Ibid.
21. Ibid., p. 503.
22. Ibid.
23. J. H. Cox, 'A Strange Play: Ibsen's *The Master Builder*', *Irish Independent*, 12 May 1908, 4.
24. Nina S. Alnæs, *Varulv om natten*: *folketro og folkediktning hos Ibsen* (Oslo: Gyldendal, 2003).
25. Eivind Tjonneland, 'Allegory, Intertextuality and Death – the Problem of Symbolism in Ibsen's *The Master Builder*', *Proceedings of the 7th International Ibsen Conference* (Oslo: Centre for Ibsen Studies, 1994), pp. 217–36, p. 228.
26. Eric Bentley, *The Playwright as Thinker* (New York: Meridian Books, 1946, rpt. 1955), p. 93.
27. 'The Gaiety Theatre / Ibsen Plays / *The Master Builder*', *Dublin Evening Mail*, 12 May 1908, 2.
28. Edward Dowden, *Essays Modern and Elizabethan* (London, New York: J. M. Dent, E. P. Dutton, 1910), p. 58.
29. Grene, *The Politics of Irish Drama*, p. 108.
30. J. H. Cox, 'A Strange Play: Ibsen's *The Master Builder*'.
31. Ibid.
32. Ibsen, *The Master Builder*, trans. Edmund Gosse and William Archer, *The Collected Works*, vol. X, pp. 187–365, p. 292.
33. Ibid., p. 293.
34. Robert S. Brustein, *Critical Moments: Reflections on Theatre and Society 1973–1979* (New York: Random House, 1980), p. 108.
35. Ibsen, *The Master Builder*, p. 295.
36. See also Richard Hornby who discusses the ambiguous nature of causality in *The Master Builder* in relation to Freud's ideas on guilt and desire. Richard Hornby, 'Deconstructing Realism in Ibsen's *The Master Builde*r, in *Essays in Theatre* 2:1 (1983), 34–40.
37. Ibsen, *The Master Builder*, p. 296.
38. Brustein, p. 109.
39. Ibid.
40. Mary Douglas, *Purity and Danger* (London and New York: Routledge & Kegan Paul, 1966, rpt. Routledge, 2002), p. 74.

41. See David Spurr, 'Myths of Anthropology: Eliot, Joyce, Levy-Bruhl', *PMLA* 109:2 (March 1994), 266–80. At a late stage of his career Lucien Lévy-Brühl postulated that the 'primitive' and the 'rational' were universal mentalities, 'both could be found in all societies, but in different proportions' (269).
42. Albert J. DeGiacomo, *T. C. Murray, Dramatist: Voice of Rural Ireland*, p. 35.
43. T. C. Murray, *Selected Plays*. Ed. Richard Allen Cave (Gerrards Cross: Colin Smythe, 1998), p. 98.
44. Ibsen, *Ghosts*, p. 294.
45. Murray, *Selected Plays*, p. 99.
46. Ibsen, *Ghosts*, p. 294.
47. Ibsen, *Ghosts*, p. 225.
48. Ibid.
49. Jorge Louis Borges, 'Narrative Art and Magic', in Jorge Louis Borges *Selected Non-Fictions*. Ed. Eliot Weinberger (New York: Penguin Books, 2000), pp. 75–82, p. 81.
50. Ibid., p. 80.
51. John Richard Northam, *Ibsen: a Critical Study* (Cambridge: Cambridge University Press, 1973), p. 102.
52. *Hundreårsutgave: Henrik Ibsens samlede verker*, vol. 9 (Oslo: Gyldendal, 1957), p. 127.
53. Ibid., p. 92.
54. Northam, p. 102.
55. Brustein, p. 111.
56. The information is from a review of the *Saturday Independent* 1917 production of *Ghosts* by Victor Lewis's company. The reviewer had a 'distinct recollection of Miss Young in the part of Mrs Alving'. Holloway commented that he did not remember this production. Holloway, *Impressions*, MS 1834, entry for 14 October 1917 (the pagination is unreliable at this point).
57. Holloway, *Impressions*, MS 1814, p. 979.
58. Martyn, '*Little Eyolf*', *Sinn Féin*, 13 July 1912, 3.
59. Shelah Richards, unpublished autobiographical piece (typescript in the possession of her son, Micheal Johnston), p. 21.
60. The première of *Little Eyolf* on 17–18 May 1912 was in aid of the Fresh Air Association; its subsequent revival on 10 December 1912 was in aid of the IWFL, as were the productions of *The Lady from the Sea* and *Rosmersholm*.
61. 'Henrik Ibsen: Feminist', *Irish Citizen*, 16 November 1912, 206.
62. Ibid.
63. Paige Reynolds, *Modernism, Drama, and the Audience for the Irish Spectacle* (Cambridge: Cambridge University Press, 2007), pp. 76–115.
64. '*Rosmersholm*', *Irish Citizen*, 13 December 1913, 245.
65. '*The Lady from the Sea*', *Irish Times*, 10 December 1912, 9.
66. Evelyn Gleeson, 'Ibsen in Dublin', *Sinn Féin*, 7 December 1912, 5.
67. Ibid.
68. See Courtney, *Edward Martyn and the Irish Theatre* , pp. 86–7; and D. E. S. Maxwell, a note on Martyn's *Heather Field* in *The Field Day Anthology of Irish Writings*, vol. 2 (Derry: Field Day Theatre Company, 1991), pp. 586–9.
69. 'Irish Productions', *The Stage*, 1 February 1912, 22; cited after Reynolds, p. 99.
70. George Moore, *Hail and Farewell*, p. 592.

71. Freud, 'Some Character Types Met with in Psychoanalytic Work', *The Standard Edition of the Complete Psychological Works of Sigmund Freud*. Ed. James Starchey, vol. XIV (London: Hogarth Press, 1957), pp. 325–31.
72. Ibsen, *Rosmersholm*, trans. Charles Archer, *The Collected Works*, vol. IX, pp. 1–188, p. 5. Hereafter cited parenthetically.
73. Margot Norris, 'Myth and Reality in Ibsen's Mature Plays', *Comparative Drama* 10 (1976), 3–15, 4.
74. Martyn, *An Enchanted Sea*, in Jerry Nolan, ed., *The Tulira Trilogy of Edward Martyn (1859–1923) Irish Symbolist Dramatist* (Lewiston, Queenstown and Lampeter: Edwin Mellen Press, 2003), p. 134. Hereafter cited parenthetically.
75. A passage in an undated typescript by John MacDonagh. Cited in Feeney, *Drama in Hardwicke Street*, p. 159.
76. Jerry Nolan, 'Introduction', *The Tulira Trilogy*, ed. Nolan, p. 16. Author's emphasis.
77. Martyn, '*The Lady from the Sea* / Ibsen in Dublin', *Irish Times*, 30 November 1912, 9.
78. Martyn, '*Little Eyolf*', *Sinn Féin*, 13 July 1912, 3.
79. Shaw to Janet Achurch, 30 October 1896, Shaw, *Collected Letters 1874–1897*. Ed. D. H. Laurence (New York: Dodd, Mead & Co., 1965), p. 687.
80. Shaw to Janet Achurch, 4 April 1903, Shaw, *Collected Letters 1898–1910*. Ed. D. H. Laurence (New York: Dodd, Mead & Co., 1972), p. 320.
81. A. F. Spender, 'Little Eyolf – A Plea for Reticence', *Dublin Review*, January 1897, 122.
82. James Joyce, 'The Holy Office' (1904), in *The Field Day Anthology of Irish Writing*, vol. II, pp. 769–71, p. 770.
83. Tysdahl, p. 44.
84. Ibid., p. 62.
85. See A. M. Leatherwood, 'Joyce's Mythic Method: Structure and Unity in "An Encounter"', *Studies in Short Fiction* 13 (1976), 71–8.
86. William Archer, 'Introduction to *Little Eyolf*', Ibsen, *The Collected Works*, vol. XI, pp. vi–xvi, p. xv.
87. James Joyce, 'An Encounter', in *Dubliners*. Ed. Hans Walter Gabler with Walter Hettche (New York and London: Garland, 1933), pp. 175–84, p. 175.
88. See Sonja Bašić, 'Book of Many Uncertainties', in *Rejoycing: New Readings of* Dubliners. Ed. Rosa M. Bollettieri Bosinelli and Harold F. Mosher Jr. (Lexington, KY: The University Press of Kentucky, 1988), pp. 13–40, p. 27.
89. Archer, 'Introduction to *Little Eyolf*', p. xii.
90. Sidney Feshbach, 'Death in "An Encounter"', *James Joyce Quarterly* 2 (1965): 82–9, 82.
91. Leatherwood, 77.
92. See Helland, p. 254; and Northam, p. 88.
93. Ibsen, *Little Eyolf*, trans. William Archer, *The Collected Works*, vol. XI, pp. 1–152, p. 17. Hereafter cited in parentheses.
94. Erich Auerbach, *Mimesis: The Representation of Reality in Western Literature*, trans. Willard R. Trask (Garden City, NY: Doubleday: 1957), pp. 1–20.
95. Ibid., p. 9.
96. Tzvetan Todorov, *The Fantastic: A Structural Approach to a Literary Genre*, trans. Richard Howard (London: Case Western Reserve University, 1973), p. 25.
97. Ibsen, *Little Eyolf*, p. 20.

98. Ibid.
99. Ibid., pp. 25–6.
100. Northam notes how the two verbs (*nage* and *gnage*), used separately by Alfred and the Rat-Wife, come together in the last words of her speech. Northam, p. 190.
101. Leatherwood, 77.
102. Tysdahl, p. 56.
103. Ibsen, *The Lady from the Sea*, trans. Frances Archer, *The Collected Works*, vol. IX, pp. 189–349, p. 240.
104. Ibid., p. 241.
105. Ibsen, *Little Eyolf*, p. 59.
106. Ibid., p. 87.
107. Ibid., pp. 88–9.
108. Helland, p. 109.
109. Brian Johnston, *The Ibsen Cycle: the Design of the Plays from Pillars of Society to When We Dead Awaken* (University Park, PN: Pennsylvania State University Press, 1992), p. 362. The term 'Ibsen Cycle' is used by Johnston in reference to the twelve plays from *The Pillars of Society* to *When We Dead Awaken* that constitute a single work unified by a complex design.
110. See Douglas, *Purity and Danger*, p. 29.
111. See chapter 6.

Chapter 5

1. Preface to *The Philanderer*, 1930. *Prefaces*, p. 835.
2. G. B. Shaw, *The Philanderer: a Topical Comedy of the Year 1893* (London: Constable, 1928). By 1911 the Ibsen club had become a reality, though its character was different from the institution in Shaw's play. The archives of the club are missing. A search in *The Times* Digital Archive has yielded a few notices of their forthcoming productions, suggesting that club was particularly active between 1911 and 1912 when they staged *The Lady from the Sea* and *Ghosts*, and planned to produce *Peer Gynt* and *Olaf Liljekrans*. That this club was different from Shaw's imaginary Ibsen club is suggested by the following untitled clipping (unearthed by Ackerman in the Huntington Collection of Cutting Files): '1912, Dec. Meeting of the London Ibsen Club: readings from Little Eyolf, selections from Greig on the piano, a lecture "Ibsen and the Fairies"'. Cited in Ackerman, p. 389.
3. 'Gaiety Theatre / Mr. George Bernard Shaw's *The Philanderer*', *Irish Times*, 11 March 1911, 8.
4. Ibid.
5. Leah Levenson, *With Wooden Sword: A Portrait of Francis Sheehy-Skeffington, Militant Pacifist* (Boston, MA: Northeastern University Press/Dublin: Gill & Macmillan, 1983), p. 79.
6. 'Gaiety Theatre / Ibsen's *A Doll's House*', *Irish Times*, 8 March 1911, 6.
7. 'Noble Suffragettes' Epistolary Comedy; Lady Selbourne, Non-Militant, and Lady C. Lytton, Militant, Bluff the London Times', *New York Times*, 9 April 1911, C2.
8. Ibid.

9. Ibid.
10. 'Suffragist Methods', *Irish Times*, 17 March 1911, 7. Published in the *Irish Times* 'by special arrangement with the proprietors of *The Times*'.
11. Ibid.
12. Ibsen, *A Doll's House*, p. 139.
13. Edmund Gosse, *Henrik Ibsen* (New York: Charles Scribner's Sons, 1908), p. 146.
14. Untitled Editorial Article, *Irish Times*, 13 April 1912, 6.
15. Ibid.
16. 'Curious Scottish Divorce Case / Disturbing Influence of a Man in the House', *Irish Times*, 3 July 1912.
17. Holloway, *Impressions*, MS 1806, p. 493.
18. *Irish Times*, 4 April 1916, 6.
19. Inghean Dubh, 'To an Irish Suffragette', *Sinn Féin*, 11 February 1911, 3.
20. Rosemary Cullen Owens, *Smashing Times: A History of the Irish Women's Suffrage Movement 1889–1922* (Dublin, Attic Press, 1984, rpt. 1995), p. 48.
21. 'L.R', 'Woman Suffrage / From an Onlooker's Point of View', *The Leader*, 1 April 1911, 161.
22. Ibid.
23. 'Current Affairs', *The Leader*, 19 March 1910, 101.
24. Maud Gonne MacBride, 'A National Theatre', *United Irishman*, 24 October 1903, pp. 2–3. Cited after *Modern Irish Drama*, vol. II, p. 81.
25. Cited after Levenson, *With Wooden Sword: A Portrait of Francis Sheehy-Skeffington, Militant Pacifist*, p. 83.
26. Ibsen, *A Doll's House*, p. 147
27. [Arthur Griffith], 'All Ireland', *United Irishman*, 17 October 1903, 1. Cited in *Modern Irish Drama*, vol. II, p. 79.
28. F. Cruise O'Brien, 'Ireland and Woman Suffrage', *Leader*, 28 January 1911, 593.
29. Ibid.
30. Hannah Sheehy-Skeffington, 'Suffragette Critics', 11 February 1911, 639.
31. 'Female Suffrage / Stormy Meeting in Dublin', *Weekly Irish Times*, 20 April 1912, 5.
32. Ibid.
33. Ibid.
34. Ibid.
35. William Archer, '*Ghosts* and Gibberings', *Pall Mall Gazette*, 8 April 1891, 3. Reprinted in Egan, p. 209.
36. Lady Gregory to Shaw 12 August 1916, in *Shaw, Lady Gregory and the Abbey: A Correspondence and a Record*, eds. Dan Laurence and Nicholas Grene (Gerrards Cross: Colin Smythe, 1993), p. 119.
37. Shaw to Lady Gregory, 22 August 1916, ibid., p.122.
38. Edward Martyn, 'A Plea for the Revival of the Irish Literary Theatre', *Irish Review* April 1914, 79–84.
39. Shaw, *Collected Letters, 1874–1897*, p. 640.
40. *Lady Gregory's Journals*, 30 June 1924, p. 557.
41. Shaw to Lady Gregory, 3 September 1916, *Shaw, Lady Gregory and the Abbey*, p. 125.
42. Ibid.

43. 'Public Amusements / Grand Opera House / Ghosts', *Northern Whig*, 9 October 1917, 3.
44. Holloway, *Impressions*, MS 1834, 13 October 1917, the pagination is unreliable at this point.
45. '"Ibsenism" Condemned / Discussion at Catholic Truth Society's Conference', *Irish Times*, 13 October 1917, 7.
46. Ibid.
47. Ibid.
48. Ibid.
49. 'Jacques' was the pseudonym of J. J. Rice.
50. 'Jacques', 'Banned Ibsen Play in Dublin / Women Predominate in the Audience', *Irish Independent*, 15 October 1917, 8.
51. Holloway, *Impressions*, MS 1834, 13 October 1917, the pagination is unreliable at this point.
52. 'Jacques', 'Banned Ibsen Play in Dublin / Women Predominate in the Audience'.
53. Ibid.
54. Ibid.
55. Holloway, *Impressions*, MS 1850, p. 1126. Cited after Feeney, *Drama in Hardwicke Street*, p. 168.
56. Holloway, *Impressions*, MS 1834, 13 October 1917.
57. Ibid.
58. Ibid.
59. Ibid.
60. James Joyce, *Finnegans Wake* (London: Faber and Faber, 1966), p. 136.
61. 'Theatre Royal / Ibsen's Ghosts', *Freeman's Journal*, 15 October 1917, 4.
62. J. H. Cox, 'Sunday Survey', *Sunday Independent* 14 October 1917, cited in Holloway, *Impressions*, MS. 1834, 13 October 1917.
63. 'Jacques', 'Ghosts in Dublin / Banned Play Witnessed by Crowded Audience', *Saturday Herald*, 13 October 1917, 1.
64. Ibid.
65. There were also revivals of the play in 1919 and 1920.
66. *Irish Times*, 29 September 1894, 5. See Feeney, *Drama in Hardwicke Street*, p. 165.
67. 'The Irish Theatre / *An Enemy of the People*', *Freeman's Journal*, 24 April 1917, 2 (also printed in the *Evening Telegraph*) cited in Feeney, *Drama in Hardwicke Street*, p. 166.
68. Holloway, *Impressions*, MS 1831, p.830.
69. A postcard from Holloway to John MacDonagh, 7 February 1918, cited in Feeney, *Drama in Hardwicke Street*, p. 198.
70. 'The Irish Theatre / *An Enemy of the People*', *Freeman's Journal*, 24 April 1917, 2, cited in Feeney, *Drama in Hardwicke Street*, p. 167.
71. Ibid.
72. Ibid.
73. Ibid.
74. Ibid.
75. Ibid.
76. *Young Ireland*, 16 February 1918, 3, cited in Feeney, *Drama in Hardwicke Street*, p. 197.

77. Ibid.
78. Interview with Martyn, *Evening Telegraph*, 6 March 1919, cited in Feeney, *Drama in Hardwicke Street*, p. 267.
79. *Lady Gregory's Journals*, 18 July 1920, p. 183.
80. 'Abbey Theatre', *Irish Times*, 12 December 1917, 5. Cited in Hogan and Burnham, *The Art of the Amateur*, p. 109
81. Ibid.
82. Editorial comment, *Daily Telegraph*, 14 March 1891, 5. Cited in Egan, p. 190.
83. 'Abbey Theatre', *Irish Times*, 12 December 1917, 5. Cited in Robert Hogan and Richard Burnham, *The Modern Irish Drama, a Documentary History*. Vol. V: *The Art of the Amateur* (Dublin: The Dolmen Press, 1984), p. 109.
84. Ibid.
85. 'Jacques', 'Scenes in Slumdom / *The Tragedy of Dublin* Staged at the Abbey / A Pamphlet in Play Form', *Evening Herald*, 12 December 1917, 3. Cited in *Modern Irish Drama*, vol. V, p. 113.
86. Ibid.
87. 'Alphabetical Ibsens', *Saturday Herald*, 15 December 1917. An unsigned clipping from Holloway's Papers. MS 23.197(3).
88. Ellmann, *James Joyce*, p. 266.
89. *Who's Who in the Theatre*. Detroit: Gale Research Co., 1978.
90. 'Jacques', 'A Look Round / Ibsen at the Abbey after a Hustle at the Queen's', *Evening Herald*, 2 July 1918.
91. 'Jacques', 'Ibsen Play at the Abbey', *Irish Independent*, 2 July 1918, 2.
92. Holloway, *Impressions*, MS 1831. 3 July 1918.
93. 'Ibsen at the Abbey', *Evening Telegraph*, 2 July 1918, 2.
94. Ibid.
95. 'Ibsen out of Favour, *Sport*, 6 July 1918, 4.
96. A discussion on 'The Abbey Theatre, Past Present and Future', Sunday 30 March as reported in 'The Abbey Theatre', *Evening Telegraph*, 31 March 1919, 2. Cited in *Modern Irish Drama*, vol. V, p. 194.
97. Ibid.
98. 'Abbey Theatre – Mr. W. B. Yeats and Mr. Lennox Robinson Discuss its Policy', *Freeman's Journal* 26 April 1919, 3. Cited in *Modern Irish Drama*, vol. V, p. 197.
99. 'The Abbey Theatre', *Evening Telegraph*, 31 March 1911, 2. Cited in *Modern Irish Drama*, vol. V, p. 195.
100. Robinson's lecture on 'Legitimate Drama' at the Abbey Theatre on 16 February 1919, as reported in 'Legitimate Drama', *Freeman's Journal*, 17 February 1919, 5. Cited in *Modern Irish Drama*, vol. V, p. 225.
101. Joyce, *Stephen Hero*, p. 88.
102. Sean O'Casey, *Juno and the Paycok*, Sean O'Casey, *Three Plays* (New York: St. Martin's Press, 1957), pp. 20–1.
103. Holloway, *Impressions*, MS 1876, p.548.
104. Ibid.
105. Ibid.
106. Yeats to Lady Gregory, 29 March 1923, *The Collected Letters of W. B. Yeats, Unpublished Letters*, Accession No. 4305.
107. Holloway, *Impressions*, MS 1876, p. 553.

108. Ibid.
109. Holloway, *Impressions,* MS 1876, p. 541
110. Holloway, *Impressions*, MS 1882, p. 1122.
111. Ibid., p. 1123.
112. 'Spealadoir' [James Cousins], 'The Plays at Molesworth Hall', *United Irishman*, 12 December 1903, 6.
113. [W. J. Lawrence], 'Irish Productions', *Stage*, 1 February 1912, 22. Cited in *Modern Irish Drama*, vol. IV, p. 216.
114. See Ivanova, pp. 135–52.
115. Lennox Robinson, *Towards an Appreciation of the Theatre* (Dublin: Metropolitan Publishing, 1945), p. 51.
116. Ibid.
117. '*A Doll's House* / Exacting Parts Well Filled by Abbey Players', *Freeman's Journal*, 23 March 1923, 4.
118. Holloway, *Impressions*, MS 1882, p. 1123.
119. Robinson, *Towards an Appreciation of the Theatre*, p. 43.
120. Ibid., p. 53.
121. Ibsen, *A Doll's House*, pp. 148–9.
122. Robinson, *Towards an Appreciation of the Theatre*, p. 54.
123. Templeton, p. 121.
124. Ibid.
125. *Freeman's Journal*, 23 March 1923.
126. Ibid.
127. Jean Chothia briefly notes the resemblance of O'Casey's heroine to 'Nora Helmer before she understands the need to leave the doll's house'. Jean Chothia, 'Sean O'Casey's Powerful Fireworks', in *A Companion to Modern British and Irish Drama 1880–2005*, ed. Mary Luckhurst (Malden, MA and Oxford: Blackwell, 2006), pp.138–50, p. 129.
128. O'Casey, *The Plough and the Stars*, in O'Casey, *Three Plays*, pp. 131–218, p. 137. Further references to this play are in parentheses.
129. See Nicholas Grene, 'The Class of the Clitheroes: O'Casey's revisions to the *Plough and the Stars* Promptbook', *Bullán*, 4.2 (Winter 1999/Spring 2000), 57–66.
130. Ibsen, *A Doll's House*, p. 137.
131. Grene, *The Politics of Irish Drama*, p. 149.
132. Ibid.
133. Joan Templeton, *Ibsen's Women* (Cambridge: Cambridge University Press, 1997), p. 122.
134. Ibid., p. 120.
135. NLI MS 29. 407. All subsequent references to the promptbook are to this typescript.
136. For a thorough discussion of the changes to this typescript made by O'Casey, see Nicholas Grene, 'The Class of the Clitheroes: O'Casey's Revisions to the *Plough and the Stars* Promptbook'.
137. See Christopher Murray, *Seán O'Casey: Writer at Work: a Biography* (Dublin: Gill & Macmillan, 2004), p. 169.
138. In order to determine whether this is the case, I compared the scribblings in the promptbook to Lennox Robinson's letters. (NLI MS 10.732, NLI MS 15395(2), and NLI MS 13267(21)). The slant of the writing, the connections

between various letters, and the tendency to separate the initial letter from the rest of the word point to the same person.

139. See O'Casey's letter to Robinson on 10 January 1926, defending the words *lowsey* and *bastard*. *The Letters of Sean O'Casey*, ed. David Krause (Washington, DC: Catholic University of America Press, [1975]–*c*.1992), p. 165.
140. This remark is underlined in pencil and marked with a V and an X; the rest of the exchange is crossed out in pink.
141. Shaw, *The Quintessence of Ibsenism*, p. 124.
142. 'The Plough and the Stars', *Irish Independent*, 2 March 1926, 7. Cited in Robert Hogan and Richard Burnham, *The Modern Irish Drama, a Documentary History*. Vol. VI: *The Years of O'Casey* (Gerrards Cross: Colin Smythe, 1992), p. 321.
143. Sean O'Casey, *The Story of the Irish Citizen Army* (Dublin: Maunsel, 1919), p. 64.
144. Hannah Sheehy-Skeffington, *British Militarism as I Have Known It* (New York: Donnelly Press, 1917), published on-line by www.wcml.org.uk.
145. 'Riotous Scenes', *Irish Independent*, 12 February 1926, 7. Cited in *Modern Irish Drama*, vol. VI, p. 301.
146. As Margaret West pointed out at a public meeting in Dublin 1912, 'Suffrage Meeting in Dublin a Lively Gathering', *Irish Times*, 21 September 1912, 3.
147. Rosemary Cullen Owens, *Smashing Times*, p. 120.
148. Ibid.
149. Sean O'Casey, 'Mr. O'Casey's Play', *Irish Independent*, 26 February 1926, 8. Cited in *Modern Irish Drama*, vol. VI, p. 317.
150. Ibid.
151. Cited in Cullen Owens, p. 129.
152. Ibid., p. 133.
153. 'Abbey Theatre / *A Doll's House*', *Irish Times* 19 December 1923, 5.
154. 'Ibsen Play at the Abbey / *A Doll's House* Staged', *Irish Independent*, 23 March 1923, 4.
155. J. W. Good, 'Ibsen Centenary / John Gabriel Borkman at the Abbey', *Evening Herald*, 4 April 1928, 3.
156. Ibid.
157. Holloway, *Impressions*, MS 1917 (3), p. 788.
158. J. W. Good, 'Ibsen Centenary / John Gabriel Borkman at the Abbey', *Evening Herald*, 4 April 1928.
159. Lennox Robinson, 'Ibsen's Influence on Irish Drama/ His Quality of Realism / Commonplace Lives', *Irish Times*, 31 March 1928, 6.
160. T. G. Keller, 'The Genius of Ibsen', *Dublin Magazine* 3, April–June 1928, 44–7. All subsequent references to Keller's ideas are from the same source.

Chapter 6

1. Yeats, 'The Circus Animals' Desertion' (1939), in *The Collected Works of W. B. Yeats*, vol. I: *The Poems*, ed. Richard J. Finneran (London: Macmillan, 1983), pp. 346–8.
2. Ibid., p. 347.
3. Ibid., p. 348.

4. Yeats, 'The Statues' (1938), in *The Collected Works of W. B. Yeats*. Vol. I: *The Poems*, pp. 336–7.
5. Ibsen, *Peer Gynt*, trans. William and Charles Archer, *The Collected Works*, vol. IV, pp. 1–271, p. 184. Hereafter cited parenthetically. The page numbers of this edition correspond to the one used by Hilton Edwards.
6. Yeats, 'The Lover Tells of the Rose in his Heart' (1892), *Collected Poems*, p. 56.
7. Yeats, 'Poetry and Tradition' (1907), in W. B. Yeats, *The Cutting of the Agate* (New York: Macmillan, 1912), pp. 187–8, p. 121.
8. AE, 'Nationality and Cosmopolitanism in Literature', *Literary Ideals in Ireland*, pp. 79–88, p. 83.
9. Tysdahl, p. 112.
10. James Joyce, *Ulysses* (London: Penguin Books, 2000), p. 606.
11. Ibid., pp. 655–62.
12. Ibid., p. 682.
13. Ibid., p. 614.
14. Cited in Brian Johnston, *To the Third Empire: Ibsen's Early Drama* (Minneapolis, MN: University of Minnesota Press, 1980), p. 8.
15. William Archer, 'Introduction to *Peer Gynt*', *The Collected Works,* vol. IV, p. xxvii.
16. Alnæs, *Varulv om natten*, p. 248.
17. Joyce, *Ulysses*, p. 627.
18. See Howard Emerson Rogers, 'Irish Myth and the Plot of *Ulysses*', *ELH* 15: 4 (December 1948), 306–27.
19. *Ulysses*, p. 17. The text is italicised in the original.
20. Gregory Castle, *Modernism and the Celtic Revival*, p. 250.
21. Meyer, *Ibsen*, p. 272.
22. Len Platt, *Joyce and the Anglo-Irish: a Study of Joyce and the Literary Revival* (Amsterdam: Rodopi, 1998) p. 158.
23. Yeats, *The Poems*, pp. 346–7.
24. Ibid., p. 347.
25. James W. Flannery, *W.B. Yeats and the Idea of a Theatre: the Early Abbey Theatre in Theory and Practice* (New Haven, CT and London: Yale University Press, 1989) p. 260.
26. Yeats, 'Preface to the first edition of *The Well of the Saints*' (1905), in Yeats, *The Cutting of the Agate*, pp. 36–49, pp. 47–8.
27. Yeats to Lady Gregory, 8 January 1910, *The Collected Letters, Unpublished Letters*, accession no. 1262.
28. See *Craig on the Theatre*, ed. J. Michael Walton, revised edition (London: Methuen, 1999), pp. 2–8.
29. 'The Hilton and Michael Show': The Story of a Famous Theatrical Partnership. Radio Éireann programme. According to the advertisement in the *Irish Times*, the programme was broadcast on 23 February 1958. The RTE Archives give the date of 31 December 1957. Courtesy of RTÉ Radio, Ireland's Public Broadcaster. Also found in Denis Johnston Papers TCD 10066/282.
30. Ibid.
31. Ibid.
32. Ibid.

33. Oscar G. Brockett and Robert Findlay, *Century of Innovation: A History of European and American Drama Since the Late Nineteenth Century*, second edition (Boston, MA: Allyn & Bacon, 1991), pp. 157–9.
34. Programme for *Peer Gynt*, An Taibhdhearc na Gaillimhe Collection at the James Hardiman Library, NUI Galway.
35. Micheál MacLiammóir, *All for Hecuba: an Irish Theatrical Autobiography* (Boston, MA: Branden Press, 1967), p. 65.
36. Ibid.
37. Bulmer Hobson, ed., *The Gate Theatre Dublin* (Dublin: The Gate Theatre, 1934), p. 24.
38. MacLiammóir, *All for Hecuba*, p. 65.
39. Ibid.
40. Ibid.
41. Frederick J. Marker and Lise-Lone Marker, *Ibsen's Lively Art* (Cambridge: Cambridge University Press, 1989), p. 13.
42. Ibid., p. 11.
43. Ibid., p.10.
44. Review reprinted in Frederick Schyberg, *Teatret i Krig, 1939–1948* (Gyldendal: Copenhagen, 1949), pp. 106–10. Cited in Marker and Marker, p. 24.
45. Tyrone Guthrie, 'Some Afterthoughts on *Peer Gynt*', *The Norseman*, 5 (1947), pp. 204–6. Cited after Marker and Marker, p. 24.
46. Hans Jacob Nilsen, *Peer Gynt: Eit anti-romantisk verk* (Oslo: Aschehoug, 1948), p. 37. Cited after Marker and Marker, p. 25. The Markers explain that Nilsen ascribed these words to the director Svend Methling.
47. Nils Beyer, *Morgon Tidningen*, 9 March 1957, cited in Marker and Marker, p. 30.
48. C. P. Curran, '*Peer Gynt*', *Irish Statesman*, 20 October 1928. The Gate Theatre Archive at Northwestern University.
49. T. G. K., '*Peer Gynt*', *Evening Mail*, 15 October 1928. The Gate Theatre Archive.
50. Ibid.
51. Ibid.
52. Curran, '*Peer Gynt*'.
53. Frederick Schyberg, *Teatret i Krig, 1939–1948* (Copenhagen, 1949), cited in Marker and Marker, p. 21.
54. Holloway, *Impressions*, MS 1921 (7), p. 692.
55. Johnston, *To the Third Empire: Ibsen's Early Drama*, p. 168.
56. C. P. Curran, '*Peer Gynt*', *Irish Statesman*, 20 October 1928.
57. Johnston, *To the Third Empire: Ibsen's Early Drama*, p. 204.
58. MacLiammóir, *All for Hecuba*, p. 68.
59. Ibid.
60. Bulmer Hobson, *The Gate Theatre Dublin* (Dublin: The Gate Theatre, 1934), p. 24.
61. Ibid.
62. Ibid.
63. Ibid.
64. Ibid.
65. Ibid.
66. Curran, '*Peer Gynt*'.

67. Dorothy Macardle, '*Peer Gynt:* Brilliant Production at Gate Theatre', *Irish Press*, 28 September 1932.
68. Marker and Marker, p 26.
69. Johnston, p. 175.
70. Hilton Edwards, *The Mantle of Harlequin* (Dublin: Progress House, 1958), p. 34.
71. Marker and Marker, p. 17.
72. *Gregory Castle*, p., 250. Original emphasis.
73. Holloway, MS 1921 (7), pp. 798–801.
74. See Tim Pat Coogan, *De Valera: Long Fellow, Long Shadow* (London: Arrow Books, 1995), p. 408.
75. Brian P. Kennedy, 'Better Sureshot than Scattergun: Eamon de Valera, Sean O'Faolain and Arts Policy', in *De Valera's Irelands*, ed. Gabriel Doherty and Dermot Keogh (Dublin: Mercier, 2003), p. 118.
76. Sean O'Casey, *Autobiographies*, 2 vols. (London: Macmillan, 1963), vol. 1, p. 548.
77. Curran, '*Peer Gynt*'.
78. Ibid.
79. Joyce, *Occasional, Critical and Political Writing*, p. 52.
80. Curran, '*Peer Gynt*'.
81. A speech to open the Radio Éireann Athlone station in 1933, in *Speeches and Statements of Eamon de Valera 1917–73*, ed. Maurice Moynihan (Dublin: Gill & Macmillan, 1980), pp. 220–3. Cited in Kennedy, p. 120.
82. 'Current Affairs / The Peer Gynts', *Donegal People's Press*, 8 October 1932; emphasis in the original. The Gate Theatre Archive.
83. Ibid.
84. Ibid. Emphasis in the original.
85. Ibid.
86. Curran, '*Peer Gynt*'.
87. Cornelius Weygandt, *Irish Plays and Playwrights* (Westport, CT: Greenwood Press, 1979), p. 163.
88. Dorothy Macardle, 'Dramatists and Movements for Nation Freedom / The Playboy in Drama', *The Irish Press,* 29 September 1932. The Dublin Gate Theatre Archive.
89. Ibid.
90. A. F., 'I Don't Care a Rap', *Dublin Evening Mail*, in Henderson's Presscuttings, NLI MS 1730, p. 81.
91. Macardle, 'Dramatists and Movements for Nation Freedom / The Playboy in Drama'.
92. Ibid.
93. Holloway, *Impressions*, MS 1921(7), p. 839.
94. *Modern Irish Drama*, vol. VI, p. 77.
95. Macardle, 'Dramatists and Movements for Nation Freedom / The Playboy in Drama'.
96. Ibid.
97. 'An International Theatre / Reasons for its Being', *Irish Times*, 27 September 1929, 4.
98. 'Nationaltheatret / John M. Synge: *Helten fra den grønne ø*', *Morgenposten*, 16 September 1927, 4.

99. '*The Playboy* Revived / Excellent Abbey Programme', *Irish Times*, 22 January 1930, 4.
100. See Jan Setterquist, *Ibsen and the Beginnings of Anglo-Irish Drama*; Diderick Roll-Hansen, 'The Playboy of the Western World: An Irish *Peer Gynt*', in *Studies in Anglo-Irish Literature*, ed. Heinz Kosok (Bonn: Bouvier, 1982), pp. 155–60; and more recently Frank McGuinness, 'John Millington Synge and the King of Norway', in *Interpreting Synge: Essays from the Synge Summer School* 1991–2000, ed. Nicholas Grene (Dublin: Lilliput Press, 2000), pp. 57–67.
101. See Maurice Bourgeois, *John Millington Synge and the Irish Theatre* (London: Constable, 1913), p. 205.
102. John Eglinton, 'National Drama and Contemporary Life', in *Literary Ideals in Ireland*, pp. 23–7, p. 24.
103. 'Synge at the Abbey Theatre / *The Playboy of the Western World*', *Irish Times* 13 March 1928, 4.
104. Ibid.
105. Ibid.
106. Adrian Frazier, '"Quaint Pastoral Numbskulls": Siobhan McKenna's *Playboy* Film', in *Playboys of the Western World: Production Histories*, ed. Adrian Frazier (Dublin: Carysfort Press, 2004), pp. 59–74, p. 71.
107. 'Symposium at the Gate Theatre / Should the Theatre be International?', *Irish Times*, 8 November 1932, 4.
108. Ibid.
109. Ibid.
110. Ibid.
111. 'The Hilton and Michael Show'.
112. Christopher Fitz-Simon, *The Boys: A Double Biography* (London: Nick Hern Books, 1994).
113. A. E. Malone, 'The Abbey Theatre Season', *The Dublin Magazine* 2:4 (October–December 1927), 30–8, 34. Malone also declared that 'the Directors of the Abbey Theatre must now keep in mind the organised timidity of which calls itself the Vigilance Committee, which they treated with defiant contempt many times in the past, and the non-literary timidity of Dáil Éireann'.

Epilogue

1. Joyce, *Occasional, Critical and Political Writing*, p. 52.
2. George Moore, *the Untilled Field* (London: William Heinemann, 1931), p. 304. Further references in parentheses.
3. The assonance of Rubek's name with Rodin's was noted by G. B. Shaw in *The Quintessence of Ibsenism: Now Completed to the Death of Ibsen* (London: Constable, 1922), p. 150.
4. George Moore, *The Untilled Field* (London: Fisher Unwin, 1903), p. 25.
5. Ibsen, *When We Dead Awaken*, trans. William Archer, *The Collected Works*, vol. XI, pp. 325–456, pp. 415–17. Further references to this play in parentheses.
6. Errol Durbach, *'Ibsen the Romantic': Analogues of Paradise in Later Plays* (Athens, GA: The University of Georgia Press, 1982), p. 141.

7. George Moore, *Hail and Farewell*, ed. Richard Allen Cave (Gerrards Cross: Colin Smythe, 1976), p. 609.
8. Durbach, p. 142.
9. Moore, *Hail and Farewell*, p. 269.
10. Shaw, *Quintessence*, p. 149.
11. Ibid.
12. George Moore, *The Untilled Field* (London: Fisher Unwin, 1903), p. 6.
13. Durbach, p. 139.
14. Moore, *Hail and Farewell*, p. 56.
15. George Moore, *The Untilled Field* (London: Fisher Unwin, 1903), p. 6.
16. This comment by Rodney appears in the 1903 American edition of *The Untilled Field*, but not in the 1903 Fisher Unwin edition. George Moore, *The Untilled Field*, (Philadelphia; J. P. Lippincott, 1903), p. 378.
17. George Moore, *The Untilled Field* (London: Fisher Unwin, 1903), p. 419.
18. Ibid.
19. Ibid., p. 420.
20. Durbach, p. 147.

Conclusion

1. Shaw, *Quintessence*, p. 29.
2. Moi, p. 3.
3. As noted by Fintan O'Toole, 'Friel Does More than Simply Translate Ibsen's Play, He Makes it Better', *Irish Times*, 13 September 2008, 7.

Bibliography

Journals and periodicals

An Claidheamh Soluis
Beltaine
Daily Express (Dublin)
Dana
Dublin Evening Mail
Dublin Magazine
Dublin Review
Evening Herald (Dublin)
Evening Telegraph (Dublin)
Freeman's Journal
Irish Citizen
Irish Independent
Irish Nation
Irish Press
Irish Review
Irish Statesman
Irish Times
Irish Writing
Leader
Lyceum
New Ireland Review
Peasant
Samhain
Scots Observer
The Times
Theatre
United Ireland
United Irishman

Manuscripts

Henderson, W. A. *The W. A. Henderson Scrapbooks, 1899–1911*. NLI MS 1729–1734.

Holloway, Joseph. *Impressions of a Dublin Playgoer*. National Library of Ireland. MSS 1794–1930.

Richards, Shelah. Unpublished autobiographical piece. The typescript is the property of her son Micheal Johnston.

Collections

Archives of the Gate Theatre of Dublin, 1928–72. Charles Deering McCormick Library of Special Collections. Northwestern University Library, Evanston, IL.
The Taibhdhearc na Gaillimhe Collection. The James Hardiman Library, NUI Galway.

Books and articles

Ackerman, Gretchen P. *Ibsen and the English Stage*. New York and London: Garland, 1987.
Alnæs, Nina S., *Varulv om natten: folketro og folkediktning hos Ibsen*. Oslo: Gyldendal, 2003.
Auerbach, Erich. *Mimesis: The Representation of Reality in Western Literature,* trans. Willard R. Trask. Garden City, NY: Doubleday, 1957.
Bašić, Sonja. 'Book of Many Uncertainties'. In Rosa M. Bollettieri Bosinelli and Harold F. Mosher Jr., eds. *Rejoycing: New Readings of* Dubliners. Lexington, KY: The University Press of Kentucky, 1988, 13–40.
Bell, Michael. 'The Metaphysics of Modernism'. *The Cambridge Companion to Modernism*. Ed. Michael Levenson. Cambridge: Cambridge University Press, 1999, 9–32.
Bentley, Eric. *The Playwright as Thinker: A Study of Drama in Modern Times*. New York: Meridian Books, 1946.
Bloom, Harold. *The Anxiety of Influence: a Theory of Poetry*. New York: Oxford University Press, 1973.
———. *The Western Canon: The Books and School of the Ages*. London: Macmillan, 1995.
Borges, Jorge Louis. *Selected Non-Fictions*. Ed. Eliot Weinberger. Trans. Esther Allen, Suzanne Jill Levine and Eliot Weinberger. New York: Penguin Books, 2000.
Brustein, Robert S. *Critical Moments: Reflections on Theatre and Society 1973–1979*. New York: Random House, 1980.
Castle, Gregory. *Modernism and the Celtic Revival*. Cambridge and New York: Cambridge University Press, 2001.
Chothia, Jean. 'Sean O'Casey's Powerful Fireworks'. In *A Companion to Modern British and Irish Drama 1880–2005*. Ed. Mary Luckhurst. Malden, MA and Oxford: Blackwell, 2006, 125–37.
Clery, Arthur. *Dublin Essays*. Dublin and London: Maunsel, 1919.
Coogan, Tim Pat. *De Valera: Long Fellow, Long Shadow*. London: Arrow Books, 1995.
Courtney, Marie-Therese. *Edward Martyn and the Irish Theatre*. New York: Vantage, 1956.
Cousins, James H. and Margaret E. Cousins, *We Two Together*. Madras: Ganesh, 1950.
Curran, Constantine P. *Under Receding Wave*. Dublin: Gill & Macmillan, *c*. 1970.
Davis, Tracy C. *Critical and Popular Reaction to Ibsen in England: 1872–1906*. University of Warwick, 1984.
———. 'Ibsen's Victorian Audience'. *Essays in Theatre* 4 (1985): 21–38.

Dean, Joan FitzPatrick. 'Bringing Abbey into Contact: The Ibsenite Theatre of Ireland'. *Hungarian Journal of English and American Studies*, 10:1–2 (2004): 33–40.
Deane, Seamus, ed. and Andrew Carpenter, Jonathan Williams, assistant eds. *The Field Day Anthology of Irish Writings*. Vol. 2. Derry: Field Day Theatre Company, 1991.
DeGiacomo, Albert J. *T. C. Murray, Dramatist: Voice of Rural Ireland*. Syracuse, NY: Syracuse University Press, 2003.
Doloff, Steven. 'Ibsen's *A Doll's House* and "The Dead"'. *James Joyce Quarterly* 31: 2 (1994): 111–13.
Douglas, Mary. *Purity and Danger*. London: Routledge & Kegan Paul, 1966. Reprinted Routledge, 2004.
Dowden, Edward. *Essays Modern and Elizabethan*. London and New York: J. M. Dent & Sons, E. P. Dutton, 1910.
Durbach, Errol. *'Ibsen the Romantic': Analogues of Paradise in the Later Plays*. Athens, GA: University of Georgia Press, 1982.
Edwards, Hilton. *The Mantle of Harlequin*. Dublin: Progress House, 1958.
Egan, Michael *Ibsen: the Critical Heritage*. London and Boston, MA: Routledge & Kegan Paul, 1972.
Eglinton, John, W. B. Yeats, AE and W. Larminie. *Literary Ideals in Ireland*. London: Fisher Unwin, 1899.
Ellis, Havelock. *The New Spirit*. London: George Bell, 1890.
Ellmann, Richard. *James Joyce*. New and revised edition. New York: Oxford University Press, 1982.
Fallon, Gabriel. *Sean O'Casey the Man I Knew*. London: Routledge & Kegan Paul, 1965.
Fay. W. G. and Catherine Carswell. *The Fays of the Abbey Theatre: An Autobiographical Record*. London: Rich & Cowan, 1935.
Feeney, William. *Drama in Hardwicke Street: a History of the Irish Theatre Company*. Rutherford, NJ: Fairleigh Dickinson University Press/London: Associated University Presses, 1984.
———, ed. *Lost Plays of the Irish Renaissance, vol. 2. Edward Martyn's Irish Theatre*. Newark, NJ: Proscenium Press, 1979.
Feshbach, Sidney. 'Death in "An Encounter"'. *James Joyce Quarterly* 2 (1965): 82–9.
Fitz-Simon, Christopher. *The Boys: A Double Biography*. London: Nick Hern Books, 1994.
Flannery, James W. *W. B. Yeats and the Idea of a Theatre: the Early Abbey Theatre in Theory and Practice*. New Haven, CT and London: Yale University Press, 1989.
Frazier, Adrian. *George Moore, 1852–1933*. New Haven, CT and London: Yale University Press, 2000.
———. *Behind the Scenes: Yeats, Horniman, and the Struggle for the Abbey Theatre*. Berkeley, CA and London: University of California Press, 1990.
———. 'The Irish Renaissance, 1890–1940: Drama in English'. In *Cambridge History of Irish Literature*. Eds. Margaret Kelleher and Philip O'Leary. 2 vols. Cambridge: Cambridge University Press, 2006.
———. '"Quaint Pastoral Numbskulls": Siobhan McKenna's *Playboy* Film'. In Adrian Frazier, ed. *Playboys of the Western World: Production Histories*. Dublin: Carysfort Press, 2004.

Freud, Sigmund. *The Standard Edition of the Complete Psychological Works of Sigmund Freud.* Ed. James Starchey. 24 vols. London: Hogarth Press and the Institute of Psycho-Analysis, 1953–74.

Gosse, Edmund. *Henrik Ibsen.* New York: Charles Scribner's Sons, 1908.

Gregory, Lady Augusta. *Lady Gregory's Journals, 1916–1930.* Ed. Daniel Murphy, Gerrards Cross: Colin Smythe, 1978.

———. *Our Irish Theatre; A Chapter of Autobiography.* New York: Oxford University Press, 1972.

Grene, Nicholas, *The Politics of Irish Drama.* Cambridge: Cambridge University Press, 1999.

———. 'The Class of the Clitheroes: O'Casey's Revisions to the *Plough and the Stars* Promptbook'. *Bullán,* 4.2 (winter 1999/spring 2000): 57–66.

Helland, Frode. *Melankoliens spill: en studie i Henrik Ibsens siste* dramaer. Oslo: Universitetsforlag, 2000.

Hobson, Bulmer. *The Gate Theatre Dublin.* Dublin: The Gate Theatre, 1934.

Hogan, Robert Goode, James Kilroy, Liam Miller, Richard Burnham and Daniel P. Poteet. *The Modern Irish Drama, a Documentary History,* 6 vols. Dublin: Dolmen Press, 1970–9. Gerrards Cross: Colin Smythe, 1992.

Hogan, Robert Goode and Michael J. O'Neill. *Joseph Holloway's Abbey Theatre: A Selection from his Unpublished Journal, Impressions of a Dublin Playgoer.* Carbondale. IL: Southern Illinois University Press, 1967.

Hornby, Richard. 'Deconstructing Realism in Ibsen's *The Master Builde*r'. *Essays in Theatre* 2:1 (1983): 34–40.

Ibsen, Henrik. *The Collected Works of Henrik Ibsen.* Ed. William Archer, 11 vols. New York: Charles Scribner's Sons, 1908–10.

———. *Hundreårsutgave: Henrik Ibsens samlede verker.* Ed. Francis Bull, 21 vols. Halvdan Koht and Didrik Arup Seip. Oslo: Gyldendal, 1928–57.

———. *Letters and* Speeches. Ed. Evert Sprinchorn. New York: Hill & Wang, 1964.

———. 'Professor Welhaven on Paludan-Müller's Mythological Poems'. Rolf Fjelde. *The Drama Review,* 13:2. Naturalism Revisited (Winter, 1968): 44–6.

Ivanova, Miglena Iliytcheva. 'Staging Europe, Staging Ireland: Ibsen, Strindberg, and Chekhov in Irish Cultural Politics, 1899–1922'. PhD thesis. Urbana, IL: University of Illinois, 2004.

Johnston, Brian L. *To the Third Empire: Ibsen's Early Drama.* Minneapolis, MN: University of Minnesota Press, 1980.

———. *The Ibsen Cycle: the Design of the Plays from Pillars of Society to When We Dead Awaken.* University Park, PN: Pennsylvania State University Press, 1992.

Joyce, James. *A Portrait of the Artist as a Young Man.* Eds. Hans Walter Gabler and Walter Hettche. New York and London: Garland, 1993.

———. *Dubliners.* Harmondsworth: Penguin Books, 1992.

———. *Finnegans Wake.* London: Faber and Faber, 1966.

———. 'The Holy Office' (1904), in *The Field Day Anthology of Irish Writing.* Gen. ed. Seamus Deane. Derry: Field Day Publications, 1991. Vol. II: 769–71.

———. *Occasional, Critical, and Political Writings.* Ed. Kevin Barry. Oxford: Oxford University Press, 2000.

———. *Stephen Hero.* Eds. Theodore Spencer, John Slocum and Herbert Cahoon. New York: New Directions, 1944, rpt. 1963.

———. *Ulysses.* London: Penguin Books, 2000.

Joyce, Stanislaus. *My Brother's Keeper: James Joyce's Early Years*. New York: Viking Press, 1958.

Kennedy, Brian P. 'Better Sureshot than Scattergun: Eamon de Valera, Sean O Faolain and Arts Policy'. In *De Valera's Irelands*. Dublin: Mercier, 2003.

Kleinstück, Johannes. 'Yeats and Ibsen'. In Wolfgang Zach and Heinz Kosok, eds. *Literary Interrelations: Ireland, England and the World*. Tübingen: Narr, 1987, pp. 65–74.

Lebowitz, Naomi. *Ibsen and the Great World*. Baton Rouge, LA: Louisiana State University Press, 1989.

Lee, Jennette. *The Ibsen Secret: A Key to the Prose Dramas of Henrik Ibsen*. New York: G. P. Putnam, 1907.

Levenson, Leah. *With Wooden Sword: A Portrait of Francis Sheehy-Skeffington, Militant* Pacifist. Dublin: Gill & Macmillan.

Levitas, Ben. *The Theatre of Nation*. Oxford: Clarendon Press, 2002.

Loizeaux, Elizabeth Bergmann. *Yeats and the Visual Arts*. Syracuse, NY: Syracuse University Press, 2003.

Marker, Frederick J. and Lise-Lone Marker. *Ibsen's Lively Art*. Cambridge: Cambridge University Press, 1989.

Martyn, Edward. *The Tulira Trilogy of Edward Martyn (1859–1923) Irish Symbolist Dramatist*. Ed. Jerry Nolan. Lewiston, NY, Queenstown and Lampeter: Edwin Mellen Press, 2003.

———. *The Heather Field and Maeve*. London: Duckworth, 1899.

May, Keith. *Shaw and Ibsen*. New York: St. Martin's Press, 1985.

McCormack, W. J. *Fool of the Family: a Life of J. M. Synge*. London: Weidenfeld & Nicolson, 2000, p. 163.

McGuinness, Frank. 'John Millington Synge and the King of Norway'. In Nicholas Grene, ed. *Interpreting Synge: Essays from the Synge Summer School 1991–2000*. Dublin: Lilliput Press, 2000.

MacLiammóir, Micheál. *All for Hecuba: an Irish Theatrical Autobiography*. Boston, MA: Branden Press, 1967.

Mercier, Vivian. 'Literature in English'. In *A New History of Ireland*. Ed. W. E. Vaughan. Vol. VI, *Ireland under the Union, II 1870–1921*. Oxford: Clarendon Press, 1996.

Meyer, Michael. *Ibsen: A Biography*. Garden City, NY: Doubleday, 1971.

Mikhail. Edward Halim, ed. *The Abbey Theatre Interviews and Recollections*. Totowa, NJ: Barnes & Noble, 1988.

Moi, Toril. *Henrik Ibsen and the Birth of Modernism: Art, Theater, Philosophy*. New York: Oxford University Press, 2006.

Moore, George. *Hail and Farewell: Ave, Salve, Vale*. Ed. Richard Allen Cave. Gerrards Cross: Colin Smythe, 1985.

Murray, Christopher. *Seán O'Casey: Writer at Work: A Biography*. Montreal: McGill-Queen's University Press, 2004.

———. *Twentieth-Century Irish Drama: Mirror up to Nation*. Syracuse, NY: Syracuse University Press, 1997.

Newey, Katherine. 'Ibsen in the English Theatre'. *A Companion to Modern British and Irish Drama*. Ed. Mary Luckhurst. Malden, MA, Carlton and Oxford: Blackwell, 2006, pp. 35–47.

Nic Shiubhlaigh, Máire. *The Splendid Years*. Dublin: J. Duffy, 1955.

Nolan, Jerry. *Six Essays on Edward Martyn (1859–1923), Irish Cultural Revivalist.* Lewiston, NY, Queenstown and Lampeter: Edwin Mellen Press, 2004.
Norris, Margot. 'Myth and Reality in Ibsen's Mature Plays'. *Comparative Drama* 10 (1976): 3–15.
Northam, John Richard. *Ibsen: a Critical Study.* Cambridge: Cambridge University Press, 1973.
O'Casey, Sean. *Autobiographies*. London: Macmillan, 1963.
———. *The Letters of Seán O'Casey.* Ed. David Krause, Washington, DC: Catholic University of America Press, [1975]–1992.
———. *The Story of the Irish Citizen Army*. Dublin: Maunsel, 1919.
———. *Three Plays*. New York: St. Martin's Press, 1957.
O'Leary, Philip. *The Prose Literature of the Gaelic Revival, 1881–1921: Ideology and Innovation.* University Park, PN: Pennsylvania State University Press, 1994.
Pearse, Padraic. *Political Writings and Speeches*. Dublin: Phoenix, 1916.
Platt, Len. *Joyce and the Anglo-Irish: a Study of Joyce and the Literary Revival.* Amsterdam: Rodopi, 1998.
Rem, Tore. 'Nationalism or Internationalism: The Early Irish Reception of Ibsen'. *Ibsen Studies* 7:2 (2007): 188–202.
Reynolds, Paige. *Modernism, Drama, and the Audience for the Irish Spectacle.* Cambridge: Cambridge University Press, 2007.
Ritschel, Nelson O'Ceallaigh. 'Shaw, Connolly, and the Irish Citizen Army'. *SHAW: The Annual of Bernard Shaw Studies* 27 (2007), 118–34.
Robinson, Lennox. *Ireland's Abbey Theatre: a History, 1899–1951.* Port Washington, NY: Kennikat Press, 1951.
———. *Curtain Up: an Autobiography.* London: Michael Joseph, 1942.
———. *I Sometimes Think*. Dublin: Talbot Press, 1956.
———. *Towards an Appreciation of the Theatre*. Dublin: Metropolitan Publishing, 1945.
———. *Selected Plays of Lennox Robinson*. Ed. Christopher Murray. Washington, DC: Catholic University of America Press, 1982.
Roche, Anthony. 'Synge, Brecht, and the Hiberno-German Connection'. *Hungarian Journal of English and American Studies*, 10: 1–2 (2004): 9–32.
Rogers, Howard Emerson. 'Irish Myth and the Plot of *Ulysses*'. *ELH* 15:4 (December 1948): 306–27.
Roll-Hansen, Diderik. '*The Playboy of the Western World* an Irish *Peer Gynt?*' *Studies in Anglo-Irish Literature*. Ed. Heinz Kosok. Bonn: Bouvier, 1982, 155–60.
Ryan, Philip B. *The Lost Theatres of Dublin.* Westbury, Wiltshire: Badger Press, 1998.
Setterquist, Jan. *Ibsen and the Beginnings of Anglo-Irish Drama*. New York: Gordian Press, 1974.
Shaw, George Bernard. *Collected Letters, 1856–1950*. Ed. D. H. Laurence. New York: Dodd, Mead & Co., 1965.
———. *Collected Letters. 1898–1910*. Ed. D. H. Laurence. New York: Dodd, Mead & Co., 1972.
———. *Collected Prefaces*. London: Paul Hamyln, 1965.
———. *Our Theatres in the Nineties*. London: Constable, 1932, 1895.
———. *The Philanderer: a Topical Comedy of the Year 1893*. London: Constable, 1928.

———. *Shaw, Lady Gregory and the Abbey: a Correspondence and a Record.* Eds. D. H. Laurence and Nicholas Grene. Gerrards Cross: Colin Smythe, 1993.

———. *The Quintessence of Ibsenism.* London: Walter Scott, 1891.

———. *The Quintessence of Ibsenism: Now Completed to the Death of Ibsen.* London: Constable, 1922.

Sheehy-Skeffington, Hannah. *British Militarism as I Have Known It.* New York: Donnelly Press, 1917.

Shepherd-Barr, Kirsten. *Ibsen and Early Modernist Theatre 1890-1900.* Westport, CT: Greenwood Press, 1997.

Spoo, Robert. 'Uncanny Returns in "The Dead": Ibsenian Intertexts and the Estranged Infant'. *Joyce: The Return of the Repressed.* Ed. Susan Friedman. Ithaca, NY: Cornell University Press, 1993, 89–113.

Sprinchorn, Evert. 'Ibsen and the Actors'. In Errol Durbach, ed. *Ibsen and the Theatre.* New York and London: New York University Press, 1980.

Spurr, David. 'Myths of Anthropology: Eliot, Joyce, Levy-Bruhl', *PMLA* 109: 2 (March 1994), 266–80.

Synge, J. M. *Collected Works.* Eds. Robin Skelton, Alan Price and Ann Saddlemyer, 4 vols. Gerrards Cross: Smythe, 1982.

———. *The Collected Letters of John Millington Synge.* Ed. Ann Saddlemyer. Oxford: Clarendon Press, 1983–4.

Templeton, Joan. *Ibsen's Women.* Cambridge: Cambridge University Press, 2001.

Theoharis, Theoharis C. 'Hedda Gabler and "The Dead"'. *ELH* 50:4 (1983): 791–809.

Tjonneland, Eivind. 'Allegory, Intertextuality and Death – the Problem of Symbolism in Ibsen's *The Master Builder*'. *Proceedings of the 7th International Ibsen Conference.* Oslo: Centre for Ibsen Studies, 1994, 217–36.

Todorov, Tzvetan. *The Fantastic: A Structural Approach to a Literary Genre.* Trans. Richard Howard. London: Case Western Reserve University, 1973.

Tysdahl, Bjorn T. *Joyce and Ibsen – A Study In Literary Influence.* Oslo: Norwegian Universities Press/New York: Humanities Press, 1968.

Vandevelde, Karen. *The Alternative Dramatic Revival in Ireland, 1897–1913.* Dublin: Maunsel/Bethesda: Academica Press, 2005.

Welch, Robert. *The Abbey Theatre, 1889–1999: Form and Pressure.* Oxford: Oxford University Press, 2003.

Weygandt, Cornelius. *Irish Plays and Playwrights.* Westport, CT: Greenwood Press, 1979.

Whitebrook, Peter. *William Archer: A Biography.* London: Methuen, 1993.

Who's Who in the Theatre. Detroit: Gale Research Co., 1978.

Woodfield James, *English Theatre in Transition 1881–1914.* London: Croom Helm/ Totowa, NJ: Barnes & Noble, 1984.

Worth, Katharine. 'Ibsen and the Irish Theatre'. *Theatre Research International* 15 (1990): 18–28.

Yeats, W. B. *Autobiographies.* London: Macmillan, 1955. Rpt. 1970.

———. *The Collected Letters of W. B. Yeats.* Eds. John Kelly and Eric Domville. Oxford: Clarendon Press, 1986–97.

———.*The Collected Plays of W. B. Yeats.* London, Macmillan, 1966.

———.*The Collected Works of W. B. Yeats.* Vol. I: *The Poems.* Ed. Richard J. Finneran. London: Macmillan, 1983.

———. *Uncollected Prose*. Ed. John P. Frayne. London: Macmillan, 1970.
———. *The Writing of the Player Queen: Manuscripts of W. B. Yeats*. Transcribed, edited and with a commentary by Curtis Baker Bradford. DeKalb, IL: Northern Illinois University Press, 1977.
Young, Ella. *The Flowering Dusk: Things Remembered Accurately and Inaccurately.* New York and Toronto: Longman, Green & Co., 1945.

Index